HOME, FOREVER.

Anna Dombkins

HOME, FOREVER.

A story of adoption, hope and the mountains we're all climbing.

PEPPER PRESS

First published in 2026 by Pepper Press, an imprint of Fair Play Publishing.
PO Box 4101, Balgowlah Heights, NSW 2093, Australia

www.fairplaypublishing.com.au

ISBN: 978-1-923236-44-8
ISBN: 978-1-923236-45-5 (eBook)

Photographs supplied by Anna Dombkins and Deborra-Lee Furness.
Cover design by Ben Hawkins
Typesetting by Ana Nedeljković

All inquiries should be made to the Publisher via hello@fairplaypublishing.com.au

A catalogue record for this book is available from the National Library of Australia.

Author's note

This is a work of creative non-fiction. Some names and personal details have been changed for privacy, and timelines altered slightly for brevity, without compromising the integrity of this story, I hope! It is a true story, recounted with the aid of journals and emails from the time, to cross-check my memory, which definitely needs cross-checking. It is our warts and all experience, and by no means a guide for others. For ease of reading, many conversations that occurred in Swahili are written here in English. It is fair to assume that most Tanzanian people featured in this book were speaking Swahili. At times, I have given both the Swahili and English translations. Where my Swahili translation is incorrect or muddled, it is because my use of Swahili is frequently incorrect or muddled.

Dedication

For my favourite little mountain climbers—Jackson, Jabari, Jemima, Shay, Charlie and Max. This is just the start of your story. You get to write the rest. I can't wait to watch. Dad and I adore you guys.

For every child waiting for a family or a safe home, and every woman fighting against poverty to keep her baby. We see you. We won't look away.

For my mum, whose quiet wisdom I miss every day.

And for you, dear reader. Keep climbing.

Foreword

The Story Before the Story

I am forever grateful to all the amazing people in our community who are creating solutions to ensure children live in a loving forever home.

The Dombkins family is one such family that has witnessed the problem firsthand, having moved to Tanzania with two biological children and then fostered and eventually adopted three children whilst living there. They took action to find solutions. They were able to take a big-picture view and understand that, with a helping hand, many of these children would not have to be relinquished. Our mission at Adopt Change and our north star is to keep families together, wherever possible. The Dombkins family align with our vision and addresses the possibilities of keeping families together through creative thinking and philanthropy.

It is so easy to be overwhelmed by the enormity of the scenario of children needing families and think that it is too hard to make even a dint in finding ways to solve this global problem. I know when I started to advocate for vulnerable children, I had no idea of how much needed to be done in order to make a change. I gained an enormous education along the way, and I am still able to keep going because of the inspiration of the Margaret Mead quote, *"Never doubt that a small group of thoughtful committed individuals can change the world. In fact, it's the only thing that ever has."*

I highly recommend Anna Dombkins' book to understand the nuances and complexities of finding 'Forever' homes for the world's most vulnerable citizens. It shines a light on the fact that we can all make a difference, no matter how large or small. Everyone is climbing a mountain, and how much easier that climb is when we do it together.

Deborra-Lee Furness

CONTENTS

Prologue

'Send them back.'

He spoke the words no adoptive parent ever wants to hear.

'What?' I questioned, disbelief flooding my mind as my heart raced.

'He said we have to send them back.' Mark's voice was panicked and shaky, like nothing I had heard in our 11 years of marriage.

Mark was in Dar es Salaam, the capital of Tanzania and a half-hour plane ride across the country from our home in Moshi where I stood, frozen in shock. He was meeting with the Commissioner for Social Welfare, the top dog when it comes to adoption. The Commissioner held our family in the palm of his hand, and his decisions would dictate our future.

'He said there's been a change of policy in Social Welfare,' Mark continued, 'and although we did everything correctly three years ago when we brought the kids home, the process has now changed,' he explained, trying desperately to calm his voice.

'So what?' I pushed back. 'It's not our fault if they've changed their policy! We did everything exactly as we should have!'

'I know, I said that, but they don't see it that way. They don't know what to do with cases that began under the old system, so they want us to send them back and start again,' he said.

I pressed my back against the concrete wall behind me and tried to take in what Mark was saying. Hot tears welled in my eyes. There was anger rising in me, a special kind of anger that our whole adoption journey had produced. It was born of fighting for life and hope and justice for abandoned children, but being constantly held back, delayed. It lived just under the surface now, ready to spill over whenever the next hurdle arose.

How could they even suggest we send them back? Our three babies came from circumstances that left them all close to death. That's why we had them. That's why they had been in our home for the past three years. How could the Commissioner possibly suggest sending them back, just to have paperwork in line with the new system?

In the next room, 13 bouncy primary school children were waiting for me—my after-school gymnastics class. Their giggles and squeals pierced my thoughts and reminded me I had to go.

'I have to teach my class,' I said to Mark. 'The Commissioner can't really make us do this. We'll fight it. We have to.'

Among my students were my two daughters. I scooped them up into a hug and squeezed them tight, holding back a fresh wave of tears. I pushed those tears and the anger that threatened to overwhelm me back under the surface. We were getting good at this, at carrying on through the normalities of everyday life in Africa, all the while preparing for the battle of our lives.

I glanced up before entering the school hall, and the clouds were parting to reveal the majestic, snow-covered peak of Mount Kilimanjaro. It had remained hidden under a thick blanket of cloud for weeks, a misty grey fog in its place. And then, silently, it appeared once again, taking my breath away with its snow-dusted crown sitting high above the treeline. I was reminded once again of all this mountain represented. Challenge. Hope. Perseverance. Faith. Overcoming, one step at a time. One glimpse could lift my mood, pulling my mind upwards, giving me a renewed perspective. *I lift up my eyes to the mountains*, those beautiful, familiar words bouncing back into my mind, *From where does my help come? My help comes from the Lord, the maker of heaven and earth.* A few seconds standing still, beholding the incredible mountain in my sight, and the promise of those words filling my mind, and I was ready to go again, ready to battle on.

Chapter 1

Faces that Stay

"We are only as blind as we want to be."
—MAYA ANGELOU

It was their little faces that first pulled at my heart. As Mark and I sat together on the couch watching the TV screen in front of us, the images we saw shocked us into silence. Rows and rows of tiny babies. Some were tied to bamboo chairs. Some lay in metal cribs, others rocked back and forth, over and over. *The Dying Rooms* is a chilling documentary. It exposes the truth of the conditions in many Chinese orphanages. We sat together crying silent tears as we watched. Beyond the rooms of countless children, there was another room. This one housed a single dying baby. This baby lay alone, dying a torturous death. Her skeletal frame was curled up; skin stretched over her bones. But it's her face that will stay with me forever. Her eyes were screaming for help, but she could barely make a sound. Her face told the story of the unspeakable tragedy we were witnessing. A child abandoned. Left to die. Alone.

My eyes travelled from the screen to the bassinet in the corner of our lounge room. Our son, Jackson, lay there sleeping soundly. The contrast was stark. Chilling. Jackson was six months old, our first baby, one of the first grandchildren for our parents, and the first baby in our group of friends. Everywhere we went, there was a line-up of loved ones waiting for their turn to hold him. He was showered in love. As all children should be.

I turned back to the TV. The dying baby had been left alone for days, with an older child sent in every so often to see if she was still alive. Eventually, and painfully, she passed away.

It was right then that we decided to do something. It was one of those moments where you know the course of your life is about to change. We couldn't live with what we just saw. We couldn't carry on as if we hadn't seen it. Something stirred in us, and we decided there and then that we would pursue adoption.

It seemed like a simple enough idea. Surely there was a well-travelled path, where others had come before us. Surely adoption was a valued process, where parentless children were matched to loving families. We all knew the statistics—there were millions of orphaned children around the world in need of a home. Surely matching these children to a family would be a top priority for governments around the world. It couldn't be that difficult to bring the two together. Could it?

As we began to research, we deflated a little, and our naivety revealed itself.

We read some concerning stories about international adoption from Australia—stories of long waiting lists, slow processing, and red tape. But as we began the process for international adoption, we expected to find ourselves in a world of people like us, people who had a heart for abandoned children, who understood the obstacles but were willing to persist through it all. What we found instead was largely a world of hostility, suspicion, coldness, and negativity. Adoption itself didn't seem to be valued, and the children in need of a home didn't seem to be the focus. It was quite a shock, and we struggled to adjust.

We pushed on, attended two weekends of training sessions, and prepared anxiously for our first assessment interview. Being assessed for adoption is a nerve-wracking process. Our whole existence was being evaluated, like bugs under a microscope. We had to prove ourselves over and over, and not in the ways we expected.

We were already parents. Our son was just a baby when we began the adoption process and would turn four while we were still waiting. We expected our parenting to be assessed. We expected they might spend time with us and our son to discover if we were raising a happy, settled, well-adjusted child. But there was not a single question about our parenting. In fact, we never moved past the very first question that was asked.

The interview was happening in our home, and we had spent the morning making sure we were as prepared as possible. House tidy, son clean, freshly baked cakes and tea set out, answers ready.

Our caseworker, Louise, knocked on the door and we let her in. We exchanged pleasantries and sat together in the lounge. Babies can be unpredictable, but I had timed Jackson's sleep so Louise could meet him briefly, see that he was a happy, healthy kid, and then I could put him to bed, leaving the adults to talk freely. It was all going well. Jackson smiled and did his best to charm Louise. After a few minutes, I took him off to bed and held my breath, hoping he would go off to sleep without fuss. He did. In my mind, we were earning points for that. We weren't.

We settled down to talk in the lounge room.

CHAPTER 1

'Tell me what you imagine your family to look like.' Louise asked.

That was it. That was the question we began with and would end with.

'Well,' I said, 'there's Mark and I, obviously, and we have our son Jackson, he's 18 months now, and we'd like to adopt a sibling group. We'd like our family to be a mix of biological and adopted children, and we'd like to have a larger family—maybe four children or so altogether.'

'I see,' Louise replied. Then she paused. I could sense the mood change. I wasn't sure what part of my answer was of concern, but she was carefully considering her next words.

'So...' she began, 'have you finished having biological children?'

'Oh, well, it was quite difficult for us to fall pregnant with Jackson,' I explained, 'and we're not sure if we would be able to have any more biological children. But if we did fall pregnant again, we would be thrilled of course.'

Wrong answer.

'I'm sorry, but we are unable to continue this interview or your assessment unless you can assure us you are not going to have any more biological children.'

'Pardon?' I asked, not sure I had heard her correctly.

'We require families to finish having biological children before they begin to pursue adoption,' she said.

'Oh,' I replied, 'I see. Well, we aren't intending to do both at the same time. But I understand the waiting list for international adoption is seven years long at the moment, so if we were to have another child in the next few years while we are waiting, I don't see that as impacting on our adoption application.'

'That's not how it works,' Louise explained. 'You need to be ready to take a child right now for us to approve you.'

'Is it possible that a child would be placed with us now?' Mark asked.

'No, it's not. You will be waiting many years. But our policy requires you to be ready now.'

'We are ready now,' I pushed. 'We don't even know if it would be possible for us to have another biological child. We just meant that if we were to fall pregnant, it would be a lovely surprise, and we would of course be very happy about it. Our choice to adopt isn't a backup if we can't have any more biological children, we want to adopt either way.'

'Well, in order for you to be approved to adopt, you'll need to show the department that you have finished having biological children. Some applicants choose to have surgery to have their tubes tied to demonstrate their commitment to adoption.'

I stared back in silence. Did she really just say that? My mind turned back to those tiny babies in China. I didn't think they would really mind if they had one, two or ten siblings, as long as someone picked them up, loved them, and brought them home.

I questioned her. 'I'm trying to understand the thoughts behind this policy. Can you explain a little more, explain why it would affect our application?'

'There's a growing body of evidence suggesting that having biological and adoptive siblings in the same family isn't a great idea,' she said. 'And certainly mixing them in birth order isn't advisable.'

In the lead-up to our adoption application, I had spent months reading and researching, and I had never come across the research she was describing. If it did exist, I wanted to read it, as it would influence our ideas and plans for our family. I was acutely aware that the whole time we were talking, we were being assessed. I didn't want to come across as argumentative. But I did want to discuss it further.

'I'm surprised to hear that,' I said. 'I haven't come across that research in my reading so far. Would you be able to send me a copy or point me in the right direction to track it down? I would be very interested to read up about this, as it certainly relates to our plans for our family.'

'Yes, I'd be happy to,' Louise replied. 'In the meantime, I'll leave you to consider your options before we proceed any further. If you decide you can demonstrate commitment to adoption and abandon any plans for further biological children, we can continue in a few months.'

We said our goodbyes, and Mark and I collapsed on the lounge, exhausted.

'What just happened?' he asked.

'I have no idea,' I said. 'That was ridiculous.'

I jumped on my computer and began searching for the research Louise had told me about. I couldn't find it. I found lots of studies about children in foster care, about disrupted birth order when children come in and out of care. But that was it.

It would be two weeks before Louise called.

'Hi Anna,' she began, 'listen, I haven't actually been able to find the research I was referring to. I'm not sure what's happened there. But anyway, anecdotal evidence from the department suggests it's not a good idea, so we stand by our policy.'

'Not a good idea for who?' I asked. 'The adopted child? The biological children? The family as a whole?'

'We just prefer there to be separation—the children won't get along if they are too close in age. Finish having biological children, then you can apply to adopt. Besides, we have no need for more adoptive parents. The waiting list is very long, and there just aren't enough orphans.'

I let her words linger in the air.

There aren't enough orphans.

I knew of some babies in China who would beg to differ.

Chapter 2

Across the Ocean

"My humanity is bound up in yours,
for we can only be human together."
—DESMOND TUTU

The next two years would bring more of the same. Meetings, discussions, waiting… more meetings, more discussions, more waiting. No progress.

Then one morning, there were two faint pink lines on my pregnancy test. We were thrilled. Jackson was almost two, and as we were no closer to being approved to adopt, we revelled in welcoming our second child. We knew what this would mean for our application: there were clear rules that applications would be "on hold" for the duration of a pregnancy and resumed once the baby was born. We called the department and let them know. Our application to adopt was now officially on hold.

Jemima Joy was born on a beautiful February morning. She was a delight from the start. She barely slept, and I barely minded. She was a bundle of giggles and sunshine, and she had me hook, line, and sinker. She nestled in the crook of my arm, swaddled in a pale pink blanket like a tiny baby burrito. Looking up at me with her deep blue eyes, an elusive dimple appeared sporadically on her left cheek, and I hugged her tighter and breathed in her sweet newborn baby smell. While all around was quiet and dark, and Mark and Jackson were sleeping soundly, she and I passed the long hours of the night together. She was almost always awake, and almost always happy, as long as I didn't try to put her to bed. I folded baskets of washing, once full of blues, greens, truck patterns and motorbikes, now sprinkled with pinks, pastels, rainbows and butterflies, while she lay in her bouncer, eyes glued to my every move.

On the other side of the world, another baby was just born. He was born into poverty. His birth wasn't registered. He didn't come home to a doting family and a decorated nursery. He came home to struggling parents in a small Tanzanian village and would learn to live with a hungry belly.

CHAPTER 2

In the first few weeks of Jemima's life, our wonderful midwife, Yvonne, came to our home regularly to weigh her, and check on both her health and ours. Across the ocean, no one was checking on him. Jemima was growing, he was not. She had enough to eat, he did not.

As I watched her thrive, I wondered what would happen if she wasn't growing, if I wasn't able to feed her, if her life was in danger. She was born into a world where this would be a crisis. Where every known medical intervention would be available to her, to bring her to health.

He was born into a different world. They shared a planet, but little else. In his world, he was the norm. Some babies lived, and some died. Some were well fed, but many were hungry. In every hut around his village, there was a child like him and there were parents like his—doing their best, on their own, to give life to their babies, and to stay one step ahead of starvation.

We had waited our nine months, being on hold in the adoption application process while I was pregnant, and now it was time to call again. I called the main reception to reactivate our application and spoke to Claire, who I'd not met before.

'We've had our application on hold for the past nine months while I've been pregnant, and now that our daughter is born, I'd like to continue the assessment process, please,' I explained.

'How old is your daughter now?' she asked.

'She's three months old,' I replied.

'I see,' Claire paused.

There's always a pause before they break more bad news. It's long enough for the sinking feeling in your stomach to begin, and your mind to race with guesses and questions.

'The department has a policy that after a child is born, the applicants wait another six to 12 months before continuing the application process. Just to be sure they still want to continue,' Claire said.

Right. Of course. More waiting. It had now been over three years since we first applied, and we were not even finished the application process, let alone started on the seven-year waiting list. I was fairly sure we would have time to rethink over those seven years and withdraw our application if we changed our mind.

'We really are sure we want to continue,' I said. 'We've already been waiting for three years, and we haven't wavered in our commitment. I can assure you we aren't wasting your time. We are serious about adoption, and we just want to get on with the application process.'

'I understand,' Claire said. 'But we have a policy we need to adhere to. If you call again in, let's say, ten months, we can continue from there.'

'Ten months?' I questioned.

'Yes, the policy is six to 12 months, so I think ten months should be fine for you.'

I racked my brain to think when or how we had met Claire. I couldn't recall interacting with her before, but it seemed as if she must know us to come up with such a specific time frame.

'I'm sorry, I'm trying to remember, but have we met?' I asked.

'No, I don't think so,' Claire replied.

'Okay, so, I'm just wondering how you've settled on ten months then, having never met us before?'

'Ten months will give you enough time to consider if you intend to continue,' Claire replied crisply, her voice becoming more agitated. I had pushed the conversation as far as I dared.

'I see,' I conceded. 'Well, I'll call again in ten months then. Thank you for your time, Claire.'

I ended the call.

It was a new skill we were learning—a delicate dance with a reluctant partner. We had to feel when to push forward, when to step back, when to tiptoe lightly and when to make a dramatic move.

Ten months. We could wait. Life would go on. Jackson and Jemima would continue to grow and be loved. Mark and I had jobs we enjoyed, a great home in a beautiful part of the world. Ten months would pass quickly for us. But ten months would be an eternity for those tiny babies in China, or that little boy across the ocean, or the millions of others like them. Ten months for them might mean life or death. Or a body and a mind that slowly deteriorates under the effects of starvation, and a spirit that loses hope in a world that has forgotten them.

Maybe it was time for a dramatic move.

Chapter 3

An Open Door

"Family is central to life in Africa...
A man without family is no one. He is nothing."
—RICHARD DOWDEN, *AFRICA*

Her weathered hands lifted another cement boulder and brought it down hard, crushing it into smaller pieces as a dust cloud rose from the dry, red earth at her feet. She continued to heave up and throw down, heave up and throw down, until the boulder was crushed into gravel. She coughed and wiped her face in an attempt to clear the dust from her eyes. The hot African sun beat down on her, unforgiving in its intensity, as she worked as hard as her 70 years would allow. Pain was a constant, her bones aching and eyes stinging, but survival pushed her onwards. She filled another bag with gravel and dragged it over to her husband. They worked as a team, filling bags together, ready to sell at construction sites. They assessed their day's work. Another hour or two would yield enough to sell for 2,000 shillings (just over one Australian dollar). With this, they could buy some rice, vegetables and a small piece of charcoal to cook with. They would eat tonight.

Approaching home as the sun was setting, they neared their small, single room. Through the dust, they saw strangers standing at their door, and the sound of babies crying reached their ears. At first unfamiliar, one of the people became unmistakable as he came into view.

'Eh! Do you see?' Bibi whispered, 'Do you see who stands at our door?' She rubbed her eyes as she spoke.

'It can't be,' Babu replied, disbelief clouding his mind.

'It's him. I know it's him,' Bibi insisted. 'What is he doing here now, after all these years?'

Babu and Bibi walked towards the small group waiting at their door.

'Son?' Bibi began. 'Is it you?'

'Yes, Mama,' replied the short, thin man standing before them, his long dreadlocked hair falling down his back. 'It's me, Mwaka.'

'And who is this?' Bibi asked.

'This is Elewa,' he replied, raising his voice above the cries of the babies around him, 'and these are your grandchildren.'

A young woman stood next to him. *Very young*, Bibi thought. Strapped to the woman's back in a brightly coloured kanga was a small child, staring into the distance, and in her arms were two tiny babies. The twin babies were wrapped in many layers and both screamed quick, sharp newborn cries. Elewa raised her eyes to meet Bibi's, but she said nothing.

'My grandchildren?' Bibi asked. 'If they are my grandchildren, you must be my son. But where have you been? What son leaves his mama to live like this?'

Mwaka dropped his eyes to the ground. It had been over a decade since they last met. The shame of deserting his parents now weighed on him.

'Mama,' Mwaka began, appealing to her heart. 'The children are sick. The twins have been born before their time. The hospital can't help them.'

'And this one?' Bibi asked, peering around Elewa's back to see the small boy still staring blankly.

'Him, he is not growing. He is sick. We can't feed him. How can we feed two more if we can't even feed this one?'

Bibi straightened her posture, standing at full height before her son, and held his gaze in silence. This son of hers had caused her deep pain. He left the family when it was his duty to work and provide. She continued to struggle for survival each day, barely making it from one day to the next. And here he stood before her.

Bibi breathed in deeply and prayed silently. '*Mungu, nisaidie*. Lord, help me.'

She opened the door and invited the young family in.

Chapter 4

Evaporation

"Even the darkest night will end and the sun will rise."
—VICTOR HUGO, *LES MISÉRABLES*

The fractured family sat on the cold, bare floor of Babu and Bibi's single room. Dark and cramped, with concrete walls that pushed them uncomfortably close, they gathered amongst the few belongings scattered around the small home.

Bibi began to prepare the meal her hard work had earned that day. Now, the meagre food must stretch to feed them all. As she peeled her single potato with a dull knife, she wrestled internally with where this path was leading. She was hurt and angry. But there was a deep kindness within her that meant she couldn't turn her family away.

They ate together, a small portion for each, from a shared pan. Elewa untied her kanga and pulled her son onto her lap. His hands reached frantically for the food before him. He scooped the rice and vegetables into his mouth, over and over, swallowing without chewing, until each grain of rice was finished. His urgency revealed the intensity of his hunger.

'When did he last eat?' Babu asked.

'We don't have enough,' Mwaka muttered. 'I have not found work. Elewa has been too weak to work. The babies are too small. We begged the hospital to help, but they sent us away. They said there's nothing they can do. He's not going to survive.' His eyes settled on his son, then moved to his twin babies, 'None of them are.'

'So why have you brought them here to us?' Bibi asked, 'What do you think we can do if even the hospital can't save them?'

'We have nowhere else to go,' Mwaka answered quietly.

Sharp cries once again pierced the air as the tiny twins stirred from their fitful sleep. Babu reached out and lifted one of the new babies, the girl. He slipped his hand under her and stared—her tiny head barely covered half of the palm of his hand. Bibi lifted the other twin, a little boy, and cradled him close to her. She could hardly feel the weight of him in her arms. Bibi caught Babu's eyes. They both knew they could not abandon these little ones. Bibi closed her eyes and breathed in slowly. The tiny stranger in her arms was winning her heart. No matter how grave the mistakes of her son, she would not neglect her duty to her family.

The cramped room housed them all overnight. Bibi spread out her few spare clothes on the floor, which provided little comfort. When the morning came, Babu and Bibi set off again to complete their day's work, leaving the young family home to look after the children and attempt to find work in a new place. It was harvesting time for the maize crops and there was plentiful work for young, strong men.

The day came and went. Babu and Bibi collected their earnings, tired from their hard labour, and overwhelmed by the prospects of supporting their son and his family. They returned home again, hoping to hear good news. When they returned, they found only Elewa and the children. Elewa looked up as they entered, her eyes red with tears.

'He's not returning,' she began, 'Mwaka has left us.' Her eyes filled with new tears as she shared the truth that tore her heart.

Babu and Bibi looked at each other. There was no surprise for them in this news. They knew this pain. They had walked this path before.

'It's too difficult for him,' Elewa continued, 'he can't face it.'

She unstrapped her son from her back, placed him down to sit on the floor, and passed the twins to Babu as she began to help Bibi prepare the meal. Silent tears continued to flow. Bibi looked over at Elewa, and it struck her again how young she was. Too young to face this pain. Her children were dying. Her husband had left. She carried the burden alone.

Once the vegetables were peeled, Elewa rose to carry the scraps outside. She collected a small pile of household rubbish and paused as she clutched it in her hands. She looked around the room, her children barely visible through her tears, and without a word she stepped outside.

Bibi continued to cook the meal. Babu cradled the babies, keeping them away from the fire. Rice bubbled in murky water, and Babu and Bibi waited. Elewa had not yet returned. The rice softened. The water evaporated. Babu and Bibi still waited, and Elewa still had not returned.

Babu set out to search for Elewa, a faint hope concealing the truth he feared. She was not at the rubbish dump. She was not talking with a neighbour. She had not been seen by anyone.

Cold rice greeted Babu as he returned without Elewa. They waited until the sun went down. It would be rude to eat without her. But the hard truth was settling on them like a heavy fog. She was not going to return. As darkness fell, they ate in silence.

The night was endless and haunting. Newborns screaming without a mother to feed them. Babu and Bibi rocked and held the babies, trying in vain to provide comfort. Bibi crushed up some remaining rice, and mixing it with water, she tried to make an edible paste. The twins gagged and rejected the offering, screaming instead for their mother, who would never return.

The sun rose on that awful night, and Babu and Bibi faced a new day, now with the responsibility of caring for three very sick children. They set out to find help, knowing that a day without work was a day without food. But they could not sit by while these children died.

Bibi, with one child strapped in a kanga to her back, and two in her arms, closed her eyes and lifted her face to the sky. She breathed in deeply and began to pray:

God, help these children! You know we are old and tired. We can't raise these babies, and we can't leave them to die. What are we to do? You must help! Please help us.

Across the ocean, I was praying too.

Chapter 5

Dreaming

"Never be afraid to trust an unknown future to a known God."
—CORRIE TEN BOOM

We were restless. We had been dreaming, hoping and waiting for so long now, and it seemed as far away as ever. Mark and I waited our ten months, and it was time to continue our never-ending application process. Only now, there was a new problem. We were applying to adopt from Ethiopia, the only African country with an adoption agreement with Australia, and now the program had closed. It closed temporarily at first, and then permanently. We were gutted. We were gutted for the children who would not find their new family. We were gutted for the families who had been waiting up to seven years for a child and now had to join a new queue or abandon their hopes for a family. We were gutted for what this meant for adoption in Australia.

As a new year was beginning, Mark and I were considering what it would hold for us. We had a four-year-old, a one-year-old, and a dead-end adoption process. Our life was wonderful, and we were thankful for an amazing family, great friends, a church we loved, and good jobs. But there was something that unsettled us. Our hearts were seeking something more, and our plans seemed at a standstill.

Mark and I walked along the foreshore of the sparkling coastline that bordered our hometown. We walked this path most days, pushing the kids in a pram, looking out at the dark blue ocean, the white boats dotted around the harbour, and the beautiful old lighthouse. We loved this place.

As we walked, this contradiction of contentment and restlessness stirred in me again. A new idea came into my mind, and the excitement of it startled me. For a few moments, I pondered whether to say it out loud. *We couldn't possibly!* I thought. *Don't be ridiculous!* But a grin was spreading across my face, and I couldn't contain the thought a second longer. I looked over at Mark, grinning like a fool.

'What?' he asked, bemused.

'What if…' I began, and paused, not quite able to say it.

'What if what?' he asked, impatiently.

'What if we just move to Africa?'

His face creased and ignited as my foolish grin infected him.

'Yes!' he said, without hesitation. 'Yes! Yes! Yes!'

His reaction was instant and emphatic. This idea, just ten seconds old, grew from nothing to all-encompassing in a matter of minutes. This was not normal for us. We weren't especially spontaneous people—we didn't just up and move internationally on a whim! This wasn't us. And yet, there was something in this idea that just grabbed us by the shoulders and shook us into action. We were all in. Immediately.

The next few months were spent madly researching, planning, dreaming, hoping and pinching ourselves to see if we were really doing this. It was thrilling for us both to consider a great new adventure. It felt like finally taking our future into our own hands, rather than enduring an endless wait in the hands of a floundering system. This move made sense to us on so many levels. Sure, we wanted to adopt, but it was more than that. The idea of living and working in Africa alone was enough to make us wild with excitement. We weren't quite sure what we would discover, or where our new path would lead, but we were ready to jump in and find out.

There was a lot to consider and, as the weeks passed, we narrowed down a profile of where exactly we were looking to move. We had two young children, so safety was our top priority. Beyond that, we needed a place to live and a job for Mark or me, or both of us. We needed a country with an adoption system that was compatible with Australian adoption law. And ultimately, we needed to find our new children. We read and researched and prayed. We believed God knew who our children were, that somewhere in the world were some precious little ones with no Mum or Dad, no home to call their own. We asked God to guide us and lead us to them.

International adoption is fraught with dangers and horror stories. We knew this well. We had heard of children being taken from perfectly good families and sold to overseas adoptive parents. We knew of families so intent on adopting that they were blind to the circumstances from which their adopted children had come. We heard of adoptive children growing up, reuniting with birth parents, only to find their birth parents never consented to their adoption. We heard of corrupt systems, fraudulent orphanages, and children gravely damaged in the process. We wanted no part in any of that. It's in response to these kinds of circumstances that many countries close their international adoption programs. It's easy to understand why. The stories are awful, and the evil behind them is unthinkable. And sadly, in the mess of it all, the children who are legitimately orphaned lose again. They've already lost so much: their birth parents, their home, their family, their community. Now they lose their chance at a permanent family.

The complexities of these issues churned over in our hearts and minds. We'd been on a long journey already of attempting to understand it all. The intersection of poverty and child abandonment is a tangled web where disadvantage, trauma, and lack of support lead to crisis for a child. In some of these circumstances, adoption is necessary. But not in all. Sometimes, often even, there are other solutions, other opportunities for a family to keep their children.

Adoption, we have always believed, can be a beautiful last resort. But it must always be a last resort.

So we had a mammoth task before us, a long list of essential items: safe country, home, jobs, compatible adoption law, ethical adoption process. And all of those in the one place.

Neck-deep in research, I floundered through oceans of information and possibilities. The task seemed overwhelming and endless at times. I could quickly rule many options out—places that didn't fit our profile. But finding that one place that met all our requirements eluded me.

And then one afternoon, the pieces suddenly started to come together. Excitement rose in me as I read and read, and checked and double-checked, and my heart filled with hope. I'd found it. I was sure.

I got all my information together, ready for Mark to arrive home. I was giddy with excitement. He came through the door, and I didn't even wait for him to set down his bags.

'I've found it!' I blurted out. 'I've found it! Come and have a look.'

He rushed over to join me on the couch, and I flicked through screens on my computer as I ran through all my findings from the day.

'It's Tanzania,' I said. 'It's perfect. It's politically safe, loads of expats live there, there are a few international schools that we could apply to work at, and their laws fit with ours. We could live, work and adopt from Tanzania. But here's the best part...'

I flicked to the next screen.

'I found this website for a baby home in Tanzania. It's called Forever Angels Baby Home, and this amazing woman, Amy, runs it. She keeps a blog, and I've spent hours today reading through it. Her thoughts and ideas about adoption are just like ours. She documents every child that comes in, and the lengths she goes to reunite children with their families is incredible. She works with the Police and Social Welfare and her own team, and they do everything possible to track a child and their family and offer help to allow them to keep their babies. It's incredible work.'

'Wow,' Mark said, trying to take it all in, 'This looks amazing!'

We scrolled through Amy's blog and read together. The stories and images broke our hearts. We read story after story of malnourished babies entering the baby home, and their transformation was breathtaking. Skeletal babies became chubby toddlers in their care. Some were only there briefly until the family was able to manage or a caregiver was found. Others were there indefinitely, their families never found. Some were reunited quickly after becoming lost, their relieved parents taking them home again. And some, after exhaustive searches turned up nothing, were adopted into new families. These were the exceptions, though, and it was clear Amy's priority was reunification of family.

We were thrilled with this discovery and filled with hope that we'd found a lead we could now follow. We were still in the dream phase, imagining and hoping what might be possible. Now it was time to make it a reality.

I set about checking through the legalities, reading late into the night while my family slept soundly. I obtained copies of the Australian adoption law and the Tanzanian adoption law and combed through both. I couldn't find another Australian family who had adopted from Tanzania, and this concerned me a little. Was it not possible? Or just not attempted? I couldn't see any reason the law of either country would prohibit it, provided we met the criteria at each step of the process. I sought legal advice to be sure, and I called the Australian embassy and talked it through with them. There seemed to be no obstacles, so long as we met the requirements along the way. There were many requirements along the way—it was clear it would be an intense and thorough process—but it was possible.

It was definitely possible.

Chapter 6

Hope

"We need hope like we need air."
—BRENÉ BROWN

Babu and Bibi considered their options for help. Where could they go? Who would be able to guide them? Especially concerned for the health of the twins, they went to the hospital. They proceeded through the back and forth of registration. They must open a file at window one, pay the fee at window two, and a long queue stretched in front of each window. Babu scraped together his remaining coins at window two. It wasn't enough. He tried to explain the situation, his voice drowned out by the screams of the hungry twins. The woman at window two accepted his offering and waved him on to window three to collect his receipt. Then back to window one, to wait in line again, and hand in his receipt.

Now they sat in the crowded waiting room. The chairs were full, and the walls and floor lined with others already waiting. The room was full of pain, of struggle, of hope for an answer. Babu and Bibi tried in vain to comfort the three children as the hours passed and the hunger deepened. Finally, their names were called, and a greying Tanzanian man led them along the hall.

'The children are sick?' the doctor asked, looking them over.

'My son has abandoned them and left them with us,' Bibi began. 'This one, he is not growing, and these twins are born too small. We can't feed them. They scream for milk, but we don't have anything to feed them.'

'You're telling me you don't have food,' the doctor began, 'but I can't help you with that. We don't provide food at the hospital. Are they sick?'

'They will not survive without food,' Babu said. 'They are not sick, they are starving.'

The doctor looked over the three.

'Babu,' he began, 'these children are not going to survive. These twins will not last even a few days. They are too premature, and you have no way to feed them.'

'And this one,' the doctor continued, 'he has been malnourished for a long time already. He may live a few more months if you can share your food with him, but I can see you don't have enough for yourself even, so how can you feed him?'

'What can we do for them, doctor?' Bibi pushed. 'You must help us!'

'There is nothing I can do for you. They don't need a doctor, or any medicine, they need food. I'm sorry, but I can't help you with that.'

Babu and Bibi left, deflated. Bibi tried again to give the twins some crushed rice paste. The twins refused it and screamed in frustration.

'We'll go to Social Welfare,' Babu suggested.

'What will they do for us there?' Bibi replied. 'They won't give us food either.'

'We have to try,' said Babu. 'There's nowhere else to turn.'

They left the hospital and walked for an hour and a half until they reached the office for Social Welfare. They had never been here before and were unsure exactly what the office was for. They joined the end of another long queue, this one snaking out the door and around the corner. Waiting with them were many women with young children on their knees or tied to their backs—each with their own story of desperation. The queue moved slowly. A woman in the queue in front watched on as Babu and Bibi struggled with the children. Realising the peril of the situation, she offered Bibi some tea. Bibi dripped it carefully into the mouths of the tiny twins, attempting again to alleviate their hunger.

When their turn came, Babu and Bibi walked into the small office. They were greeted by a stern, middle-aged Tanzanian woman named Mama Manessa. The deep crease between her eyebrows told the story of the many concerning cases that had come through her office door, not just today, but for years.

Bibi once again explained the situation and implored Mama Manessa to help. Mama Manessa sat back in her chair.

'What is it you think I can help you with?' she asked.

'We don't know what else to do,' Bibi said. 'The hospital won't help us, we can't feed them. What can we do?'

'What did the hospital tell you?' Mama Manessa asked.

'The doctor said they will all die,' Babu replied. 'But how can we just take them home and wait for them to die? We won't accept that. You must help us.'

'You know,' Mama Manessa began, 'in Tanzania it is illegal to abandon a child. Now these babies have been left to you, you must care for them, or you will be jailed.'

'How can we care for them?' asked Bibi, becoming more agitated. 'Listen to them scream! I can't feed these babies. No one will help us. We are here to save them, and you must help us.'

Mama Manessa again leant back in her chair. Her many years in this role, hearing stories like these, had desensitised her to the pain of those who came into the office each day. But there was something about this story that resonated with her. She found herself unable to send them away.

'There is one place that may be able to help,' Mama Manessa began. 'An orphanage that can sometimes care for babies in circumstances like these. But they are full, and I cannot place another child with them. However, I will call and see if they can come to your home and bring some formula milk for you.'

Mama Manessa picked up the phone and, after a short conversation, she placed the receiver down and turned back to Babu and Bibi.

'She can help you with a small amount of formula milk,' Mama Manessa said. 'She will come to your home this afternoon and show you how to prepare the milk and bottle-feed the babies. Now, you know, formula milk is very expensive in Tanzania, and she can't give you a lot, so you will have to find work and find another way to feed them all.'

'Thank you, Mama Manessa, thank you very much,' Bibi said.

Babu and Bibi rose to leave and walked to the door, relieved to know they had a reprieve, if only for a day.

'Mama Manessa?' Babu asked, turning back briefly. 'What's her name?'

'Who?' replied Mama Manessa.

'The lady coming to help us. What's her name?' Babu asked again.

'Amy,' Mama Manessa replied. 'Her name is Amy.'

Chapter 7

The Next Right Thing

"Hope begins in the dark, the stubborn hope that if you just show up and try to do the right thing, the dawn will come."
—ANNE LAMOTT

Amy bounced side to side in the seat as her small 4WD lurched along the worn dirt road. During the wet season, the rain fell onto the hard land, forming thin rivers that carved deep crevasses in the roads. These roads were travelled mostly by foot, as residents of these areas didn't own cars. And today the roads were unforgiving as Amy pressed on in search of Babu and Bibi's house. Her sister, Zoe, sat beside her. Zoe was visiting from the UK and had agreed to help with this unusual visit.

Babu and Bibi stood out the front, waiting hopefully for their guests. Amy and Zoe travelled as far as possible by car, then parked when the road thinned too much to allow them to pass. They continued on foot. Unsure of exactly where to go, they considered asking some neighbours, but then the screams of newborn babies reached their ears. They followed the piercing sound to find Babu and Bibi.

Amy was familiar with the hardships facing so many families in Tanzania. She had moved here from the UK with her husband Ben seven years ago, originally as a schoolteacher. But her heart pulled her in a different direction. Ben and Amy adopted their first child after arriving in Tanzania, and through this process became aware of the dire hardship facing so many mothers and babies. Amy founded a baby home soon after this to provide care for abandoned babies. She named it Forever Angels Baby Home, and it became a sanctuary and a lifeline for the poorest of the poor in Tanzania. Amy's compassion, determination, strength and persistence made her a powerful force in this city. When all other options for a family failed, there was Forever Angels. When a child was found abandoned on the side of the road, there was Forever Angels. When a mother died in childbirth, leaving a baby without milk, there was Forever Angels. And on this day, when Babu and Bibi had exhausted all other options, there was Forever Angels.

Amy and Zoe greeted Babu and Bibi and entered the single room that was their home. It looked like many others Amy had encountered; it was small, dark and crowded. Every possession Babu and Bibi owned was on view, their few cooking and washing items pushed back against the wall. Amy carried with her a small supply of powdered baby formula and some bottles. She planned to teach Babu and Bibi how to boil their water to clean it, sterilise the bottles, prepare the formula and feed the newborns. Assessing the situation, she became quickly aware that this was not going to work. Babu and Bibi had not been able to work today, so they had no money for charcoal. Without charcoal, they could not make a fire. Without fire, they could not boil water. Without boiled water, they could not make clean formula, and the babies would die anyway.

Amy had come with two bottles prepared, knowing the newborns would need feeding immediately. She and Zoe carefully cradled one of the twins each and began to feed them. Although Amy was used to tiny babies coming through the baby home, she was surprised by how minute they were. Gently cradling one of the twins in her arms, she lifted the bottle to his tiny mouth, and he guzzled and spluttered, finally feeling his tiny tummy fill up with milk. Zoe did the same, the little girl in her arms gratefully drinking. The room became quiet, the newborn screams finally silenced, and a wave of relief swept over Babu and Bibi. Knowing their tiny tummies wouldn't hold much, and being careful not to overfeed them, Amy and Zoe finished feeding the babies as they drifted off to sleep, exhausted after the trauma of their last 24 hours.

Amy's mind had been racing through any options and ideas she could think of to help this family. Their immediate needs should be addressed first. Babu, Bibi and the little boy quietly waiting by the door still hadn't eaten today. Amy called an older neighbourhood child over and sent him off with some money to purchase some charcoal and enough food for a meal.

'Babu,' Amy began, 'Mama Manessa has asked me to bring you this formula milk and teach you how to prepare it. It's very important that the water must be boiled until it's clean, and the bottles boiled too, so the babies don't pick up any germs. Do you think you can manage that if I show you how?'

'We can do our best, but we don't have charcoal every day. How are we going to work and look after these babies?' Babu asked. 'I don't know how we can manage.'

'I'm afraid I don't know either,' Amy replied.

While they waited on the neighbourhood boy to return, Amy and Zoe stepped outside and began talking through the situation.

CHAPTER 7

'How is this going to work?' Amy began. 'There's no way the babies can survive here.'

'I can't see how Babu and Bibi can possibly keep everything sterile in this environment,' Zoe replied.

'Yes, and even the smallest contamination will be enough to kill them. They aren't strong enough to fight off any infection or bacteria.'

'And how can Babu and Bibi go to work?' asked Zoe. 'They can't take the children with them. At least one of them will need to stay home to feed the babies, and the other can't crush enough rock alone to provide for the family.'

'Yes, I know,' Amy sighed. 'I really don't think there's much hope for them at all.'

The neighbourhood boy returned, and Bibi began making a meal.

'Amy, don't we sometimes look after babies at the baby home for a short period of time until the parents are able to care for them again?' Zoe asked.

'Yes, sometimes we do,' replied Amy. 'Usually in cases where the mother has died in childbirth and the father can't feed the baby, and will lose his job if he stays home, and the whole family would then be unable to eat.'

'Well, isn't this a similar situation?' Zoe pushed.

'Yeah, I know, but I can't take any more babies. We are already overfull, and Mama Manessa has to give permission for every child who comes into Forever Angels. She hasn't sent me here to take in the babies, just to bring milk for them.'

'Well, Mama Manessa isn't here!' Zoe said. 'She can't possibly expect us to leave them here. Anywhere else in the world these babies would be in intensive care in a hospital!'

'Yes, but we aren't anywhere else. We are here. And Mama Manessa constantly reminds me that we can't help them all.'

'Mama Manessa will just have to understand. You've helped her out by coming here, and now it's in your hands. They're only tiny—they won't take up much space!' pleaded Zoe. 'We'll just explain to Mama Manessa later.'

Amy loved her sister; they shared the same passion for helping those in need, and they were a great team. Despite her hesitation, Amy agreed with Zoe. She knew taking the babies to Forever Angels was their only hope for survival. It was the only hope for the whole family.

Amy and Zoe stepped back inside the small room as Bibi was finishing up preparing the meal. Amy looked again at the little boy sitting at the door. He looked no more than six months old, although she knew he must be older. He stared blankly out the door, his eyes vacant, his face immobile. The skin on his arms was loose and wrinkled, and his thin legs folded up underneath him had clearly never held his weight. His belly was swollen and protruding, although it contained no food. He had remained here in this same position for the duration of their visit.

'Amy,' Bibi began, 'we thank you very much for bringing milk today, but what are we going to do to survive? Where else can we go for help? We don't want to abandon our grandchildren, but we can't continue like this. What can we do?'

Amy took a deep breath, knowing her heart wouldn't let her walk away.

'Well,' she began, 'there is a way we could help, but I don't have permission from Mama Manessa yet, so I really shouldn't be offering this, but I don't see any other option.'

'Please,' Bibi replied. 'Please, anything you could do.'

'Sometimes we take in babies at the baby home for a short period of time—just until the families can cope with raising them, and the children are strong enough to survive the hardship of life here, and then the babies come home again,' Amy said.

'Oh yes,' Bibi said. 'Please, you must take them. They might survive with your help.'

'It would only be for a few months, and then they would return to you,' Amy explained, 'and you would be able to come and visit them at the baby home, so they maintain a relationship with you, and know you when you bring them home again.'

'Could you take all of them?' Babu asked.

'No,' Amy replied. 'I can only take the twins. I'm sorry, but I am already full and really shouldn't take any of them. In fact, Mama Manessa may send them straight back to you tomorrow. At least the older boy is eating solids, and you can take him to work with you. He will sit and watch while you work, and you will be able to earn enough to eat. I know it will be very hard on you, but this is the best I can do.'

'We are so grateful,' Babu said, his eyes starting to brim with tears. Hope was rising in him, a small ray of light emerging through the dark fog of the past few days. It was an unimaginable pain they were living, watching their grandchildren starve before their eyes. And at this moment, relief rushed over him. There was a chance the babies would live.

Amy talked through the details of this arrangement with Babu and Bibi: she would take the babies now, so she could feed them every hour through the night, and they agreed to meet together with Mama Manessa the following day.

CHAPTER 7

Amy cradled the babies in her arms and looked again at their tiny faces. They were gorgeous and still sleeping. She looked across at the little boy in the doorway. Her heart hurt for him, too. He would have to be strong enough, brave enough to face the reality of life in poverty. If he survived, it would be a miracle. But there was another factor at play that Amy had learned through all her years caring for abandoned children—although he wasn't coming to the security of the baby home, he would keep something the twins would lose. He would keep the loving care of his grandparents.

Chapter 8

Lift-off

"I've heard tell that what you imagine sometimes comes true."
—GRANDPA JOE, *CHARLIE AND THE CHOCOLATE FACTORY*

Back in Australia, our decision to move to Africa was met with some interesting reactions from our family and friends, and rightly so. This had come out of nowhere. We had two small children, and it seemed like a wild thing to do. It was a shock to hear we wanted to move so far away. Many were concerned about safety, but mostly our friends and family just loved us and were going to miss us. It was bittersweet to share excitement about a new adventure, and sadness at the thought of leaving.

We began applying for jobs at different international schools—primarily for Mark as a maths teacher. He was given a number of interviews, and the process was both thrilling and gut-wrenching. He did interviews over Skype, and I giggled at him sitting on the lounge wearing his shirt and tie on top, visible to his potential employer, and tracksuit pants on the bottom, out of sight. Mark is an amazing teacher, and I knew any school would be lucky to have him. But most of the international schools taught a different system to the one Mark was teaching, so he was a risk to hire. The stakes were high for us, and our hopes pinned on success in one of these interviews.

Professionally, I worked as a child and adolescent counsellor. I'd worked in schools, jails and community organisations, and loved my work dearly. Childhood trauma is a special area of interest for me, and helping small people face big challenges is my passion. My students inspired me with their determination, and witnessing them heal and transform was an incredible privilege that I treasured dearly. Although we looked for school counsellor jobs, they were rare, and finding a maths teacher position for Mark was much more likely.

After a few knockbacks for Mark, we started to worry we might not find an opportunity for work. There was one school in particular that we hoped for—it was in the same town as the baby home and seemed like a perfect fit for us. We prayed and hoped and put everything we had into Mark's application.

We didn't get it. And we were devastated. We wanted it so badly, and it just wasn't happening. We had to start considering we might not get to go, and it knocked the wind out of our sails completely. Then a few weeks later, another ad appeared. It was for an international school that was, unfortunately, on the other side of the county to the baby home—but it was still in Tanzania. We both applied—Mark for teaching high school maths, and me for the school counsellor position and a job as a boarding parent. The school looked great for us—it was a secure campus, we could live on-site, and the salary package meant we could afford a life there.

We interviewed for the jobs over Skype; we sent off our references and paperwork, and we prayed and waited. It was an excruciating wait. This was the last school we could apply to as there are only a few international schools in Tanzania, and no others were hiring. This was our last hope to make this crazy plan happen.

We checked our email constantly, waited on phone calls that didn't come, and agonised over if or when we should call the school ourselves. Once it was well past the given timeframe for a response, and we hadn't heard either way, we decided we should call. Maybe they were having a problem with calling our mobiles from Tanzania. Maybe they'd tried to get through but couldn't. Maybe things just happened slowly in Tanzania. We didn't want to be pushy, but we didn't want to let the opportunity go either. I came home from work one afternoon to find Mark crouched on the coffee table in a little ball of stress. He'd called the school. It didn't go well. They hadn't been trying to contact us. They just hadn't got around to completing their process yet. Mark regretted the call, fearing it made him seem pushy and impatient.

And then, after a long enough wait to make us assume we had missed out, we got our jobs. We jumped and squealed and danced around the lounge room, and hugged each other tight. Then we screamed and danced some more, and laughed and pinched ourselves and double-checked we weren't dreaming. It was hard to believe, but it was really happening—we were going to Tanzania!

Getting these jobs then set into motion the mammoth task of picking up our life and moving it across the world. The months that followed were a flurry of organisational tasks and logistical nightmares. But the excitement within us could not be dampened, and we pushed onwards.

We packed up our home, gave away or lent out anything we could, and locked up the rest of our furniture and belongings in storage. We packed boxes with the essentials we thought we would need in Tanzania and had them shipped ahead of us. How on earth we could know what we might need, or not need, in our new country was an impossible and amusing task.

Mark finished up work, reluctantly leaving his Year 12 students before their final exams. We checked and double-checked that we had all the documents we would need for our travel, our new employment, and our adoption process. I'm a checklist kind of girl, and I had a list for everything. One by one, I checked the items off my list.

Our last few days in Australia were a mad rush of final tasks, peppered with goodbye meals and teary farewells. It came down to the wire—Mark was literally running through town on our last day, sorting international drivers' licences and trying to complete the final tasks before take-off.

After an absolute whirlwind few days, we found ourselves sitting at the airport, surrounded by family, with nothing to do but say goodbye. A mess of conflicting emotions flooded us—the excitement of our upcoming adventure was intoxicating, but there was very real pain in leaving our loved ones, and especially in taking our children far from their grandparents. In the bustling airport food court, we pulled tables together and sat down for one final coffee. Jackson and Jemima gave each grandparent a children's book—one half of a matching pair. The kids had the other book packed with them, so they could share bedtime stories with their grandparents on Skype, each with their own copy of the book in hand. We hugged and cried and hugged again, then gathered our bags and walked through to our gate.

We stood at the window, watching baggage handlers load final items onto the aircraft that would carry us to our new life. A 27-hour trip from Australia to Tanzania ahead of us, with a one-year-old and a four-year-old, a strange assortment of belongings; and our hopes and dreams for expanding our family and sharing a great adventure clutched tightly in our hopeful little hearts.

We were off!

Chapter 9

Shanty Town

"I always get where I'm going by walking away from where I have been."
—A. A. MILNE, *WINNIE THE POOH*

Our journey to Tanzania was surprisingly smooth. Jemima slept most of the way, thanks largely to the baby bassinet hanging precariously from the front of the bulkhead in front of my chair, which was a godsend. The small rectangular cot was barely bigger than her, but she curled herself up like a cat and snoozed her way across the Indian Ocean. Her peaceful slumber was a shock, since she hated sleep, and a blessing for the poor souls in the seats surrounding us. Jackson happily watched movies and enjoyed the adventure of being on an aeroplane. Mark and I finally exhaled. After a frenzied few weeks, we were sitting down at last, with nothing more to do. I squeezed his hand in mine and closed my eyes.

There was no direct route to travel from Australia to Tanzania—it required three flights, no matter which way we chose to travel. We travelled from Sydney to Dubai, then through Nairobi and finally to Kilimanjaro in Tanzania.

Upon landing at Kilimanjaro airport, we collected our bags and stood together around our luggage trolley. I looked up at Mark. This was it. The four of us, and our four bags—all we needed in the world was right here. What lay before us was completely unknown, but the thrill of the adventure was intoxicating. Mark and I grinned at each other, squeezed the kids into a group huddle, then walked out of the airport and into our new life, hoping like hell that someone was there to collect us.

We were overjoyed to find there actually was someone waiting for us, and we were greeted at the airport by Peter, another staff member from our new school. As Peter and Mark loaded our luggage onto the roof of his Land Rover, I took in my first few moments on African soil. The air smelt different—it was earthy and sweet and dusty, and I closed my eyes to breathe in and try to identify the scents that I was yet to recognise. It was warm, despite the late hour, which thrilled me. It was after 10pm local time, and completely dark. I was struck immediately by how different the 'dark' was. In the absence of streetlights, or even the lights from homes or businesses in the surrounding area, it really was pitch black. I could see very little beyond the Land Rover in the car park, and I wondered what new sights the dark concealed.

With our car loaded and the kids buckled in, we were off. Peter's car had headlights, of course, which illuminated the road ahead, but looking out the windows to the side, there was nothing but deep, endless darkness to see. Looking ahead, on the other hand, was highly entertaining. Despite the dark, the roads were alive with people walking from place to place. There were donkeys hauling heavy loads on trolleys, there were men pulling rickety timber wagons piled high with anything from furniture to sticks, there were women chatting together with babies strapped tightly to their backs, and even the occasional child walking alone beside the road. *Where are they going?* I wondered. *And how can they see anything in the dark!*

It was clear from the start that life was about to change, and it was thrilling. At times, a little too thrilling. After travelling for an hour or so, a small truck travelling from the opposite direction suddenly swerved in front of Peter's car, making a U-turn in front of us. Peter slammed on his brakes, pulled off the road to the left to avoid colliding with the truck, and we lurched up a steep embankment. The truck sped off in front, and we lurched back around and rejoined the road.

'Woah!' Mark breathed, 'What was that guy doing?'

'Yeah,' Peter said. 'You've gotta learn to expect the unexpected. Driving around here is an extreme sport.'

We were anxious to see our new home, as we had not seen any photos of it yet. We had been told the homes provided by the school were modest but comfortable, and we wondered exactly what that meant. The school was located in a suburb named Shanty Town, which sounded slightly concerning, but as we neared our new home, we turned onto Shanty Town Road and found it was a sealed road with gorgeous Jacaranda trees growing along each side and meeting in the middle to form a canopy high above the street. This was clearly not a shanty town after all, and even just by Peter's headlights, we could see paved driveways leading to brick homes.

We turned into the school driveway and paused in front of a tall, metal gate. Peter honked his horn, awaiting action of some kind. A school *askari* (guard) scurried out, looking sleepy, and he opened the gate to allow us in. A second *askari* jumped into action and opened a boom gate immediately in front of the metal gate, by leaning his full body weight onto the heavily weighted end of the boom. The first *askari* ran ahead to the second boom gate, just five metres past the first, and similarly jumped onto the boom, like a teenager riding a shopping trolley, causing the gate to open and allow us further into the school. I was immediately pleased by the level of security on campus, even if the *askaris* were half-asleep. It was almost midnight, after all.

A short drive through the campus along a gravelly road and we pulled up in a small gravel parking area in front of our new home. A sprawling single-level boarding house stretched before us, painted white with beautiful large timber windows and a tall jacaranda tree that reached its arms over the dark green roof. A side-section extended to the right, and this would be our new home.

We were pleasantly surprised when we entered. It was larger than we expected, with a lounge room big enough for board games, reading and dancing, a dining room with an eight-seater timber dining table, a small but adequate kitchen, plus three bedrooms and a laundry. The floors were concrete, painted a brownish-orange colour, with a large crack running through the lounge room. There were lovely, large timber windows, which were all fitted with black metal bars for security. There was a welcome hamper in the kitchen with food and other essentials to get us started, and the school had provided bedding and kitchen utensils for us to borrow until we unpacked and the rest of our boxes arrived.

The main bedroom was large, with built-in wardrobes and a king-sized bed with a large mosquito net cascading from a suspended ring in the centre of the room. I sat on the bed and got a shock.

'Oh,' I said to Mark, 'there's no mattress on here.' I lifted up the bed covers to look underneath and was surprised to find there was, in fact, a mattress. It was just so firm it felt like plywood.

'We'll have to add a new mattress to our shopping list!' Mark laughed as he lay down on the wood-mattress. 'What's happening at the end?' he asked as he felt around with his feet. He pulled up the sheets at the end to find the wood-mattress didn't actually extend all the way to the end of the bed, so the last 30 centimetres was stuffed with cushions and pillows to fill the gap. 'Innovative, I guess,' Mark laughed as he tucked the sheets back in.

I tucked the kids into their beds in their new room, across the hall from us. We set up our portable cot for Jemima, tucked Jack into a single bed (thankfully complete with a soft foam mattress), and kissed them goodnight for the first time in our new home, before pulling mosquito nets over them. I stopped for a minute at their door, looking at their trusting little faces. *How does this play out for you guys?* I wondered, fearful for a moment about how challenging this may be for them. It's an incredible responsibility, raising little people, and while we hoped and believed this adventure was going to be valuable for all of us, there were certainly moments of doubt. I closed my eyes and prayed over them, asking (or maybe begging) God to protect and guide us.

Completely exhausted after 30 hours of travel, even the nerves and excitement of the unknown world that lay ahead didn't keep me from sleeping soundly on our cushion-end wood-mattress.

Chapter 10

Washing Up

"Tomorrow is always fresh, with no mistakes in it yet."
—L. M. MONTGOMERY, *ANNE OF GREEN GABLES*

Over the next few days, we slowly learned about our new world. We explored the school campus (now our home) and found it entirely more comfortable and well-equipped than we were expecting. The school campus was quite beautiful, with huge old jacaranda trees forming a canopy over the buildings below. Concrete classroom blocks in long rows stretched out across the grounds, many painted with bright colours or framed with pin boards covered in children's artworks. The campus had a swimming pool, tennis courts and two large sporting ovals. But the most magnificent thing of all was the incredible view of Mount Kilimanjaro towering majestically above the school, its snow-capped peak rising above the cloud line. The sheer scale of its size in comparison to all else made it a commanding presence, and the different shades of light reflecting off its glacial summit gave it a magical beauty. It stopped me in my tracks with every glimpse.

It was an international school, with a diverse population of students from around the world. Many were Tanzanian, children of local professionals who were financially well-off and could afford a private school education for their children. Others were from all over the world. Some were children of expats now living and working in Tanzania, while others had families living back in their home countries.

Mark would be teaching high school mathematics, while I would be running a boarding house that adjoined our own new home, along with working as the school counsellor. Counselling was my love. This role was entirely familiar to me, and I looked forward to getting started with my new clients. My boarding parent role, however, was completely new and I had no idea how it was going to go. The structure suited us well, as Mark would be working during school hours while I was home, and I would start work with the boarding students after school and into the evenings, meaning one of us was always home with the kids. Living on campus gave us lots of great perks—like excellent security, access to the pool, tennis courts and sports fields, and eating our meals with the boarders in the dining hall.

Settling into our new life was wild and wonderful. Everything was different. Foreign. It was exciting and unnerving at the same time. We were navigating a new world where nothing worked the way we were used to. We were the visitors, and we had to learn to adjust and accommodate the way things were done. Usually, this meant slowly. Everything happened slowly. But we enjoyed the challenge and became chameleons—blending into our new environment. Over weeks and months, the change in us was palpable.

Every day there was new learning, and we were putting our foot in it constantly. Trying not to make the same mistake twice became our basic aim, and the days often ended in Mark and I comparing stories of who'd done the dumbest thing that day. Mark took an early lead in this contest, after he met his head of department for the first time, shaking her hand and introducing himself eagerly before feeling the unmistakable sensation of nausea rising suddenly, and turning to vomit in the grass next to her. Something in the water wasn't agreeing with Mark's belly, and he made quite the first impression! But not to be outdone, I was soon to make many blunders of my own.

My boarding house was filled with gorgeous young girls who lived on campus with us, and I tried so hard to get to know each one. There were 30 or so living in the boarding house connected to our home, and another 30 or so living in the dorm across the clearing, which I was also responsible for while on duty. There were a lot of students to get to know, and I wanted to learn their names and as much as I could about them quickly, to show my care for them.

Many of the girls had incredibly intricate designs braided into their hair. I knew nothing about Tanzanian hair, and I marvelled at the varying styles—tiny cornrows curving tightly in spirals, brightly coloured individual braids held in ponytails or flowing freely, stylish soft curls hanging in a long bob, and elegant short-shaved styles that highlighted a classic African silhouette—there was so much variety, and it helped me remember each student. I often went to bed reminding myself of each student's name and hairstyle to make a link that would help me get it right the following day.

Then there was a weekend and lots of the girls went home, or to town and got their hair done. They returned to campus with completely different hairstyles, and I suddenly had no idea who some of them were! I had no idea that many of them were wearing long weaves, which were not their natural hair, or that it was possible to braid long extensions into hair that had only been a few centimetres long the day before. They were beautifully kind to me and had a good laugh at my shocked face before reminding me who they were and teaching me the wonders of African hair.

Countless times, I messed things up. My boarding parent role was testing new parts of me. I loved my boarders and wanted so badly to do a wonderful job. But these kids were different to the students I was used to working with, and it took me time to really understand their experiences and to be the kind of boarding parent they needed.

One evening, as I was walking through the dorm room by room and saying goodnight to the girls, I came into a room with one standing in front of the mirror. She looked disapprovingly at herself as she turned side-on, then flicked around to see herself from the other side.

'Miss Anna!' she moaned. 'Why am I so thin? When is my body going to grow fatter?' I stopped in the doorway, stunned. Never in my years of working with teenage girls in Australia (in the pre-Kardashian era, of course) had I heard one of them complain about being too thin! The sweet, young girl before me was gorgeous—she was 16 years old, and practically Beyoncé. She was tall, curvy and stunningly beautiful. I pulled her into a hug and said, 'You're perfect' as I gave her a squeeze. 'Now, get into bed!'

I began to realise how much I had to learn—how my assumptions about what these students might be thinking, feeling, or going through were often completely off. I needed a lot of time with them to listen and see the world from their perspective before I could be much use to them.

We ate meals in the dining hall, but the students would sometimes make a snack in our boarding-house kitchen. The other boarding parents and I were fighting a constant battle in the dorm with some messy students cooking in the kitchen and leaving their mess everywhere. Most of my dorm was filled with senior boarders, but I also had a group of M1 students in their first year of high school. These sweet girls were only 11 years old and had already been boarding as primary school students. They were impressive in their independence, but nevertheless, they were usually the messiest.

They loved two-minute noodles and would cook them, then leave packets, pots, bowls, forks and stray noodles all over the kitchen. One Saturday, I came into the kitchen to find it a mess and asked the girls to come and clean it up. They looked a little disgruntled, as if they were expecting me to clean it up for them, or to wait for the maid to come and do it. Most of the students were from wealthy families and had grown up with housekeepers who did that. But I wanted them to learn to look after themselves, and it wasn't the cleaner's job to clean up that kind of mess.

The girls came into the kitchen and began cleaning up. I joined in to help them, chatting as we went. One of the students went to the sink to wash up. She turned the tap on just a little, a thin stream of water running limply out of the tap. She picked up a bowl and ran it under the water. Watching her, I thought to myself, *This child has never washed up anything in her life.* Without another moment's thought, I said to her, 'Has no one ever taught you how to wash up? Here, let me show you.'

I proceeded to find the plug, fill the sink with hot, soapy water, put the dirty dishes into the water, wash them, and put them in the dish rack to dry. She watched me as if I was doing the strangest thing. 'I've never washed up like that,' she said. 'I just run things under the tap.' I left the encounter believing I had introduced this child to the *real* way of washing up. Because there was only one way, in my mind, to wash up, and now she knew how to do it properly.

A few weeks later, Mark and I were visiting some American friends for dinner. After the meal, we helped clear the table and take the plates to the kitchen. I'll never forget walking into that kitchen to see one of our friends washing up. He held a plate under a thin stream of water, exactly as my student had done. I stopped in my tracks for a moment and watched to see if he was just rinsing the plates, or if this was, in fact, his way of washing up. He placed the plate on the rack to dry.

'Is that how you wash up?' I asked.

'Uh, yeah,' he said. 'How do you Aussies wash up?' I proceeded to explain the sink—full-of-soapy-water method and he laughed. 'That's kind of weird,' he said. 'Aren't you just washing everything with the same dirty water?'

I was so unnerved by the discovery that not everyone washed up the same way I did that I started asking other expats. A few nights later, we had some friends around to our house. The group included people from countries all over the world. None of them washed up the way I did.

It was such a trivial and ridiculous thing, but it struck me deeply. It intrigued me that I had never thought to imagine there might be another way, or that my way might not be the best way. When I saw someone act differently, my reaction was to correct and teach the *right* way, rather than to take an interest in their way and see what I could learn.

The experience of seeing old things in a new way became a daily occurrence. At first, it was disconcerting. Nothing was predictable. There was no "right way" or "wrong way". It made me realise how much safety I found in familiarity; in believing there was a right way, and that I knew it. My arrogance showed itself to me repeatedly over these first few months, highlighted by the comparative graciousness of those around me. The expat community was so beautiful in its diversity and its curiosity about other cultures and traditions. There was appreciation and interest in the different ways we all approached life, but no judgement. It was refreshing and fascinating.

We found ourselves often in the company of wonderfully intriguing people. Each one had turned up in Tanzania following their own path of adventure, and so any given group of friends was full of people from different cultures with different experiences and faiths. Conversations in groups like these were diverse in content and respectful in approach. The point of a conversation was never to be right or to prove another wrong—it was to learn. To learn about another's thoughts and how they arrived there, to understand a person more deeply and see the world through their eyes for a moment. It didn't mean everyone agreed—far from it! But the point was never to agree, it was to understand. Someone disagreeing with your opinion was not a threat, it was an opportunity to discover more about that person. I enjoyed watching these dynamics play out, and I learned so much as these once-strangers became dear friends.

The next chance I got, I found those lovely noodle-loving students and apologised for the way I had behaved. They graciously forgave me, and we made a new deal—they could wash up however they liked, as long as they washed up!

Chapter 11

A Perfect Storm

"I know up on top you are seeing great sights, but down here at the bottom we, too, should have rights."
—DR SEUSS, *YERTLE THE TURTLE AND OTHER STORIES*

As we slowly settled into our new life, Jackson started pre-school, walking out our front door just 50 metres across the school grounds to arrive at his new classroom. A brightly coloured playground with swings and a slide out the front made it immediately appealing, and a large undercover play area with tables and chairs, wooden blocks, dress-ups and a toy microscope sparked Jackson's interest. We hung up his bag on a bright red hook with his name above it, and he joined his new friends.

Lining up at the classroom door, the students were greeted by their new teacher, Miss Amelia. As she moved down the line of four-year-olds, her kind, joyful face met each child at eye level as she bent down to introduce herself and her puppet monkey, which draped around her shoulders. She tucked her short honey-blonde hair behind her ear as she reached Jackson.

'Hello Jackson, it's so nice to meet you,' she said in her thick Brazilian accent.

'Excuse me,' Jackson jumped right in, 'did you know this is Mount Kilimanjaro on the badge of my school shirt?' Skipping the intros to get straight down to business, he held out his badge to show Miss Amelia. 'And that is actually Mount Kilimanjaro right there, too,' he continued, pointing to the mountain behind him. 'But don't worry, it's a dormant volcano. It's not likely to erupt today.'

Miss Amelia's eyes lit up as he spoke. She was the kind of educator who oozed enthusiasm and joy, and I knew right away she was a perfect match for Jackson. He was inquisitive and intensely interested in everything. The dull or mundane in life was a treasure trove of fascinating learning for him. She valued his love of learning and gave him endless opportunities to grow his mind and ponder his thoughts. Jackson adored her and loved going off to school each day. He talked non-stop and had entertained me from day dot with the hilarious things that came out of his mouth.

Like most four-year-olds, Jackson was full of endless questions. I tried my best to give him satisfactory answers, but quite often his face told me I wasn't hitting the mark. One afternoon, he asked me, 'Mum, what is the internet?' and I rambled on for a while trying to explain. 'But what exactly IS it?' he replied, indicating I was not answering the question to his satisfaction. I had another go and thought I had done an okay job until he came home from school the next day with a textbook from the school library called *The Internet, For Beginners.*

This became a common occurrence. He and I both loved the library, and as his reading improved, so did his memory bank of facts and information, stored forever in his mind, ready to bring out should the right moment present itself. Tanzania was a wonderful place for a mind like his.

Our days were busy and long. An average day for me looked a bit like this:

5:30am—Wake up and get dressed.

5:45am—Open up the boarding house for students who go running before school.

6:00am—Wake up the other boarders, make sure they were up and getting ready.

6:30am—Wake up our kids and get them dressed for the day.

6:40am—Breakfast in the dining hall. Make sure our own kids plus my 30 boarders are dressed, ready for school and in the dining hall on time.

7:30am—School starts. Drop off Jackson at school, check the boarding house is empty.

8:00am–11:30am—Play at home with Jemima.

11:30am—Pick up Jackson from school.

12:00pm—Lunch in the dining hall.

12:30pm—Play at home with Jackson and Jemima.

2:30pm—Mark home from work. I start afternoon duty. Boarders return. Monitor boarding house and activities.

6:00pm—Dinner in dining hall.

7:00pm—Study hall with boarders.

9:00pm—Evening snack for boarders, and free time before bed.

10:30pm—Curfew. Boarders return to boarding house.

10:45pm—Lights out. Lock the dorm.

11.00pm—Go to bed myself.

A few times a week, I would get up once in the night and check the boarders were all still there and hadn't gone out the windows to visit the boys' dorm, pop into town, or roam the school during the night. They were usually all there, sleeping soundly in their beds... but not always!

Never far from our minds, as we settled into our new home, were our hopes for adoption. We continued reading, learning and trying to understand as much as we could about the adoption world, and international adoption in particular, so we were careful to avoid the pitfalls of those who had come before us. Of all the voices on adoption that were out there, the voices of adult adoptees were the most significant to us. We read many personal testimonies of the experiences of others who had been adopted internationally as babies and were moved to tears by the joys and struggles they faced. I'm forever grateful for the strength and vulnerability embraced by these storytellers—to return again to the hard places of their lives, to allow others like me to peer inside and listen to their words of advice and of warning. Their voices shaped our story. Their experiences became our lighthouses—standing strong and tall on the shore, directing our ship away from the dangers of the rocks below, as we sailed on through the foggy night. Ringing loud and clear through every story was one truth—that adoption must only ever be considered as a last resort.

Our great comfort was that Amy held our same convictions about adoption. We had been in contact with her over email for the past few months. She knew we were hoping to adopt a child or a sibling group who had no other alternative to a family but through adoption, and one quiet afternoon I found an email in my inbox from Amy. It told a tragic and moving story that would change my life forever.

There was an elderly couple—Babu and Bibi.

They had an estranged son.

He arrived on their doorstep with a young woman.

In her arms were newborn twins.

In desperation, they left the babies.

They didn't return.

Their story broke my heart. It was a perfect storm of circumstances that let down every member of this family. Poverty. Lack of support. Premature birth. Lack of access to medical care. The trauma of watching children starve. Family separation. And the result was twin babies who lost their biological parents.

Babu and Bibi's strength and persistence to get help had saved their lives, and for the past ten months, the twins had lived at the Baby Home, with Babu and Bibi coming every week to see them. With around-the-clock feeding and care, the tiny preemie babies grew bigger and stronger, ever so gradually, and were now healthy ten-month-olds—sitting, crawling, and pulling themselves up to stand on chubby little legs.

They had all hoped that the babies would soon be able to return to Babu and Bibi, but it had become clear to all that this wouldn't be possible. Bibi had become sick with stomach cancer and did not expect to live beyond the next few years or even months. They wanted their babies to have parents young enough to raise them. Babu and Bibi both loved the babies dearly, but had come to Amy in the months prior and asked her to find a permanent family for them. Amy had resisted, saying she could work with Babu and Bibi to care for them–that she could find a way to support them to keep the babies at home. She even offered them a home to live in and a job at the baby home so they could support and house themselves while they raised the babies. But Babu and Bibi, with tears in their eyes, explained that this may last a year or so, but once they passed away the babies would be orphaned once again. They wanted a family for the babies they loved so dearly.

Amy had spent the past few months working with Social Welfare and the Police, tracing relatives, searching for the biological parents, and attempting to find another solution for these babies. There were no other viable options.

'Please Amy,' they had asked, 'can you find a family that wants them both and will keep them together? They've lost so much, but they could keep each other.'

'I think I may know just the family,' Amy replied.

Chapter 12

Happy Tears

Mad Hatter: "Have I gone mad?"
Alice: "I'm afraid so. You're entirely bonkers. But I'll tell you a secret. All the best people are."
—LEWIS CARROLL, *ALICE IN WONDERLAND*

Jemima and I travelled the winding, bumpy dirt roads from the airport to the baby home. We'd taken a scenic flight across Tanzania from our home in Moshi, over the Serengeti, to Mwanza in the north-west of Tanzania on the shores of Lake Victoria, to visit the baby home and meet the beautiful twins Amy had told us about—Shay (Shalom) and Charlie (Charles). My stomach was twisted in knots. There was so much uncertainty before us. This was a moment I had dreamed of for years, and yet nothing was certain and there were many hurdles still to leap over. Giant hurdles. I squeezed Jemima a little tighter on my lap and tucked my head in beside hers, kissing her chubby little cheek. Her response in the next few minutes and hours was a huge unknown. Was she ready? How would she react to me holding other babies? How would she interact with them herself? How would pursuing this path impact the rest of her life? For now, her response was our litmus test. We knew that if this was going to work for our family it would have to work for all of us. Jackson was ready, and we could see his excitement, but Jemima had always struggled with sharing me. If she wasn't ready, it wasn't the right time for us.

And then there were questions spinning through my mind about the twins. How would I feel seeing them? What if they didn't *feel* like mine? What if they did? I tried to prepare myself for an emotional tightrope walk—balancing precariously between falling in love and keeping a distance that might protect my heart if it all fell through; between hope and self-preservation; between dreams coming true and another let-down.

I paid my taxi driver and stepped out onto the dusty, red earth. With Jemima on my hip, I looked up at the building before me. Forever Angels Baby Home. My mind flicked back for a minute to the first time I'd seen a picture of this place—it seemed a world and a dream away. And now here we were.

Stepping through the front door, we were greeted by the sight of three or four beautiful Tanzanian ladies, with mops and buckets in their hands, dancing and laughing as they cleaned the floor and grooved along to the music flooding the hallway. Their joy was infectious. I grinned, and Jemima giggled as I bounced her on my hip and gave her a spin while we dodged mops and walked towards Amy. Countless emails had been exchanged between us, and it was so wonderful to finally meet. Amy wore a long, patterned skirt with a short-sleeved T-shirt, in keeping with respectful dress for women in Tanzania, her sandy brown hair tied up in a loose bun, and she greeted me with a warm hug, as if we'd been friends for years. We chatted for a while before she said, 'Come on then, let's go meet them.'

We walked outside to an undercover outdoor area, with colourful woven mats covering the concrete floor, and about 15 crawling babies scattered around, chasing toys and clapping their hands to the music. Several Baby Home staff—all Tanzanian mamas—sat around with the babies, singing, beating toy drums and playing. Each of the mamas had two or three babies crawling on their laps, jostling for position. I put Jemima down and watched her closely. She smiled and bounced along to the music and happily found a toy. I scanned the room quickly, looking at each baby, and found Shay. She wore a purple T-shirt and lay with her head on the thigh of the outstretched leg of one of the mamas. The rest of her body was sprawled on the floor, with one thumb in her mouth and her other hand twisting her hair around her fingers. She was so gorgeous. She was little and super-chubby, with big brown eyes and a gummy smile with two bottom teeth peeking out.

Looking across the room, I found Charlie. He was banging a toy drum with a stick at lightning speed and stopped to squeal and look for a reaction from the mama nearest him. He was unbearably cute with a cheeky grin and soft fuzzy hair sticking straight up.

As I watched, another child crawled up and pulled herself up on my leg. I lifted her up and she giggled and kicked her legs with excitement. I looked over at Jemima and waited for her to see me holding this baby. When she saw me, she smiled and said, 'Look Mumma! All the babies!' She tickled one under the chin and giggled. I leant forward to return the little one in my arms to the floor, and as I set her down, the baby cried immediately.

'Mumma,' Jemima said, 'baby sad! Pick up baby!' As I lifted the little girl up again, her cries stopped, and my fears evaporated. Jemima had never let me hold another baby without screaming objections and climbing into my arms herself. But not today. Today she was ready.

Amy was moving a few toys and a mat over to the side, separated a little from the others, and called us over. Jemima and I sat on the mat and Amy brought Shay and Charlie over to sit with us. Jemima crawled over to Shay and said, 'Hello baby!' and planted a soft kiss on her cheek. Shay grinned and Jemima softly patted her back, peering around to look in her eyes. It was a precious moment that has never left me—the beginning of what would become a beautiful friendship.

Charlie crawled over to my lap. He was agile and quick, and cute as a button. He held my hands and pulled himself up to stand in my lap—his strong little legs holding his weight. He looked at me with intense fascination—staring straight into my eyes, as if trying to determine my intentions right then and there. *Don't get too attached. Don't get too attached,* I repeated over and over in my mind, my feeble attempts to guard my heart waning as the minutes passed.

I thought back to the story I had read of the beginning of their life. It was hard to believe these were the same two preemie babies that barely survived. Here they were—strong, healthy, happy and climbing all over me. We sat and played together and as I watched them, I realised they *did* feel like mine. There were babies all over the place, but there was something about these two. A calm settled over me. I had prayed for this moment—that God would show me who my children were, and that I would know it when I saw them. And at this moment, I knew it. There were mountains ahead, and nothing was for certain yet, but with Shay snuggled in my right arm, and Charlie tugging at my left earring, I knew deep in my heart—these were my children.

Later in the afternoon, Jemima and I walked the short distance to Amy's house—not far from the baby home—and sat with her on her front porch. The afternoon heat finally subsided as the light softened. I watched Amy's own five children play together—a few bouncing on the trampoline, one lying on the porch reading, another two giggling and chasing each other. It was a beautiful picture. Jemima wandered around the garden, stopping here and there to pick up something of interest, and Amy and I chatted the afternoon away. I wanted to find out everything I could about Shay and Charlie, to hear the story again, in person, and to ask the myriad of questions that remained in my mind. I could see how much Amy loved Shay and Charlie. She and her team had raised them from tiny babies into bouncing toddlers, and she was deeply connected to them.

I asked Amy to tell me again the story of when she had first met them, and as quickly as she began, she stopped and said, 'Oh, there's actually something I haven't told you about the twins.'

'What's that?' I asked, my hairs standing on end, the familiar fear returning in anticipation of bad news.

'They actually have a brother. He's not much older than they are, and he still lives with Babu and Bibi. He's terribly malnourished and his survival has been uncertain for a long time. We just didn't have space to bring him into the baby home, so we had to leave him behind.'

'They have a brother?' I repeated, trying to take in the story, my mind spinning as to what this might mean.

'Yes. His name is Jabari. Babu and Bibi can't keep him either, and they would like them to stay together, so how would you feel about adopting all three?'

A thousand questions flooded my mind. Of course I wanted to say we would take all three. Our purpose from the beginning was to keep a sibling group together. But that would take our total to five kids altogether. Mark and I had never spoken about having five. In fact, I had always thought parents of five were a little nuts! To me, four kids seemed like a fun, busy family, but five tipped it over the edge. Five was entering crazy land.

There were a thousand things to consider, but the only thought that flooded my mind was '*Mark will never say yes.*'

'Wow,' I spluttered. 'Okay, wow.' I felt like I was pregnant having an ultrasound, and the technician had just told me I was having triplets. 'I need to call Mark; I have no idea what he will think about this.' I asked a few more questions, trying to get enough information to tell Mark, and then made the call. Amy left me alone to speak with him.

'Hi!' he answered the phone with enthusiasm. 'How's it going? I've been dying to hear from you!'

'It's amazing,' I started, 'Everything has been amazing—the twins are gorgeous, and Jemima is so relaxed, and she loves them, and I've had the best day.'

'Oh, that's so wonderful!' Mark replied. 'Tell me all about the kids!' I talked him through our day, describing every detail, knowing he would want to see it all through my eyes. He was as thrilled as I was. So many of our concerns were now calmed.

'So... I'm just at Amy's house and she's been telling me more about their story, and she's told me something pretty huge.'

'What?'

'They have a brother. He's only little, maybe just under two years old. He was left with Babu and Bibi on the same day as the twins, but the baby home couldn't take him. Babu and Bibi still have him, but they can't keep him. He's awfully malnourished and might not survive. They want them all to go to the same home.' I finished and held my breath. I was preparing myself for him to say no. For this to be another dead end, and for us to go back to square one and start again. I squeezed my eyes shut while I waited for him to speak. Quick as a flash, his voice came back.

'Okay, so I guess we're taking three!' he replied. My eyes sprung open and a huge grin spread across my face.

'Really?' I asked, checking that I hadn't imagined his response.

'Of course!' Mark said. 'We can't leave him behind!'

I loved Mark more than ever at that moment. It was the goodness of his heart that I first fell in love with. His rugged good looks helped of course, but his heart was the thing I loved the most. He was just so *good*. This moment reminded me of that again. The whole situation was overwhelming, and big fat tears swelled in my eyes and flooded over.

'Are you sure?' I sniffed. 'He might not survive, and I don't know what to do with a malnourished baby! We'd have five kids! Five! We've never really talked about having five!'

'We'll just give it our best shot,' Mark said. 'We have to at least give that little guy a chance! Whaddya reckon? Can we do five?'

I looked around the garden again, Amy's five little ones still running and playing and giggling in the sun. Jemima wandered among them, her little face lit up as she watched them play.

'You know,' I said, 'I think maybe we can!'

We talked the situation through a little more, and I hung up the phone. I sat back in my chair, trying to take in all that had just happened, tears still sliding down my cheeks. Jemima toddled over to me, and looking at my face, she said, 'You sad, Mumma?'

'No, baby,' I said, scooping her up in my arms, 'I'm not sad. These are Mumma's happy tears. I'm very, very happy.'

Chapter 13

Heart Pieces

"The best and most beautiful things in all the world cannot be seen or even touched—they must be felt with the heart."
—HELEN KELLER

Following the excitement of deciding to adopt all three of the children, a host of questions remained, and the afternoon gave way to early evening as I heard more about the past year for Amy and the twins.

We had come to Amy in the first place because we knew how hard she worked, with Social Welfare and the Police, to find the very best outcome for each child in her care. In the year the twins had spent at the baby home, Amy had worked tirelessly to chase any path that would lead to a permanent home. She had tracked down distant relatives and followed every lead.

From her research, Amy had found three possible options. The children could return to Babu and Bibi, they could go to live with their only other relative, Aunt Git, or they could be adopted into a new family.

Amy had first tried to find a way for it to work with Babu and Bibi. She had offered them a quiet job at the baby home, and a house nearby to live in, if they would take the twins back to live with them. It must have been an enticing offer. Babu and Bibi were living a hard life—their work was physically exhausting and painful, they struggled to make enough money for food, and they lived in a single room. Amy's offer would provide comfort, relief, and security for them for the rest of their lives. But they turned it down. They turned it down because they knew they were elderly and could not care for the children long term. In a few years, they would pass away, and the children would be left alone again. Once more, their dedication to their grandchildren came first, and they turned down Amy's offer, knowing the children needed parents and a home that would last.

Amy then investigated the children's only other relative, Aunt Git. She lived in a rural village, hours away. Amy learned that she was a single mum with 15 of her own children. Fifteen! She was struggling to survive as it was, with only one income and so many children to feed, but Amy still asked her if she would be able to take the children. She declined. Taking three more would leave her with 18 children. She knew she could not feed any more.

With the first two options ruled out, all that was left for the three children was adoption. Amy, like us, firmly believed in adoption, but only when there was no possible way for a child to stay with family. In this case, after a year of searching, adoption was the only remaining path.

Listening to Amy tell these stories and discuss the lengths she had gone to, to find any other path, gave me so much confidence that the children were genuinely in need of adoption. This was vital to us.

Jemima and I spent a little more time in the baby home before returning home. It was the kind of place I'd always imagined I would love. I had always loved babies and being around small children. I babysat as a teenager and worked as a nanny while I was at university. But although I tried to convince myself otherwise, the truth was that being in the baby home was both beautiful and excruciating for me. The quality of care that was provided was exceptional, the staff were amazing, and these little ones were being looked after to the highest standard. But it broke my heart that each little one here didn't have a mum or dad to call their own. I just couldn't fathom how this was possible—how this was not a front-page news story that required immediate action around the world. Had we just come to accept that this was okay? That some kids didn't have families, and that was fine?

There are certain things in the world that just strike a chord in a particular way for a particular person, and this was it for me. Babies without families. It was so painful. I'm sure it was compounded for me by being a mum to young children. I knew the depth and breadth of what these little souls really needed. I knew the importance of attachment, of how vital it was in the early days, weeks, months, years and forever. I knew that having someone hold them, stare into their eyes with joy and connection, and lovingly meet their needs was the only way to grow healthy little people.

So, sitting in a room full of babies, with big deep brown eyes, dimpled smiles and cheeky grins, I couldn't help but wonder what the future held for each one. I looked over at Jemima again. She was swaying side to side with a bounce, tilting her head one way and then the other to the beat of the soft drum being played by one of the mamas. As I watched her, I wondered what it would take for her to find herself in the situation these babies were in. It was so far from her reality, and the thought of it made the extent of the poverty faced by these children so clear.

If, by some tragedy, Mark and I were not able to care for Jemima, I could name a hundred people who I knew would step in and raise her. Probably more. For her to end up abandoned, it would mean everyone we knew must also lack the resources to raise her, or that we were so isolated that we lacked the connection and support of family or friends who would love her. These babies were all in this very situation. How could it be that there was not one adult in their life that could step up and take them in? This was poverty in the flesh.

Jemima and I flew back across the country to our home, but a little bit of my heart was now left behind in Mwanza. I had done quite poorly at my attempts to prevent getting attached. The trip had confirmed so much for me. Jemima was ready. She and I both had an obvious connection with Shay and Charlie, and even with the crazy bombshell news of a third child (beautiful little Jabari) thrown in, it all somehow felt right. Although there was bound to be a long, difficult process ahead, I felt a peace that this was it, and from this point on, it felt as though half my heart and mind was with me in Moshi, and the other half was wandering around without me in Mwanza.

It was a lot to prepare for without a scrap of certainty. We were nowhere close to this being a sure thing. We were not even in the same galaxy. There were a zillion possible obstacles, and it felt silly and unwise to place too much hope in this possibility. And yet, those little faces stayed with me and were never far from my mind as our life went on.

Walking across the school grounds that evening, I stopped in my tracks once more as the clouds had lifted and there was Kilimanjaro towering above me, with an orangey-pink glow reflecting from a fresh dump of snow on her peak. I stood for a moment, just absorbing the beauty before me and contemplating the verse that always came to my mind as I beheld this view:

I lift up my eyes to the mountains.
From where does my help come?
My help comes from the Lord
The maker of heaven and earth.
Psalm 121:1–2

Chapter 14

Hot Springs

"There's something about everything that you can be glad about, if you keep hunting long enough to find it."

—ELEANOR H. PORTER, *POLLYANNA*

I was slowly adjusting to my role as boarding parent. As I got to know and understand my boarders more, I relaxed into the role a little and felt slightly more like I might be able to do this job.

One of my responsibilities was to organise weekend activities for the boarders to do on weekends. I worked every second weekend and had to produce a full program of events for them to enjoy, from Friday midday until Sunday evening. Being new, I asked around to see what had been done in the past, and what was typical for a weekend at boarding school. The students came up with a great list for me, with some new ideas and some old favourites that they'd like to do again. They told me there was a natural hot spring nearby, where they visited each year to swim. I checked it out with other staff, and it all looked great. So, on my first weekend responsible for the program, I booked a trip to the hot springs. I booked buses, enlisted the help of Sabini—the school swimming teacher/lifeguard, and looked forward to the adventure ahead.

Not long before we left, I was sitting at lunch in the dining hall when the Head of Campus casually mentioned to watch out for crocodiles. Naturally, I assumed he was joking and had a giggle. He didn't join me. He looked seriously at me and said, 'Oh no, I'm not joking. A few years ago, we lost a volunteer at the hot springs.'

'What?' I asked, astounded. 'What do you mean 'lost'?'

'I mean a school volunteer was taken by a crocodile at the hot springs and died,' he said simply.

I sat with my mouth agape.

'This same hot springs?' I asked, 'The same one I'm about to take 100 children to?'

'Yes,' he answered. 'Same one.'

Moments like this were surreal, and all too frequent. Nothing in my experience could make sense of what I was hearing. I came from a world of risk assessments, safety checks, and filling in forms to mitigate even small risks. And here, on this strange new planet, there was none of that. But there were crocodiles! And eaten volunteers! And it didn't seem to register as a problem!

'So…' I began, searching for words, 'we still go back there? Even though we've lost someone before?'

'Well, yes, we do go back,' he answered, sensing my confusion. 'There really aren't that many places to go. So, if we stopped going everywhere after an incident, we'd be left with nowhere to go.'

I stopped short of asking what other 'incidents' had occurred that I might want to be aware of, but I did ask what we might do to make sure no one else was eaten.

'Oh, well you're taking Sabini,' he said. 'He'll climb a tree and watch out for crocodiles.'

Needless to say, I was intensely uneasy about the whole thing. I asked around to see what other staff thought about all this—and they were all equally relaxed. 'Yeah, that was awful,' was a typical response, 'but I've been twice and never seen a crocodile.'

I wasn't convinced. Nevertheless, we corralled 100 students onto two buses, and off we went to the hot springs. Sabini climbed a tree and watched for crocs, and the kids swam and climbed and dived into the water without a care in the world. I, on the other hand, was terrified the entire time. Terrified, and yet somehow enjoying myself immensely at the same time. This place was magical. Miles from anywhere, surrounded by the African bush, it was a scene straight out of *The Jungle Book*. Tall trees with arching branches, hanging vines, and crystal clear, naturally warm water. Children swung from the vines, flipping in the air before splashing gleefully into the deep pool, challenging themselves to climb higher and jump further, and revelling in the beauty of their surroundings. I got lost in the joy of witnessing the raw, free, adventurous life these students were living, and then the danger of crocodiles would flash back into my mind and the terror would return. I counted children and counted again, and the relief I felt when we got back on that bus, with all students accounted for, was immense!

This was boarding life. It was strange and wonderful, and then more strange and more wonderful. We lived on a whole new set of rules, and I struggled often. It was hard to let go of the familiar. My challenge became to pick my battles—to fight for the things I really thought were important, and to let go of the others. Sometimes, the lines were blurry. Was it really important? Or just my preferred way? Is there a great reason it's done differently here? Or is the school just behind the times? Every situation was different, and it stretched me in many ways to navigate the new waters we sailed.

Our new school took just as much getting used to. Everything was done so differently, and we really needed to just stand back and absorb the way things were and give everything a chance.

One afternoon, Jackson came home chatting about the triathlon that was coming up. I commented that this must be for the older kids. Jackson was four and was one of the only students in the class who could swim without inflatable arm bands, and even then—he could only swim about 20 metres. He was convinced it was for the entire school, and I let him chat about it, sure in my mind he was mistaken.

Once again, it was I who was mistaken. The triathlon was in fact for the entire school. Every child, from three years and up, would participate. I grinned when I heard this news—I was starting to enjoy watching on and seeing how the school would navigate this.

The triathlon day was beautifully warm and sunny, and the kids sat excitedly, dressed in their swimsuits, ready to race. There was a practice run, so the students could run through the course and make sure they knew what to do and where to go. I watched in amazement as the three- and four-year-olds lined up to practice. It was the most precious thing. They lined up with their floaties, kickboards, and whatever they needed to use to get across the pool. There were teachers in the pool ready to carry the ones who couldn't swim at all.

And off they raced. Giggles and splashing and flotation devices of all kinds filled the pool. Jackson doggy-paddled his way across with a great grin. Out they climbed and ran with their chubby little legs through the ropes, around the playground, and over to the tennis courts. There, a whole row of tricycles awaited them, and they jumped on and scooted their way around the court to the finish line, grinning from ear to ear. I was so impressed. There was not a nervous, reluctant child in sight—everyone participated, in whatever way they could, with whatever support would help them succeed. I was an instant fan. There was no pressure, no intense competition, no anxious parents barking tips at their kids. There was just the fun of the race and the challenge for the kids.

As the other age groups warmed up, Jackson and his friends played in the grass beside the pool, while the parents chatted next to them. I heard a loud gasp followed by a scream and looked over to see Jackson on the edge of the pool, blood streaming from his mouth. Mark was there in a flash, scooping him up and I ran over to join them. Jackson screamed and cupped his hands under his chin, his little eyes wild with pain.

He had fallen and bashed his teeth on the concrete corner of the pool edge. There was so much blood, it was hard to see what the damage was. We took him into the nearby bathroom and tried to wash some of the blood away. It was a gruesome sight. His two front teeth had been pushed backwards into the centre of his mouth, and parts of his gums had been severed, falling out of his mouth into my hands. Realising it was not an injury we could fix for him at home, we frantically asked around to find out what to do. There was a dentist in town, but only occasionally. We waited, holding Jackson and trying our best to comfort him while our friends called the dentist. It was an intensely frightening experience—looking at our son, seeing his pain, and knowing we were in a place with limited medical care.

What are we doing here? I found myself thinking.

Amazingly, the dentist was in town that day. It was a great relief, but still unnerving. We weren't sure what this dentist would be like, what he would be able to do for Jackson, or how traumatic this was likely to be. I was on duty at school and couldn't leave, so Mark took Jackson to the dentist. Neither of them has ever forgotten that day—the details don't bear repeating, but Jackson had his two front baby teeth removed, with Mark holding his hand, wiping both their tears.

I walked around campus in a daze, to the soundtrack of my own thoughts: *Why are we here? What are we doing to our kids? What possessed us to move to Africa? Everyone back home was right—it's not safe, we shouldn't have left Australia. What kind of dentist works in this town anyway? What is he doing to my kid's mouth right now? We should just go home. How soon could we get back home? We are the dumbest parents ever. We shouldn't even be allowed to raise kids. We definitely shouldn't be allowed to raise anyone else's kids! This is all a massive mistake.*

My thoughts have a tendency to get carried away. But just as I was ready to find flights online and start packing, Mark arrived home and carried Jackson through the front door. Jackson grinned through a toothless, messy, bruised mouth and held up a lollipop.

'Ith okay Mum, dentiths here have lollipopth too!' he said with a new lispy voice. I wrapped them both up in a hug.

'Are you okay?' I asked.

'Yep!' he answered. 'Do you think the tooth fairy can find me in Africa?'

'For sure, buddy.' I replied, as Mark lowered Jackson to the floor, letting him run off to show Jemima.

I looked up at Mark. 'How was it?' I asked.

'It was awful. I can't even talk about it,' he answered, shaking his head. 'But that kid is amazing!' He pulled me into a hug. 'He's going to be fine. Two more teeth are damaged and will fall out on their own in a few weeks, but they're all baby teeth. He'll be gappy for a few years until his new teeth come down, but he's fine.'

This day was like many in the weeks and years to come. We could swing from 'I love this place' to 'I hate this place' in a matter of seconds. Our doubts were fairly constant. There was so much that we loved, such growth that we saw in our kids and ourselves, but it was hard to let go of the safety of home.

Chapter 15

Goose Man

"A little nonsense now and then is relished by the wisest men."
—ROALD DAHL

We met some new friends, Dusty and Marlaina, at a school event for staff and their families. I noticed them quickly on arrival, as they stood by the drinks table.

'Would y'all like a drink?' Marlaina called out to us, her blonde hair skimming her shoulders as she turned towards us, smiling kindly.

'Sure!' Mark replied, taking Jackson's hand and bringing him towards the table while I carried Jemima on my hip.

'Oh my word,' said Marlaina, softly brushing Jemima's cheek. 'Dusty, look at this sweet girl! I mean, is she not the most precious thing?'

Dusty greeted us with a handshake and introduced himself, his thick southern accent matching Marlaina's.

'Oh man,' he said, looking at Jackson and Jemima, 'y'all need to meet our son, Imani. He's going to love you guys.' He turned behind him and called out to Imani, who stood in the garden with a stick in hand, rolling it between his palms to make it spin. Imani looked no older than Jemima and was beautifully dressed in a collared shirt and dress pants. He toddled over to us, bouncing on his tiptoes with a huge grin, his little white teeth contrasting starkly with his dark Tanzanian skin.

'Imani, this is Mr Mark and Miss Anna,' Dusty told him quietly. 'And this is Jackson and Jemima.'

'Myyyy-ma,' Imani drawled, a sweet grin spreading over his face as he looked at Jemima. I lowered her down from my hip and the two of them wandered into the garden, Jackson following along behind.

We hit it off immediately, and there was a lot we had in common. Marlaina taught Year 6 at our school and Dusty worked on microfinance projects in some of the poorest villages in the area. They had lived in Tanzania a lot longer than us. They spoke Swahili fluently and had a depth of local knowledge to share with us. We could barely believe it when they shared their story of adopting Imani from a baby home in Mwanza called Forever Angels.

They scooped us up into their lives as if we were family, and we spent many of my weekends off staying over at their place. The intensity of living on campus, surrounded by staff and students in such close proximity, was overwhelming at times, and we took every opportunity to get away. Dusty and Marlaina lived 200 metres down the street from our school, but nevertheless, we would pack our bags for the weekend, load up the car, drive 30 seconds down the street, and move into their home. We laughed at the seeming ridiculousness of it, but just getting off campus felt like a breath of fresh air, and we loved their company.

When a long weekend in September came, we made plans to go on a trip together to a little village named Lushoto. Nestled into a mountain at about 1,400 metres above sea level and a three-and-a-half-hour drive away, it was set to be a wonderful change of scenery. Dusty, Marlaina and Imani drove in their Toyota Landcruiser, and we followed behind in our Honda CRV. We had bought this car before we even landed in Tanzania—with very little knowledge of what we might need. Feeling super prepared and proud of ourselves for finding and purchasing a car before we even arrived, we enjoyed having it waiting for us on arrival. We began to notice that others around us had significantly larger, sturdier 4WDs than we did. However, our CRV was doing its job, and we were grateful to have the freedom to travel as we wished.

All was going well for the beginning of our trip—we settled in for a long drive and enjoyed the classic scenes of Tanzanian life out the windows as we went. We passed through bustling village markets, dodging donkeys and wooden trailers. We travelled long stretches of dusty, open road with flat plains either side of us and herds of cattle scattered here and there, tended to by young Maasai children with large sticks. As the road ahead of us climbed higher, we found ourselves winding carefully through changing vegetation. The sheer mountainside moved closer to the side of the car as the way narrowed and the drop on the other side increased, revealing a magnificent valley below. It was stunningly beautiful. The sun was setting, and we were enjoying the view immensely, climbing higher and higher, until we noticed a steady puff of steam coming from under the bonnet of our car.

We pulled over, realising our engine was overheating, and Dusty and Marlaina pulled in to help. Our trusty CRV just wasn't going to make it. As darkness was approaching, we knew we didn't have a lot of time to wait for it to cool down. Dusty set off in his car to find some rope so he could tow our car to the nearest *fundi* (mechanic). He returned quite swiftly with a rope and directions. He even sent someone ahead of us to let the *fundi* know we were on our way. We were, once again, so grateful for Dusty's knowledge and resourcefulness.

Before long, we were hooked up to Dusty's car with a short rope, and we had a 17-kilometre journey before we reached further assistance. We set off—Dusty towing us, Mark's foot carefully hovering over the brake ready to apply pressure if we bounced too close. It was comical and stressful at the same time. We laughed at once again finding ourselves in a situation like this, and Mark tried to concentrate on the road ahead, which he couldn't see in the dark, to anticipate the need to brake. The road continued its unforgiving path rising and falling, winding around the mountain, with its perilous drop looming beside us. I had visions of us being swung over the edge after taking a corner too quickly, but Dusty and Mark were managing well. We made it 16 kilometres along the road when we entered a small village, and while negotiating an intersection, Mark accidentally put his foot on the brake as Dusty accelerated. The rope pulled forward, and the force ripped our front bumper bar right off. We came to a halt once again.

Although it was 8:30pm and pitch-black outside, the village was abuzz with people everywhere, and within seconds, we were surrounded by local men who helped push our car out of the intersection and onto the side of the road. I laughed as I saw one man approach our car, carrying a goose under one arm. He used a few fingers on his free hand to 'push' the car, in a token gesture of support, as the goose looked in the back window. Jackson and Jemima giggled at the goose man and were soon surrounded by the faces of village children looking in the window at them.

Dusty once again went ahead to the *fundi*, who was still waiting for us, and returned with a new rope. He hooked us up again and we were ready to continue, but not before dealing with the crowd of men awaiting compensation for their assistance. Mark, having faced similar situations before, found the eldest member of the crowd, left a generous tip with him in thanks for their help, and asked him to distribute it among those who assisted us. As Mark went to return to the car, Goose Man approached him, asking for an additional payment. Mark laughed and told him, 'You're carrying a goose! How much could you really have done?!' He directed him to his elder, who would decide who should be compensated and by how much.

We set off again with just a short distance to travel, and were soon approaching the *fundi*. Ahead of us, Dusty slowed when the driveway for the *fundi* came into view. He indicated right, for us to cross the oncoming lane of traffic, waited for the traffic to clear, and turned into the driveway, beeping his horn for the gate to open. But the gate didn't open, and this left us precariously placed behind him. Dusty jumped out to open the gate, and found it locked. Our car, still attached to Dusty's, was now stopped halfway across the road. Without streetlights, visibility was terrible, and Mark and I jumped out to direct traffic around our car. Stretched between the two cars, the tow rope was pulled tight 30 centimetres off the ground, and we directed the oncoming traffic around the back of our car to avoid a collision.

As Dusty continued trying to get the gate open, we saw a *piki piki* (motorbike) coming down the hill towards us, carrying two passengers. Seeing an opportunity to overtake the cars in front, the driver swerved out of line and instead of proceeding around our car, he came straight towards us, intending to slip between our car and Dusty's. The driver, oblivious to the rope that connected our cars, hurtled towards us. No amount of yelling and waving from us could deter his attempt at a shortcut, and he continued his trajectory. He whizzed past us and hit the rope at speed. We watched in horror, like a movie in slow motion, as the bike caught on the rope and flipped forward, throwing its startled passengers into the air. They hit the ground hard, scraped along the gravel, and scrambled to their feet. They looked around, shocked, still unsure of the cause of their sudden calamity. A few onlookers shouted and pointed at the rope, and realisation flooded their faces. They collected their scattered belongings, checked over their *piki piki* for damage, and raced away into the dark. Relieved that no one was seriously injured, we carried on directing traffic until the gate swung open. We could finally proceed through to find our *fundi* and have our trusty CRV repaired.

We left the car with the *fundi* for the weekend, piled into Dusty and Marlaina's car for the remaining few kilometres to reach our destination, and enjoyed a wonderful long weekend in Lushoto. The air was cool high up the mountain, a stark contrast to the heat of Moshi, and we rugged up in front of a fireplace, played cards, and watched the kids lie on the floor and roll toy trucks around the rug.

As we attempted our trip home, the CRV revived itself long enough to cruise down the mountain, before returning to a boiling mess once we hit flat ground. With 190 kilometres still to travel, it wasn't looking good. Once again, Dusty and Marlaina hooked us up to their car (with a rope Dusty 'purchased' from a village nearby by exchanging it for some car oil and brake fluid) and towed us home. As we sat in the front seat of the CRV, travelling at 90 kilometres per hour with a short rope between us, Mark and I laughed at this visual representation of our life—Dusty and Marlaina towing us through Tanzania. They were our lifeline and our sanity, and we were so thankful to be living this adventure with them.

The mighty CRV never really recovered from this trip, but it was totally worth it. You'd think we would have learned our lesson and upgraded our car to a stronger 4WD before attempting any more long trips, right? Well, we didn't. The school holidays were coming, and we had grand plans for our time off.

Chapter 16

Simba

"He had been through a good deal in the course of the Great Quest—he had seen beautiful things and horrible things—but up until now he had not known that one and the same creature can be both, that beauty can be terrifying."

—MICHAEL ENDE, *THE NEVERENDING STORY*

We crawled into the holidays, farewelled all my boarding students, locked up the dorm, and celebrated surviving our first term. We had been dreaming of our first real safari, and this was our chance to get away and see it all for ourselves.

Tarangire National Park was only a few hours' drive from us, and our plan was to drive there Sunday morning, get to our tent camp by lunchtime, spend the afternoon in the National Park, and then return to our tent for dinner. Of course, this is not even close to what happened.

First, we took a wrong turn and made it a good way towards Kenya before realising we were going the wrong way. That wasted some time, but not to worry, we thought. We backtracked and found the right road.

As we got close to Tarangire, we began looking for the turn-off to the tent camp. We had instructions from the website and attempted to follow them. At some point, the paved road ended and we found ourselves on a terrible gritty, bumpy road with dust cyclones everywhere—the worst road we had driven on so far in our time in Tanzania. They weren't the big, fun kind of bumps—they were the small, sharp kind that make you feel like there's a jackhammer under your car.

We followed this road for a while, looking for the turn-off to our camp. It never came. We asked many people for directions, but no one had ever heard of the camp, although some gave us directions nonetheless, and we travelled down other small side roads that also went nowhere.

So, we turned back and drove the length of the horrendous road again, back to the turn-off point to find somewhere else to stay. Somewhere that actually existed. Looking for a silver lining, I said to Mark, 'Well, at least the car hasn't broken down!' Sure enough, a few minutes later, the car broke down. It really wasn't the best car. In fact, we were beginning to hate this car. It was nothing personal. I'm sure it's great for other purposes—it just wasn't made for roads like this, or maybe for drivers like us.

The engine had overheated, again. Perhaps the disaster of our trip to Lushoto should have put us off attempting another long trip with the same car. I guess we were slow learners. The radiator cap blew off, high in the air, and disappeared completely. We poured more water in, waited a while for it to cool down, and drove to the next town. We found a local *fundi* and got a new cap. He cleaned dust out of something, fussed around with other things, and all the while, the kids, who had been sitting still in the hot car for eight hours now, were poked and prodded by curious local children.

Then, there was some more messing around, no solid answers, and we looked for different accommodation. The car had cooled once again, and the *fundi* gave us instructions to proceed slowly, watching the temperature gauge carefully, and stop in the shade as soon as the temperature started to rise. It seemed simple enough. Ready to set off again, we had one last look at the map and realised we had been reading it wrong. We were looking for a turn-off 20 kilometres past the wrong small town. We had come way too far. Nice one.

We travelled back to the previous small town, and we found a clearly labelled turn-off—just as the directions said it should be. Five hours later, we finally drove into the tented lodge. Our children had become incredibly patient travellers, and we were so grateful for their tolerance, and their fascination with the wonders they watched out the windows along the way.

The tented camp was wonderful, the food was great, the people were lovely, and we were so glad we finally found our way. Tired after a long day, we happily went off to sleep, just after receiving these instructions from our hosts: 'There are many elephants around camp at night. They like to drink water from the showers. If you hear animals in the night, we strongly advise you to stay inside your tent.' Right. Good to know.

At about 3am, I woke up to some strange sounds—thudding footsteps, scratching sounds, something brushing against the side of the tent, and moving in circles around us. I lay still, trying not to make a sound, while quietly freaking out. The canvas tent was looking pretty thin at this point. All I could think of was an elephant tripping on a tent rope and falling on us. I woke Mark, and he quickly joined me in my panic. We just lay there frozen, trying to imagine what we would do if something actually attacked. I looked over at the kids—apologising to them in my mind for bringing them here and vowing to myself that if we got out of here alive, I would be a better mother. What were we thinking coming here?

As we lay there, fearing for our lives, Mark started shifting uncomfortably. Then squirming a little. I knew that squirm. Mark didn't have the greatest bladder capacity known to mankind, and many a long car trip featured that squirm. That squirm meant he was busting.

'Don't even think about it!' I whispered to him.

'I've gotta go!' he urged.

'You can't!' I hissed. 'The elephants will hear you, and the man said they're attracted to the shower water!'

There was a toilet in the bathroom area at the back of our tent, next to the shower, but we both feared making a sound in case the elephants came closer, or smelled humans and decided to attack. We really had no knowledge of the habits of African animals at this point, a reality made clear to us in this moment. Why hadn't we done any research before plonking ourselves in the middle of a Tanzanian National Park with nothing but a tent?

'I've gotta pee!' Mark screech-whispered. 'It's either the toilet or this bed!'

The bed was looking like a better option to me. If it was a matter of life or death, I was going to go with the bed.

'Just pee in the sheets,' I whispered back, irrationally. 'We'll blame one of the kids when we take the sheets to the laundry in the morning!'

Mark looked at me like I had lost my mind. Or maybe like he wished he wasn't married to a nutcase.

'I'm not doing that!' he half-giggled in disbelief. 'I'll just try to hold on,' he concluded, finding a new level of bladder capacity appeared when his life depended on it.

An eternity later, the sun came up, the sounds stopped, and eventually Mark slowly opened the tent and peered out. There was a Maasai man, an *askari* (guard) standing by a tree not far away, dressed in the bright reds and purples of a traditional Maasai shuka, and holding a spear. Mark had a chat with him in Swahili.

'*Je, kulikuwa na wanyama hapa jana usiku?* Were there animals around camp last night?' Mark inquired.

'*Ndiyo!* Yes!' The askari said, excitedly.

'*Tembo?* Elephants?' Mark asked.

'*Hapana, hakuna tembo hapa jana usiku.* No, no elephants last night,' he said.

'*Simba!* Lions!'

'*Simba*?' Mark asked, 'Lions?'

'*Ndiyo!* Yes!' Mr Askari said.

'*Walikuwa karibu kiasi gani?* How close were they?' Mark asked.

'*Hapa hapa, kuzunguka hema yako*. Right here, around your tent,' he replied. '*Lakini usijali, nilikuwa hapa.* But don't worry, I was here.'

I wanted to run up and hug the brave Maasai warrior man! I wondered how he was even able to protect us, armed with nothing but a spear and a flashlight. We would learn in the days to come that this was entirely normal. All kinds of curious animals frequented tented camps across the many safari parks in Tanzania, but they never attacked the tents. Nor did they attack when guests used the toilet in their tents, funnily enough. The theory is that the lions view the tents as a solid rock—not realising they are hollow and could contain tasty humans. This would have been wonderful information to know the day before! We would come to love those sounds—the power of a lion's roar in the wild, just a few metres from your head, is just incredible. Terrifying, but incredible.

In the morning, we tentatively made our way through the camp to the breakfast tent and then packed up and went on our way to Tarangire National Park. We were hoping, of course, to catch a glimpse of lions. We could have just opened our tent!

We made it through our first safari, eyes wide with wonder at the incredible sights. We pinched ourselves, sitting in our car just metres away from so many incredible creatures in the wild.

To our delight, we did come across a pride of lions, lying in the shade of an acacia tree. A magnificent male lion lay in the dust at full stretch, while a female lion and her three cubs slept close by. The pride was just metres from our car, and we sat, glued to the windows, as they lay about paying no attention to our vehicle.

After a few minutes, the male lion lifted his head and yawned widely, revealing his full set of sharp teeth, before shaking his glorious mane and looking around. He stood slowly and wandered over to the female lion, licking her face affectionately to make his intentions known before proceeding to show her even more affection.

Jackson watched, wide-eyed through his window, as the lions began mating right next to us. The particular angle we were at gave him quite a graphic view.

'Ummm, excuse me Mumma, what's happening here?' he asked with concern. Mark and I looked at each other, trying not to laugh, wondering what was appropriate to tell our four-year-old.

'Well,' I began, figuring this was as good a time as any to begin a "birds and the bees" conversation, 'the lions are mating. That's the daddy lion and the mummy lion, and this is how they make a baby lion grow.' The lions continued to give an explicit demonstration as I described exactly what they were doing, answering Jackson's questions as they continued. It was not at all how I imagined this conversation might one day occur, but everything about our life at this point was not at all how I imagined it might one day occur, so at least it was fitting.

'Is that how all creatures make babies?' he asked.

'Not exactly, but lots of animals make babies like this,' I replied.

'Is that how humans make babies?' he asked.

'Yes, but it's a bit different for humans,' I responded.

'Because we don't live in the dirt?' Jackson asked.

'That's true, we don't live in the dirt,' I answered, trying clumsily to follow his lead and give him enough information, but not too much for his little mind.

This was a particularly spectacular biology lesson, one of many like it as we drove around the national park. I loved what our kids were experiencing and learning. Jemima was still too young to really know what she was seeing, but Jackson was the perfect age to be absorbing every scrap of information. I loved watching his wide eyes as he rested his chin on the window ledge and enjoyed the incredible sights he was witnessing. We lay in our tents that night and listened to the guttural sounds of a lion's low growl, thunderously loud albeit barely a roar, as it walked through camp, its panting breath on the other side of our canvas wall. Beauty and terror dancing together. I held my breath once more, this time revelling in the thrill of the moment.

A few months after this trip, Jackson came home from school one day and sat next to me on the lounge while I sipped a cup of tea.

'Mumma,' he began, 'when you and Dadda did mating to make me, did he try to bite off your ear towards the end?' I nearly spat out my tea as a laugh escaped.

'Um… no buddy, Dadda didn't try to bite off my ear. Why do you ask?'

'Well, I was at school today and I was looking at the teacher, and I know she has children, so she's definitely done mating, but she still has both her ears,' he said.

'Why would you think she wouldn't have both her ears?' I asked him, struggling to follow his train of thought.

'Oh, because when the lions were mating, the man lion tried to bite off the lady lion's ear towards the end,' he said. 'I don't think I'd like the taste of ears, so I don't want to bite off my wife's ear one day,' he finished. I burst out laughing.

'Don't worry buddy, you don't have to bite off anyone's ear! Remember I told you it was a bit different for humans?'

'Yeah,' he replied.

'Well, there's no biting off ears for humans,' I assured him, to his obvious relief.

Our safari adventures had been mesmerising and fascinating, and we immediately started planning and dreaming of our next chance to get away. An experience that began with fear for our lives quickly became thrilling and compelling, and we found ourselves feeling right at home in the national parks.

Our car, however, was clearly not right at home, and it became painfully obvious we needed a larger, stronger 4WD. Besides, we might have a few more passengers joining our family sometime soon. We traded in the not-so-trusty CRV for a Toyota Prado and never looked back. It was like trading in a toddler 4WD for its grown-up equivalent. And importantly, it had eight seats.

Chapter 17

The Choice

"You never really understand a person until you consider things from his point of view—until you climb into his skin and walk around in it."
—ATTICUS FINCH, *TO KILL A MOCKINGBIRD*

Since we decided we would take all three children, things moved alarmingly quickly. On Amy's end, she was working with Social Welfare and Babu and Bibi to thoroughly sort through the possibilities.

Mama Manessa, who had graciously approved the twins to enter the baby home almost a year ago, had now given Babu and Bibi a deadline to make their decision: November 27th. On this day, the twins would be required to leave the baby home.

They faced an unimaginable decision. They were already living with the pain of watching one grandchild starve in their care. I can't imagine there are many more awful situations to be in than this. The helplessness they must have felt, the despair, the deep sadness. I held them in such high regard for their strength and their integrity throughout their struggle. Having turned down the job and home offered by Amy, Babu and Bibi were firm on their choice—they wanted their grandchildren to have a family, and a childhood where they were allowed to be kids, not obligated to work. It was an enormous decision, and everyone involved wanted them to think it through again and again—to mull it over and consider every possibility.

Mama Manessa had been clear with both Amy and Babu and Bibi that, in this case, she agreed with Babu and Bibi that an adoptive family should be found. This was a rarity. In fact, it was the first time Amy had felt a relinquishment was the best option for a child in her baby home.

Mama Manessa, ever thorough in her work, wanted Babu and Bibi to think it through once more. She wanted to look over the options again—to meet the children's Aunt Git and ask her in person if she would take the children in herself. Although Aunt Git already had 15 children to look after, Mama Manessa knew that remaining with family was always the best option for a child where possible. Mama Manessa also wanted Babu and Bibi to meet with her and a local lawyer to discuss the implications of adoption. If they chose that path, she wanted to ensure they fully understood what this would mean. Mama Manessa was thorough and diligent, and her experience and no-nonsense approach gave us confidence in her opinion.

In the days leading up to November 27th, we had many updates back and forth about what may happen in the days ahead. We offered to fly across to Mwanza to meet with Babu and Bibi if they felt it would help guide their decision. We couldn't imagine making such a decision without first meeting the people who may adopt their grandchildren. But we didn't want to pressure them either. Their choice was harrowing. We left the decisions up to Amy, Mama Manessa, Babu and Bibi.

As possibilities were talked through once again, it became clear once more that the only real option for the children was adoption. Aunt Git made it clear she was not coping with raising her own 15 as a single mum, let alone taking on three more. She would not consider it. Babu and Bibi didn't want support to keep them—they were tired, and Bibi was unwell, and they knew the children would be orphaned once again when they passed away. They were unwavering in their wishes for the children. They wanted a family for them. A family who could keep them all together, who could raise them as siblings, who could provide for them, and parents who would live long enough to see them grow up.

In the days leading up to November 27th, we waited and wondered, knowing there was a deadline that would force a decision for the children. Mark had left for a school hiking trip—he was part of a group that took students through hiking expeditions that would culminate in an attempt to summit Kilimanjaro in the years to come. This time, they were climbing Mt Meru, another favourite of ours that rose above the city of Arusha—the next major town to the west of Moshi. Mt Meru is no easy feat for untrained climbers, standing 4,565 metres above sea level with an impressive crater at the centre and steep, unnerving ridges to navigate in the four-day climb to the summit.

It was while Mark was up the mountain that we got the call. Babu and Bibi had asked to meet us.

November 27th was rapidly approaching. Shay and Charlie had become unwell, and Amy had decided to admit them to hospital. They were battling stubborn high fevers and had become lethargic, refusing their bottles and sleeping through the day. It was terrible timing for sickness to strike, and Amy knew that in a few days' time, they would leave her care and either come home to us, or return to life in the village. Shay and Charlie had become dehydrated, and the hospital staff hooked them up to drips in the hope of rehydrating them and strengthening them in case they were about to face the hardship of life in poverty once more.

During her visits with Babu and Bibi, Amy had become even more concerned for Jabari as well. His development had progressed no further than when she saw him one year ago. He was terribly small and often unresponsive. He was slowly starving.

Jabari's life, too, was about to change. If Babu and Bibi decided to bring Shay and Charlie home, the little they had would be stretched to feed the five of them. With one week remaining until the 27th, they had brought Jabari to stay at the Baby Home too. At least for the next week, he could be fed and hydrated and given the best chance of surviving the next chapter of his story.

Mark and I left Jackson and Jemima in the capable care of Dusty and Marlaina, the excited laughter of three children in a paddling pool still audible from the car as we left their driveway to head to the airport. I chatted Mark's ear off the entire way, telling him again every detail I could remember of my last visit. On landing, we went straight to the Baby Home. Once again, we were unsure what to expect—our hearts held in the balance again between hope and self-protection. We could return home tomorrow with three new children, or we could return alone.

We stepped into the Baby Home, the first time for Mark, and were greeted by the hustle and bustle of the afternoon routine. A group of little ones grinned and waved at us, bopping along to the music playing in the background as they crossed the hallway from the playroom to the bathroom. Each child's towel hung from a hook with their name on it, and a shelf above held a separate cup, toothbrush and bar of soap for each child. The level of organisation and individual care for each little one was impressive.

Amy gave Mark the full tour before giving us the latest update on what was happening. Tomorrow, Babu and Bibi would meet with us and then meet with Social Welfare to make their decision. Shay and Charlie were still in the hospital, but we could go there and visit later today. For now though, we had another little person to meet.

We had seen a few photos of Jabari by himself and with the twins, and we hoped we would recognise him. We entered a playroom where 15–20 babies crawled around, waiting for their bath time, or being dressed in their pyjamas.

I spotted him straight away. He sat close to the wall; his head turned towards the cold concrete. I watched him for a few moments before walking over. While the other babies crawled, played, laughed, sang and interacted with each other, Jabari sat still and stared at the wall. There wasn't a sound or movement that caught his attention, he just sat. His eyes were blank and distant, like he was looking through the wall rather than at it. He was tiny. Significantly smaller than the others in this group, and his body was out of proportion—his head and belly quite large, but his limbs very thin.

I walked over and quietly sat down next to Jabari. His head turned to register my presence, then he returned to his wall-watching position.

'Hi buddy,' I said quietly. I knew he didn't speak or make any vocal sounds and had no exposure to English yet. I didn't want to frighten or overwhelm him. I figured he might be staring at the wall because the rest of the room was too much for him, with the busyness, noise, colours, and social interaction. So for a few minutes, I just sat. I stared at the wall with him.

His left hand rested on the floor beside me, and I gently traced down his pinkie finger with my finger. His fingers quickly recoiled, and I worried I had scared him. His head turned back to me, expressionless. Then he moved his hand closer to me and put it back on the floor. I traced his finger again and waited for his response. He kept his tiny hand there this time, and I traced his next finger.

Amy brought over a bottle of milk for Jabari and handed it to me. Quick as a flash, Jabari scooted sideways towards me and I pulled him up into my lap. I laid his head in the crook of my left arm and fed him his warm bottle of milk. He kept his eyes on mine and guzzled that milk like his life depended on it. As he drank, he made a soft, rhythmic gurgling sound, almost like a cat purring. It was like every mouthful was overwhelmingly joyful, like it was filling a deep void in him that had been empty for far too long.

Mark put his arm around my shoulder and pressed his face against mine, and we looked into those deep brown eyes until his milk was finished. I prayed as he drank that it wasn't too late for this little guy. Although we'd been warned he may not survive, I wanted so badly to believe he could make it. I passed his sleepy, relaxed little body into Mark's arms. Jabari lay there, sleepily staring into the distance, his full tummy now looking five times the size it should be for his little body. It was nap time. Mark carried him to his bed and laid him in one of the cots that surrounded the walls of the Toddler Room, alongside the other babies his age. Jabari's head turned once again to watch the wall.

'I don't want to leave him there,' Mark said as we tiptoed out of the room.

'I know,' I replied. He wasn't ours yet, although we knew he may be soon. This land of in-between was strange and agonising.

We drove to the hospital next to see Shay and Charlie. They lay tummy-down beside each other on their hospital bed, with drips in their wrists. They were both awake, but they lay lethargically in place—vastly different to the energetic little bunnies I had met weeks earlier, scooting around the room and banging away on a drum. Mark spoke to them quietly and stroked their hair.

'You can hold them,' Amy said, and gently lifted Shay and passed her to Mark, carefully navigating her tubes and bandaged arm. He held her up against his chest, and she snuggled her head under his chin and sucked her thumb, as if she had belonged right there forever.

I gently lifted Charlie, his warm sleepy body relaxing into my arms, and cradled him close. I leant into Mark's side, and we just held them and watched their tired eyes half-close. They seemed so helpless. It was hard to imagine how they were going to cope if they were, in fact, going back to the village. We held them and stroked their little heads for as long as we could before it was time to go.

After an hour with Shay and Charlie, we were off to meet Babu and Bibi. This was a moment it seemed impossible to prepare for. What exactly are you supposed to say and do in this circumstance? Mark and I had spent days planning, writing out our ideas on paper, and achieved nothing more than a pile of scrunched-up pages in the bin. The language barrier felt insurmountable. It was the nuances that mattered, and they were so difficult to get right in another language. I felt such deep respect for them—for the pain they had been through, for the integrity of their choices, and for the struggle they endured in facing everyday life. I mostly wanted to hug them and tell them I wished life was different.

As unprepared as we were, the time had come, and Amy drove us to their village. It was in a hilly area of Mwanza, where the dirt streets rose up in irregular bumpy mounds and single-room dwellings made of concrete or mud bricks lined the streets in bunches. The muted tones of earth, concrete, timber and corrugated iron were broken up only by the brightly coloured fabric kangas worn by the women who walked the streets carrying heavy loads or stood behind makeshift stalls selling fruit and vegetables. We went as far as we could by car until the roads became almost impassable, then parked when the streets became too thin for a car to squeeze through. We walked from there, passing mud-brick huts with thatched roofs, children playing in small groups, and stray dogs sniffing through debris in search of food.

On our right, we came upon a large rubbish dump. Piles of rotting trash formed large, rounded hills as the warm breeze tossed papers into the air and brought the foul stench to our noses. Beyond the dump, we turned to the left and followed Amy towards an area of denser housing. Looking behind, I noticed we had started to attract a following. A handful of children and a few teenagers had gathered, kicking up dust with their feet as they grinned and elbowed each other as they followed along a few metres behind. We were obviously a strange sight in this little village. A few more turns down narrow dusty pathways between precariously built living areas, and we arrived at a small open clearing surrounded by single-room dwellings. A few makeshift clotheslines crisscrossed above the bare earth, with brightly coloured kangas flapping gently in the warm breeze.

Babu and Bibi stepped out of one of the single rooms and greeted us gleefully with wide grins and outstretched arms. Babu was tall and thin, with a broad, gappy smile. He wore a brown suit jacket but lacked a shirt underneath, and his visible ribs told the story of the hardships they were facing. Bibi was tiny, dwarfed by Babu's height, and wore a grey, stained T-shirt tucked into a yellow and black kanga tied firmly around her waist. Her thin, greying hair was trimmed short, highlighting the silhouette of her head in classic African style. We hugged, as if old friends rather than the strangers we were, and sat down on low timber logs in front of their room. Our crowd of followers had grown, and the small outdoor area began to resemble an amphitheatre with spectators sitting, squatting or standing in a semi-circle behind. Babu and Bibi were unfazed by the crowd, so we tried to ignore the oddity of the situation and focus on Babu and Bibi.

With some help translating, to ensure our clunky Swahili didn't cause any confusion, we listened to their story intently and shared with them about our own family. Babu and Bibi shared that they had been hoping and praying for a family to come for the children since the day they were left with them. Bibi was sick with what they believed was cancer, and didn't have high hopes for her life expectancy from this point. Babu was her second husband, so no blood relation to the children, although he had fought for them as if they were his own grandchildren. It's not easy to be elderly and poor in Tanzania. There are no nursing homes, no pension, no support for people other than what their family can provide. Bibi had been abandoned long ago by her son, whose place it was in their culture to care for parents in their old age.

Their days were long and hard, and there was no possible way to care for the children. We asked them, although we knew others had asked already, if they would consider Amy's offer of a home and a light job at the baby home; if this would allow them the support they needed to keep the babies. They were so thankful for the offer and shared it was incredibly tempting. That life would be immensely easier and more comfortable. Someone would care for them. They wouldn't need to spend their days crushing rocks, hoping to earn enough to make a meal. But more than all this, they wanted a family for the kids. A permanent family. A family who could keep them all together.

Their sacrifice brought tears to my eyes. I believed them. And I knew that if they chose us to raise their grandchildren, I would make sure those children would always know how loved they were, and how their grandparents gave up their own security and comfort for their grandchildren's chance at a permanent family.

They chose us.

Chapter 18

Coming Home

"The ache for home lives in all of us. The place where we can go as we are and not be questioned."
—MAYA ANGELOU

The next day, we woke up, knowing today was the day we would bring three more children home. It was the most bizarre, unrecognisable feeling. Maybe it would be akin to booking in for a C-section, to have triplets, only you don't have nine months to prepare—you only have a day, although you've been hoping for this moment for five years but you weren't really sure if it would ever happen, and you wanted to believe it would, but you couldn't be sure until today, and you really only thought you were having twins, but then there was a surprise third, and he may not survive, but you hope he does, and you're about to find out. Maybe it was a bit like that.

My head was pounding from the moment I woke up—presumably because thinking about today was making my head explode. I took some Panadol and tried to focus on getting us organised. It was so very exciting, and so very terrifying. I had a bag ready to take to the baby home, with no real idea of what I needed. I like to plan and control my way around stressful situations, which is rarely an effective coping strategy, but nonetheless I was trying! I had three outfits packed in there for the babies, and some backups in case they didn't fit or needed to change. I had nappies, wipes, snacks, drinks and toys—all the things I'd usually pack in a nappy bag, only I was used to packing for babies I knew. For Jackson and Jemima, I knew what special toy would calm them down, which brand of dummies they liked and which they would spit, how much water they drank, and which snacks would bring an excited glint to their eye.

Today, I was getting on a plane with three one-year-old babies who I knew very little about. They didn't own anything—even the clothes on their backs would be new to them. They would only have their own bodies and each other—nothing else would be familiar. Shay and Charlie were used to wearing cloth nappies, and Jabari was used to being naked from the waist down. I had a bag full of disposable nappies. Voicing my doubts and concerns as I went through the bag, Mark could see me spiralling. He came over, gently took the bag out of my hands and hugged me close.

'We can't know everything they want or need,' he said. 'We're just going to have to be okay with learning as we go.' I closed my eyes as small tears began escaping. The nappies and the toys weren't the thing, and I knew it. The thing was that we were about to put these beautiful babies through another trauma. Although it was leading to a path we hoped would be full of life and hope and healing, there was first going to be another trauma. We were taking them, once again, from everything they'd ever known, to start over in a new family—and we would be their fourth home. In their short lives, they had already passed through the care of their birth parents, their grandparents, the baby home, and now us. I knew they couldn't stay in the baby home, so one way or another, there was going to be another trauma, but taking those babies in my arms, knowing the hurt and confusion it would cause in that moment was making me sick.

We went to the baby home and met Babu and Bibi there. We spent some time in the toddler area with the kids. They had a lot of goodbyes to say today, although their capacity to understand what was happening was so limited. Amy and the mamas who had raised Shay and Charlie until now were enjoying their last moments with them, and their deep devotion to them was so evident. They shared such joy that the children would now have a family and a future together, and they were used to these goodbyes, but the love and connection were real, and parting wasn't easy. They presented each of the children with a 'life book' containing pictures and stories of their time at Forever Angels, and wiped tears as they hugged one last time.

We wanted to take a family photo with Babu, Bibi, Shay, Charlie and Jabari, and sat the children on their laps for the photo. They had visited the baby home regularly while Shay and Charlie had been here, but nevertheless all three cried and screamed while we tried to take a photo. Needless to say, it isn't the best picture! Babu and Bibi had a wonderful sense of humour about it and said their goodbyes with repeated expressions of gratitude and hope for this new beginning. One thing we were all sure of was that nothing could change Babu and Bibi's importance in their life. They would visit and see the children grow and very much remain their grandparents, even as they became Dombkins children.

I changed the babies into the clothing I'd packed and returned the outfits they had been wearing back to the baby home mamas, ready for another child to wear. My size predictions were pretty good, and their clothes fit well. They immediately looked different in smart, clean clothes and it was at this moment that it began to feel very real. I had chosen clothing that had previously belonged to Jackson and Jemima, and it felt symbolic to me to remove their baby home onesies and clothe them anew in beloved Dombkins family items. They were coming home.

We stood to leave and collected ourselves and our new babies. Mark lifted Shay up and she tucked her head under the right side of his chin, resting her chubby cheek on his chest, thumb firmly in place in her mouth. He bent down to scoop up Charlie and he sat upright on Mark's left hip. I picked up Jabari and gathered our other belongings. I looked at Mark, with a baby either side and smiled, thinking of how this would be standard now for both of us. Once we were back with Jemima, we'd each need to carry two babies to go anywhere!

I turned and looked at the children all around me on the floor. They played and squealed and crawled around me as I watched. We were leaving with three. We literally had our arms full of babies. But standing there, looking at all the little ones remaining, three seemed like nothing. There were over 50 more in this one baby home, and countless others across Tanzania.

What about all the others?

The thought first appeared in my mind at this moment. Unlike some thoughts that come and go like the wind, this thought would become a regular visitor, eventually moving into my mind and making a home.

What about all the others?

For now though, the best I could do was close my eyes quickly and pray for them. Some prayers are said with words, but there are those times when I can't find words that are powerful enough to even begin to describe what I think and feel. In those moments, when there are no words, I just breathe in deeply and imagine my hands picking up the contents of my heart and holding it out. I hand this confused, messy, beautiful bundle of heart-prayer over to God and trust Him with it. Sometimes, in moments like this, that's all I can do.

Mark and I carried our new babies out the door and piled into a taxi together. The kids must have been terrified. We were two strangers taking them to a new life and a new home and removing them once again from everything they knew.

They didn't cry. Not one of them. They sat on our laps, looked intently around and out the windows, but there was not even a whimper. I imagined what Jemima might do if a pair of strangers took her away from her home in a car without me—she would scream bloody murder.

In a way, we were grateful they weren't screaming, but I wondered what was happening on the inside. Were they screaming in their minds? Were they terrified but unable to express it? Or was it just so normal for them to be with different carers? Was this what it looked like for a child to have never had a strong attachment to loving, stable parents?

Throughout the trip, they travelled incredibly well. We held them and fed them and read stories and played—trying to anticipate their needs and meet them quickly. Once we boarded the plane to fly back across Tanzania, I rested my head on the seat behind me. My headache was back, and I wished I'd taken some more Panadol before we took off. The children fell asleep as we held them, and Mark and I held hands and watched the mountain of sleeping babies curled around each other on our laps. They were so beautiful. I was overwhelmed in this moment, with gratitude that we could keep them together. Of all they had lost already in their short lives, they had at least kept each other.

Chapter 19

Malaria

"A person's a person, no matter how small."
—DR SEUSS, *HORTON HEARS A WHO*

The pain stabbed through my forehead and travelled in ripples outwards, down my face, intensifying at the back of my neck and flowing quickly down my body. Piercing, intense pain that paralysed me. I assumed yesterday's headache was born of the intensity of the day—the hope, the relief, the excitement, the millions of rushing thoughts, the overwhelming joy—and forgetting to stop and breathe. But through the night, the dull pain grew claws and fangs, and this morning I lay in bed, unable to even lift my head. I had never felt sickness like this.

Somewhere beyond my room, I could hear Mark with the kids. I tried to listen through the pain. There were beautiful sounds of new siblings waking up at home together for the first time. There were delighted squeals, curious questions, and giggles from everyone. The pain of missing these moments was almost worse than the physical pain ripping through my body. *I've been waiting for so many years for this moment,* I thought, *and now I can't even pick up my head to look at them. I must be dying.*

As it turns out, the pain had a name—malaria. Malaria is a ruthless illness. The severity of it depends on how quickly it's identified and treated. The possibility of malaria was the furthest thing from my mind with the excitement of our new children, and we didn't catch it early. By the time I had been tested, confirmed it was malaria and started treatment, those vital first few days had passed, and I suffered the consequences. There are simple pinprick home tests for malaria that are readily available in Tanzania, and following this experience, we kept a ready supply and tested ourselves at the first hint of a headache. How I wished we had known this earlier!

The confounding factor with malaria is that the side effects of the treatment medication are almost as bad as the illness itself. You have to get worse to get better. I was utterly crushed to be missing these first beautiful moments for our new family. I mean, what were the chances that I would get malaria on the very day we brought our new children home?!

Mark was an absolute champion. We went from two children to five overnight, and he was dealing with them alone. Worse than alone—he also had me to look after. He had two weeks' leave from school, but his students were doing exams, which he needed to create and mark. He was waking up at 4am each morning, writing the exam for that day, printing it off and taking it into the school, then returning home to get the day started with the kids. Jackson and Jemima needed to get up, get ready and off to school, and the three "newbies", as we began to call them, needed constant attention. He fed them, changed them, played with them, put them to bed, fed them again, changed them again, and played with them again. He did school pick-up, afternoon playtime, fed them all dinner and put them to bed. Once the children were down for the night, he ran down the street to stock up on Pepsi and worked until midnight marking the exams his students had completed that day. At midnight, he crawled into bed and crashed, ready to start it all again the following day. He was utterly exhausted and utterly amazing.

As my health improved, I finally got to join in. Life with five was a wild ride. We had one four-year-old, and four one-year-olds! There was so much to learn about these three little people who had joined our family. It was so different to welcoming a newborn baby—they already had their own little personalities, preferences, habits and fears—there were so many fears. I had spent years reading and learning about this moment—about what would be happening in their little hearts and minds, and what they might need from me. Although I felt like I'd been preparing for this for years, I had barely scraped the surface in my understanding, and in fact, we were just at the beginning of a long journey of learning to deeply know our new children.

From the very beginning, there was a stark difference between Shay and Charlie, and Jabari. The events of their lives so far had taken them along very different paths, and each path had its own beauty and its own trauma.

From the outset, we knew that Jabari's health was a huge concern. The trauma of his path was so visible—one look at him and anyone could see it. We were sobered by the responsibility of caring for a child who was so severely malnourished. We had no experience with this, but he had no other options, so we were his best hope for a chance at life. All we could do was give him our best attempt to preserve his life. We sought advice from everyone we could. Amy, who had nursed countless children back from near starvation, was a deep well of knowledge and wisdom. In addition, we took Jabari to our closest hospital and sought advice there, and we spoke to doctors back home in Australia. And we prayed. We prayed that God would heal this little body we held in our arms.

Jabari looked like a malnourished African child you would see on the news during a famine. He was tiny. His legs were shrivelled and weak, and had never held his weight. His belly was swollen and protruding, with tight skin stretched around it. His head looked proportionally too large for his body. His face was expressionless, and his eyes stared far into the distance. He didn't respond to noise or movement around him or take an interest in any toys or people in front of him. He made no speech sounds at all. He didn't baby-babble or cry or attempt any communication. He couldn't crawl or stand. He could shuffle on his bottom a little towards the door where he liked to sit—staring outside, blankly. There was so much he needed, and so many hurdles before him.

We began a long, careful mission to draw him out of his quiet, solitary shell and into our world. We carried him against our bodies as much as possible, which he loved, and we tried to anticipate every need—slowly building his trust and attachment to us. We bottle-fed him, and as we did, he started to make the soft, almost purring sound he had made when we first fed him at the baby home. These were the first moments of real connection with him—staring into his smiling eyes while he drank his milk and "purred". It was beautiful.

Something that struck me deeply in our first few weeks with Jabari was the challenge of holding him. It turns out that being held is a learned skill, and to hold a child who had so rarely been held is a steep learning curve on both sides. When we picked up Jabari and carried him on our hip or against our chest, he would suddenly swing his head around and accidentally headbutt us! It was as if he had no ability to predict or sense where our heads were in relation to his. It had never before occurred to me that babies learn this as they are carried in their parents' arms and sat on their hips. It just happens naturally when a child is held from birth. But holding Jabari was a whole different adventure. He loved being held. His little arms shot straight up in the air whenever we approached, and then we braced ourselves for the swing of his head. Of course, we persisted. We carried him in a sling, in our arms, on our backs in a kanga, and gradually we worked each other out. Eventually, he learned how to be held, and the headbutts faded.

One evening, not long after we brought the kids home, I gave Jabari a worming tablet. We kept a ready supply of little chocolate worming squares, and every few months I gave them to all of us. Before bed one night, I gave one to Jabari, Shay and Charlie as a matter of routine, not expecting any particular reaction. The following morning, Jabari woke up screaming. He barely ever made a sound, and

I ran into his room to find him writhing around in his cot, as if trying to escape his own body. I picked him up to comfort him, but he wouldn't calm down. He pushed me away and kept trying to rip his clothes off. I undressed him quickly, searching for the source of his distress. I took his nappy off, and there in his nappy was a large, pink roundworm. It was wriggling around, alive! It was as thick as a pencil, over 20 centimetres long, and it was angry. Jabari stopped screaming immediately, and he and I stared at this vile creature in amazement. I scooped that little boy up in my arms and hugged him tight. The thought of that worm living in his belly and eating even the small amount of nutrients he had been given made me so mad. I squeezed him tightly and rocked him in my arms. I pulled back to look in his eyes and told him, 'It's okay buddy, it's all gone now. It's all gone now, and you're never going to have a worm like that again.'

I took great pleasure in killing that worm. That worm copped the wrath of all my anger at how a beautiful child could exist in this state. There were moments like this when the sadness and reality of a child living in poverty overwhelmed me to my bones. How could we let this happen to any child? How can our world accept this? Poverty, in concept, is incredibly complex. But when you look in the eyes of a child who has lived it, it's so simple. It's simply unacceptable.

The following night, I was bathing the kids before bedtime. Jabari was sitting next to Jemima in the bath, and the size difference between the two of them struck me once again. Although we didn't know Jabari's age exactly, we knew he was older than Jemima—probably only slightly. And yet, sitting there in the bath together, she dwarfed him, and she wasn't even a tall kid! I asked Jemima to stand up, and although Jabari wasn't able to stand yet, I held him up next to her, with his little feet on the bottom of the bath. He was half her height. He looked like a six-month-old baby next to an almost two-year-old.

'Jemima,' I said, 'did you know that Jabari is your BIG brother?'

'He not big!' she giggled. 'He little!'

'Well,' I said, 'you just wait. He's going to catch up to you!' She kissed his cheek and said, 'Love you, Jabari,' before plopping herself back down to play.

The contrast between these two struck me constantly in those first few months. Born a month or two apart from each other, their lives could not have been more different. Now, she was running, jumping, climbing, and talking. He was trying his best to stand up, to start making speech sounds, and to hold his weight on all fours. He was just learning to smile, and when he did, it shocked him so much he grabbed his cheeks in surprise. When he smiled, his usually blank expression erupted, and tiny dimples appeared all over his face. He discovered his face could move and spent hours moving his mouth, his eyebrows, his cheeks and wriggling his nose.

He started trying to speak. At first, he just blew air from his lungs and out his mouth. Then he started blowing raspberries. He spent weeks repeating a sound that alternated between a raspberry and a hiss.

'Pffffft… Tssssssst. Pffffft… Tssssssst. Pffffft… Tssssssst. Pffffft… Tssssssst.' He went on and on. Making this sound was enough to bring on his dimply smile—he was so impressed with himself. Then he started baby babbling, as if he was three or four months old.

We tried to teach him to laugh after we noticed him watching the other children laugh, with interest.

'Jabari,' I said, 'that's laughing! You try it! Like this: ha ha ha.'

He looked at me intently and I repeated the sound over and over. I placed his hand over my mouth and repeated it again, letting him feel the movement and air. I placed his hand on my throat and repeated it again, and then on my belly, showing him all the places that helped make that sound. Eventually, he had a go. A deep, serious voice emerged from him, slowly saying, 'ha ha ha.' It was so funny-sounding that we all burst into laughter, and his face burst into a smile, which shocked him, and he grabbed his cheeks with his hands again.

It was fascinating to watch him. He had such a lovely temperament and didn't seem to get upset or frustrated by the things that held him back. He just kept trying. Watching him, we realised that laughter isn't a given for every child—many live in a world without it. Jabari found his laugh that day and never looked back.

One night at bedtime, Jemima was playing a game on our iPad where she matched sight words together. I carried Jabari in, and she handed the iPad to him for a turn. I put him down next to her on the bed as the screen auto-locked. Jabari caught a glimpse of his face in the reflection of the dark screen and threw himself backwards in a fit of laughter. I grabbed my phone to video his laugh. He grabbed the iPad again and stared at his reflection, before pulling a face and cracking himself up again. Jemima tried to put her game on for him to try, but all he wanted was to look at his face and try to make it move. She was matching sight words, and he'd never seen his own face. Developmentally, they were a world apart. But there was already so much love between them. She laughed with him, tickled him and kissed his cheek. He gazed back at her with smiling eyes.

Jackson took great joy in helping Jabari learn new things. He made it his mission to teach Jabari to walk and spent hours sitting in front of Jabari on the floor, slowly pulling him up to stand and lowering him back down to sit. As

Jabari's legs grew stronger, he began to balance for a few seconds on his legs, before sitting back down in a mess of giggles. Jackson and Jabari laughed and worked, and laughed and worked, and ever so slowly, Jabari grew more stable on his feet. Jackson started taking him by the hands, holding him carefully as he walked before him, pulling Jabari forward to take a step. With each step, Jabari would burst out laughing and fall down again in a fit of hysterics. The hardest part was getting him to stop laughing long enough to take another step! After a lot of hard work from the two of them, Jabari began to walk, and Jackson could not have been prouder.

The trauma of the path Jabari's life had taken was so apparent, but there was a beauty deep underneath that we could sense also. Although poverty had ravaged his mind and body, he had the benefit of a strong attachment to Babu and Bibi. He had primary caregivers who loved him deeply and did all they could for him. Because of this, when he came to us, he was able to transfer that attachment to us. He quickly came to understand we were his parents, and he wanted to be near us. If a stranger came to the door, he would cling to us. If he was sad, he would come to us. If he was happy, he wanted to share it with us. His mind didn't know how to walk or talk, but he knew relationships, he knew connection, and this was the beauty of the path he had walked.

By comparison, Shay and Charlie looked like healthy, bouncy one-year-olds from the outside. Their trauma wasn't visible, but it revealed itself to us quickly. Their interactions with us and other adults were almost the exact opposite of Jabari. While they loved to be hugged, held and played with in ways that appeared normal at first, we began to notice that they interacted in the same way with any adult. If a person came to visit that they didn't know, they raced to greet them, lifted their arms to be held and put extraordinary effort into charming the socks off our visitors. Similarly, if we were in a park and they fell, they would cry and crawl to the nearest adult for comfort. It didn't matter at all to them who the adult was, or if they had met before, they just found the nearest legs and reached up. They were completely indiscriminate. It took a very long time—many years actually—before they really understood that Mark and I were their parents, before they came to us first, before they stopped trying to follow any stranger home.

We understood, of course, how they developed this way. Almost from birth, they didn't have primary carers. They had a wonderful, committed group of caring mamas at the baby home who provided such high-quality care, but they didn't have parents. Any of the mamas were a source of comfort to Shay and Charlie. If they were sad, or hungry, or wet, or hurt, someone was there—someone who really loved them. But it was a staff of 50 women on rotation. No wonder they had such broad trust in any adult they came across.

The development that happens in a child's brain during their first year of life is just astounding, and when a child's brain is wired a little differently from the start, it takes time to rewire. We would see the effects of this start to life on our little ones for many years to come.

Chapter 20

Pink Milk

"If you want to change the world, go home and love your family."
—MOTHER TERESA

We began to settle into life with five kids, four of them one-year-olds. In many ways, it was so ridiculous it was funny. Getting anywhere at all was quite a challenge, as we had so many children who couldn't walk yet. I couldn't even carry all of them by myself. So we stayed home a lot, which was helpful anyway in their understanding of their new life.

We had four children in nappies, and cloth nappies were our only option, as disposables were incredibly expensive. We went through 20–30 cloth nappies a day, and of course, these all needed to be washed and dried. Each nappy consisted of a cover and two or three thick inserts. We didn't have a washing machine when we first arrived, but the onslaught of nappies quickly had us hunting in town for a machine. We found an old twin-tub machine, which needed to be manually filled with a hose on one side, set to wash and drain, then I had to transfer the washing to the other side to spin. It was slow and labour-intensive, but it was a thousand times better than hand-washing dirty nappies.

Once the nappies were washed, a process that often required several trips through the machine, they needed to be dried. In Tanzania, there is a delightful little insect called a mango fly. It lays microscopic eggs in wet fabric, which then transfer to your skin when you wear your clothes, burrow under the surface of your skin, and hatch into maggots. The undetected maggots grow under your skin, forming a boil, and eventually, a disgusting maggot crawls out of you alive. The thought of it alone was enough to make me sick. The way to avoid this is to either iron all your clothes for 10 minutes to kill the eggs with heat, or to not hang your clothes outside. I was not about to spend hours a day ironing 30 nappies and 60–90 inserts! So, we had to hang them inside. Our windows had metal bars stretched across them, for security, and these became our new washing line. Each day our house was covered in nappies and liners, hanging from any available surface. It was not my favourite outlook, but one of so many necessary new adjustments.

Once dried, the nappies needed to be re-stuffed, by putting the liners back inside the covers, and folded ready for use the following day. Mark and I spent countless evenings on the lounge room floor, folding nappies as we chatted about the day.

After many months of living like this, my Mum sent over an amazing gift—money for us to buy a proper automatic washing machine and dryer! It was a dream. Once we brought them home, those machines were on 24/7. Although they gave out on us regularly (from sheer exhaustion, I'm sure) and the washing machine *fundi* (mechanic) became a regular visitor to our home, we loved those machines dearly. Still today, when I push the button on my washing machine at home, I remember life with cloth nappies and no automatic machine, and by comparison, everything is easy.

In our whole time living in Tanzania, we only experienced one mango fly. It had burrowed into Mark's elbow, and sure enough, once we realised what it might be, I squeezed the welt and out came a wriggling maggot. It was as disgusting as you imagine it would be!

We went through nine litres of milk each day to fill all the babies' bottles. We could buy cartons of UHT milk down the road, but the sheer quantity we needed made it too expensive. Thankfully, the children were all old enough to drink cow's milk. We became painfully aware at this time of the plight of mothers in Tanzania who are unable to breastfeed, or fathers who are left to look after their baby after the mother has died in childbirth. Even for us, formula milk was unaffordable. It was totally beyond the reach of most Tanzanian families. This weighed heavily on our hearts and stayed with us over the years.

For us, cow's milk was possible, but the only affordable way to get it was to have it delivered straight from the cow. Each morning, a young man would ride up on his *piki piki* (motorbike), unstrap two huge drums of milk, and bring them to our door. I would bring out our massive cooking pots, and he would pour our nine litres of milk straight from the filthy drums into the pots. Along with the milk, there were often some bonus bits of dirt, rocks or leaves.

The milk was unpasteurised and full of who-knows-what, so it went straight on the stove where we pasteurised it ourselves. This involved bringing the milk to the boil and cooking it for 30 minutes, or letting it boil up and cool down three times. It sounds simple, but if you've ever heated milk, you'll know it tends to suddenly rise up and overflow, especially when you have four toddlers to tend to at the same time. We often ended up with milk all over the stove, but hey—at least we had milk.

After pasteurising, we then had to let the milk cool, push it through a sieve to remove the aforementioned rocks, dirt, and leaves, and pour it into our jugs ready to use. Just getting the milk ready to drink was a task in itself. The three newbies had bottles three times a day, so after cooling the milk and keeping it in the fridge, we had to reheat it. We filled their bottles, set them in a pot of warm water to heat, and our three little ones happily gulped down their milk before we started the process all over again.

Holding and bottle-feeding all three newbies at once was one of my favourite times of the day. I sat on the floor with my legs stretched out in front and lay the three of them there on my lap, so I could look each one in the eyes and smile at them as they drank. Often, they found each other's hands and held tightly to each other. They were precious moments.

Jemima was a milk-lover too, but she struggled to adapt to the change from the toddler formula she drank back in Australia to the cow's milk we pasteurised ourselves at our new home. I couldn't really blame her—she saw the dirty drum it came out of each day. We struggled for a while trying to get her to try it, but she just cried for her old milk. Then one day I saw a little bottle of incredibly overpriced strawberry topping at a shop in town and bought it home. I hid in the kitchen and put a few drops into Jemima's bottle with the pasteurised cow's milk, and brought it out to her, saying, 'Look Jemima! Mummy found pink milk!' And it was the beginning of a beautiful friendship. Jemima and 'pink milk' became inseparable, and since we were largely just trying to survive life with five, we didn't care one bit.

Chapter 21

Grace

"The humblest tasks get beautified if loving hands do them."
—LOUISA MAY ALCOTT, *LITTLE WOMEN*

When we arrived in Tanzania, we were advised by many that we needed a "house worker". The idea didn't sit well with me, since Mark and I were working at alternating times, so one of us would always be home with the kids. It didn't seem necessary. We resisted at first, but were reminded by many that it was expected, and that not hiring a house worker was offensive to the local community. If we could offer employment, we should. The last thing we wanted to do was offend our local community, so we relented and saw it as an opportunity to provide an income for a local family. Our neighbour's house worker knew of a lady named Grace who was without work and was unable to send her children to school. We met Grace and gave her a job.

It was uncomfortable for me from the start, and despite loads of advice from our new expat friends on how to go about managing a house worker, I just struggled. When we first met Grace, she looked down at the floor shyly and curtsied when she shook our hands. She didn't speak a word of English, and at that stage, Mark and I both had limited Swahili, so I couldn't imagine how we were going to get by.

What troubled me most was her feeling of inferiority. I wanted to include her like a member of the family, and it made her incredibly uncomfortable. I was obviously not the kind of employer she was used to. I was doing it wrong, and I knew it, but I couldn't stand to function in any other way in my home. She expected to bring lunch to the kids and me at the table, and leave us to eat. I expected to make the lunch myself and have her join us at the table. She expected to do all the housework, but I couldn't just sit there while she worked. I wanted to do it together, but she responded with such embarrassment at the concept that I could see I was offending her and getting in the way. Dusty and Marlaina gently reminded me that I was making her uncomfortable by trying to make myself more comfortable, and that I needed to get out of her way. It was a great job for her, and I needed to let her do it.

Slowly, over time, we forged a way to work together. Grace was lovely, with a heart of gold. She wanted to work hard for us and would jump at any chance to be of assistance. She had a great sense of humour, which emerged as her shyness dissipated, and she worked really hard to connect with the kids.

Jackson and Grace developed a great relationship. Their conversations were hilarious. Four-year-old Jackson thought that if he put an 'ie' sound at the end of an English word, it would sound like Swahili, and Grace might understand. So he would say things like, 'Gracie, lookie at the bookie,' trying to show her something, and no matter what he said, Grace would respond, 'Okay, Jackie.'

At first, I spent most of the day with an English/Swahili dictionary in my hand, trying to look up every word so we could communicate. It quickly became apparent that this was of little help. But we laughed a lot and became good at charades!

There were many things Grace did each day that were a huge help to us. The one I was most grateful for was washing shoes. In the wet season in Tanzania, the mud is so thick and sticky that one walk outside leaves a pair of shoes caked with two inches of mud. Our little ones had two or three pairs of plastic crocs each, and every day they came home caked in mud. Grace would collect them in a bucket, take them out the back and scrub the mud off each one. I loved her for it.

There were many frustrations too that came with having someone in our home all day. I learned how much I need time by myself. We kept shortening Grace's hours, without reducing her pay, just to give ourselves some time in the morning before she arrived, and some time in the afternoon after she left. A lot of the time, I needed to put things away before she arrived that I didn't want her to clean, and return things at the end of the day after she left. Grace was so thorough she would try to wash everything in our home every day. She would daily strip all the beds and wash the sheets, quilts and pillowcases. To me, it was overkill. They didn't need washing every day, and I wanted the kids to learn to make their own beds in the morning, not leave it a mess for someone else to come and make for them. It was a great test of my personality—I had to let go of the thousand things that didn't really matter, and most of them didn't really matter.

Having Grace in our home gave me so much more time to just sit and play with the children, and this was an incredible gift. We had so much lost ground to make up. I had missed their crucial first year of life, and what they needed now to develop an attachment to us was hours upon hours of what we called "eyeball time". Us, with the kids, eyeball to eyeball. When they were awake, one of us was there, sitting on the floor, singing, playing or building block towers while we really built a connection.

Sometimes, however, the challenges were legitimate. One afternoon, Charlie was finishing his lunch at the table when he threw up all over himself and the floor. I scooped him up and carried him to the bathtub to wash him off and passed Grace in the hallway who had noticed what happened and was coming with a mop and bucket to clean the floor. *'Oh, how lovely of her,'* I thought to myself, as I began washing Charlie. When he was sorted, we returned to the living room to find Grace dutifully mopping the floor. She had cleaned up Charlie's mess, which was great, but she had then continued to mop all the concrete floors in the house with the same bucket of dirty vomit water. I could see bits of vomit from corner to corner. I sighed as I set Charlie back down in his chair.

At moments like this, having Grace was so close to being helpful, and yet so far. These were the situations I struggled with. I felt awful criticising the work she was doing—she was in my home cleaning up my child's vomit! And her intention was so good. But, as many expat friends told me, I should be communicating with her and showing her how I'd like her to do things, rather than cleaning up vomit scraps after she left. Most of the time, I let things go and just waited until she'd finished for the day before I re-did the job myself. It was a rod for my own back, and entirely my own fault.

Most expats also used their house worker for childcare. It was a great set-up for many families and gave them a lot of freedom to work, or go out with friends, while the children were being cared for. But again, our situation was different. We had three new children, and we wanted to spend as much time with them as possible. We were trying to show them that we were their parents and to build a trusting relationship with them by knowing them deeply and meeting their needs. Having someone else step into that role would have been completely counterproductive, so we were clear from the start that the kids were our job, not Grace's.

Grace really understood this and worked hard to help with other home tasks but left all the kid duties to us. She navigated a tricky space where she was always around, but never providing direct care for the children. She laughed with them and let them show her things and sang them songs as she worked, but she didn't try to step in to comfort them, feed or change them, carry them or dress them. She left this to me, even when all three needed attention at once, and I appreciated this about her immensely. Over time, we learned to work together, and Grace became like a member of the family.

Chapter 22

Mama Uriah

"Well begun is half-done."
—MARY POPPINS

Not long after the kids came to live with us, we connected with the social worker in our region. We made an appointment to see Mama Uriah, the senior social worker in Moshi, and met her at her office in town. We parked in the rocky, unsealed car park behind the building. Our shoes gathered dry dust as we made our way to a long, concrete block with six or seven offices lined up in a single row. A narrow, covered porch stretched out along the row, and a winding queue of women and children snaked its way along the porch and around the corner. The mood was solemn and the voices low. Small toddlers with vacant stares and swollen bellies sat on their mothers' laps. Sharp cries came from tiny hungry mouths, and strangers in line helped each other manage their heavy loads. It was clear everyone here was in significant need or distress. I hadn't thought at all about what may greet us when we arrived and was taken aback by the scene. We had a 3pm meeting time, but looking at the queue, I was guessing that didn't mean much.

We stood for a minute, wondering what to do. Should we join the line and wait? Was there a window or reception to put our name on a list or register our arrival? Looking around, I doubted a system of any kind was in place here, and we stood quietly at the end of the queue. The posture of the women around us indicated this queue was not moving anywhere fast. Many had settled down to sit on the concrete edge, breastfeeding their babies, or setting down baskets of belongings they would later carry home on their heads. Standing at the end of this line, we were obviously out of place. After some quizzical looks, a kind woman indicated we should approach the door. We did so and knocked tentatively.

Mama Uriah sat back in the wooden chair behind her desk and waved us in as she finished off a phone call. Her preoccupation gave us a few minutes to take in our surroundings. The single-room office was dark, even though the bright sun was beating down outside. The small windows and low porch roof barely let in any light, but our eyes adjusted as we waited. Mama Uriah's desk sat in the centre of the room. Surrounding her on all sides were piles and piles of manila files with loose-leaf papers inside. The piles stretched from the desk almost to roof height, and hundreds of folders were piled high on low benches that surrounded every wall. The files balanced precariously on top of each other, leaning to the left or right as the towers threatened to fall. I stared around the room in stunned silence, barely believing this was a functioning office. I could not imagine any possible way of locating a file in this room. I could see no labels, colours or systems, just unidentifiable files piled in every available space. Mama Uriah, dwarfed by her mountains of paperwork, ended her call and turned her attention to us.

'*Shikamoo Mama Uriah*,' we greeted her using the respectful Swahili greeting reserved for showing respect to elders or those in authority. *Shikamoo* literally means 'I hold your feet' and must be said by the younger or more junior person to initiate a conversation.

'*Marahaba!*' Mama Uriah gave the traditional reply, accepting our offering of respect. She looked pleased, and it was a good start. We knew that developing our Swahili was going to be important in showing our commitment to Tanzania and to our children, but we were only just beginning. Just four months into our life in Tanzania, we always reached a point in conversation where our Swahili ran out, usually as the speaker increased their pace and used language unfamiliar to us. We were hoping to give a basic conversation a good go, especially not knowing if Mama Uriah spoke English, and if so, how well.

Mama Uriah continued the greetings in Swahili, a back and forth exchange we had prepared for as we tried desperately to keep up our side of the conversation.

'*Hamjambo?* How are you?' She called.

'*Hatujambo.* We're fine,' we replied, a little proud of ourselves for knowing to use the plural *Hatujambo* ('We're fine') rather than the singular *Sijambo* ('I'm fine'). I was hoping we scored points for that.

'*Habari gani?* Any news?' she asked.

'*Nzuri.* Everything is fine,' Mark answered. '*Na wewe?* And you?'

'*Salama tu.* Only good news,' she responded. '*Habari za kazi?* How is your work?' She continued our test.

'*Safi sana.* Very good,' Mark replied without skipping a beat.

'*Hiya. Habari za nyumbani?* What's news from home?' she asked.

'*Nzuri kabisa.* Completely good,' Mark replied again. Mama Uriah looked pleased with our progress, then with a small grin, she continued.

'*Hiya, Habari za kuku na ng'ombe*?' she asked. We paused. We'd been working hard on our Swahili, but this one confused us. It sounded like she asked us how our chickens and cows were.

'*Nzuri tu.* Only good,' Mark replied cautiously. Mama Uriah erupted into laughter and broke into English.

'Really? Your chickens and cows are doing well, are they? How many do you have these days?' she continued to laugh. 'Your Swahili is coming along, but I like to test you. Anyone can answer '*Nzuri*' to anything, but I like to check that you know what I'm asking you!'

I don't know what we were expecting of Mama Uriah, but a cheeky, belly-laughing woman with a good sense of humour was not it. I liked her immediately. She wore a blue and yellow traditional Tanzanian dress, tightly fitted around her round frame, with a matching head scarf tied beautifully around her pulled-up hair. A large gap between her front teeth, a wide, open smile and a glint in her eye all added to her endearing nature.

Mama Uriah changed gears seamlessly to discuss the reason for our visit, using English to ask us about the children and how they came to us. Eager to impress, Mark responded in Swahili, telling the story of the children, the baby home, the grandparents, and inviting Mama Uriah to visit our home and begin her assessment of our family in preparation for our Court process in the years to come. Mama Uriah was visibly impressed by Mark's insistence on speaking Swahili. I thought he did an excellent job, stumbling at times, but always finding a way to express the story in Swahili. I was thankful he was telling the story, and not me, as he was spending each evening studying while I was on duty in the boarding house. His Swahili was much better than mine at this point. Mama Uriah sat back and let him speak—following along until Mark finished his story.

'Mark!' she began, speaking English once more, 'your Swahili…' she paused, and I expected her to congratulate or affirm his use of language, 'you are *struggling*!' she finished. I could feel Mark deflate from her words.

'Mama Uriah, I'm learning as quickly as I can—I'm studying every night when the children are in bed and my students at school are helping me. I'll keep working, we're both really committed to speaking Swahili well.'

'Yes,' Mama Uriah responded, seemingly in agreement, but then added with even more emphasis than before—'you are *struuuuggling*!'

The meeting was an overwhelming success. Mama Uriah agreed to come to our home and observe us and the children and begin our assessment. We liked her a lot and held out hope that we would develop a great relationship with her over the next few years. But her comment to Mark was a lingering slight on our progress that we didn't forget easily. It was excellent motivation to continue learning the language but also became an ongoing joke. If ever Mark stumbled over his words in Swahili, I would shake my head at him with a wink and say, 'Mark... you are *struuuuuggling*!'

Chapter 23

Hot Showers

"I am not lost, for I know where I am.
But however, where I am may be lost."
—WINNIE THE POOH

We were excited to bring Babu and Bibi to Moshi to visit the kids and see them in their new home. We'd spent hours discussing the best way to get them across the country, and each option presented some difficulties. We thought flying them would be the quickest and easiest path, but they had never been on a plane and just the thought of it was too much for them. They were familiar with catching buses, although they had never travelled further than Mwanza, so we settled on booking tickets for them to take a coach ride from Mwanza to Moshi. This would be a long journey—around 16 hours from start to finish—but it would be a safe, comfortable ride and, most importantly, Babu and Bibi felt comfortable with this.

Mark had purchased a budget Nokia phone for them to keep in contact with us throughout the journey. However, it was stolen from them before they set off, so our communication strategy was ruined. As long as they stayed on the bus (apart from scheduled toilet and meal breaks) until they reached Moshi, it wouldn't be a problem.

We received word from Amy that Babu and Bibi had boarded the bus and were on their way to Moshi. We prepped the kids and looked forward to welcoming their grandparents that evening. Mark went to the bus depot in Moshi well before the scheduled arrival time to make sure he was there to meet the bus, and he waited. He waited and waited, and no bus from Mwanza arrived. Mark went from driver to driver asking if they had any news of the bus from Mwanza, but could not find any information. He stayed at the depot late into the night, hoping the bus was just delayed. But it didn't arrive. Mark came home in the early hours of the morning, devastated to not have found Babu and Bibi.

'Okay, let's talk through the possibilities,' Mark said, pacing back and forth across our bedroom.

'Well, we know they got on the bus,' I began, rubbing my eyes and willing my tired mind to come up with a helpful thought.

'It could have been the wrong bus,' Mark responded. 'They could be anywhere in the country.'

'Amy put them on the bus. I'm sure it was the right bus. It must have broken down or...' I paused, not wanting to say my thought out loud. We both knew an accident was possible. We'd witnessed many tragic road disasters in our time here, many involving buses. They were often unroadworthy and generally piled high on top with all sorts of belongings—bags, sacks of grain, piles of buckets, and even pieces of furniture tied onto the roof in teetering towers. We'd chosen a reputable bus company for Babu and Bibi, but an accident was still a likely possibility. The thought of this was unbearable, and neither of us wanted to entertain the idea.

'It's probably broken down,' Mark concluded. 'So, what would have happened to them? If the bus broke down somewhere between Mwanza and here, where would they go and how are we going to find them?'

We sat up together through the night, trying to imagine what had happened and what we should do to find them. They were out there somewhere—someplace between Mwanza and Moshi. But we had no idea where. It was the most helpless, awful feeling. Surely we couldn't have lost our kids' elderly grandparents!

Mark went back to the bus depot in the early hours of the next morning, before the first buses of the day started arriving. He once again started asking other drivers if they knew anything about the bus from Mwanza. Could they find out? Could they use Mark's phone to call other drivers? Could anyone recall seeing an elderly couple looking a little lost? The drivers gave in to Mark's persistence and made some calls. Someone thought the Mwanza bus had gone to Arusha instead. Someone else thought it wasn't coming to Moshi at all. Another driver thought it would arrive that morning. And then one driver had confirmation of a Babu and Bibi sighting. The Mwanza bus had gone to Arusha last night and an elderly couple had remained on the bus. They didn't want to get off in an unfamiliar city, so they slept on the bus and told the driver they must not get off until they reached Moshi. The bus was on its way.

As the coach pulled into the depot, Mark held his breath and crossed his fingers and toes as the passengers disembarked. Weary travellers climbed down the bus steps in a steady stream, and then the stream stopped. There was a pause long enough to make Mark feel sick, and then he saw Babu appear at the entrance and slowly descend the stairs, gripping tightly to the railing.

'Babu!' Mark screamed and ran towards him. Babu's face lit up at the sight of Mark, and after helping Bibi down the final step, the three of them embraced in one big joyful hug. The relief was intense. We hadn't lost them after all. They were here safe and sound, if a little weary, and we couldn't wait to bring them home. But first, they needed a long sleep after such an ordeal.

Mark took them to their hostel to check in. We had agonised over the best place to have them stay during their visit and had settled on the Lutheran Hostel down the road. It was simple, but clean and comfortable, and had a restaurant that served excellent local food. We hoped it would be the right balance of comfortable and special—not so fancy that they felt unwelcome, but a treat nonetheless.

Mark checked them in and took them to their room. He showed them around, briefly pointing out the bathroom. Babu peeked his head in and turned back to grin at Bibi—a glint of wonder and excitement in his eye. She rushed to look in the small, simple room, and they squealed excitedly, with child-like joy. Mark soon realised what was happening—Babu and Bibi had never before used a shower or a flushing toilet! They giddily turned taps and pushed buttons and exploded in excitement when hot water slowly emerged from the faucet.

Babu turned his gaze to the toilet.

'Mark,' Babu said, looking with caution, 'please will you show me. Show me how to use this.'

'Umm,' Mark began, finding himself in a situation he had not prepared for. 'Sure. Okay, so… here's where you sit,' he said, gesturing towards the seat. 'And here's the paper to wipe, and then press this button when you finish,' Mark concluded, hoping this was enough detail.

Babu moved closer to the toilet and lifted one foot up onto the seat.

'We squat here like this?' Babu said, preparing to stand on the seat.

'No, no!' Mark interjected, 'Feet on the floor, feet on the floor!' Babu's confused expression told Mark he was going to have to actually demonstrate. No adoption book had prepared him for a moment like this. He stood in front of the toilet, motioned to imitate removing his pants, then sat himself on the toilet seat.

'Like this,' he said, before continuing to demonstrate the use of toilet paper, putting the paper into the bowl, and flushing it away.

'Ahh, okay, okay,' Babu said, satisfied with the demonstration, to Mark's great relief.

They moved on to learning about the shower. This was clearly the most exciting of all the many wonderful new things in the bathroom. Babu and Bibi peppered Mark with shower-related questions. When could they shower? How much water was there? How many times were they allowed to shower? Mark had a giggle and broke the happy news that they could shower whenever they liked, for as long as they liked. This was brilliant, almost unbelievable news to Babu and Bibi.

After all bathroom functioning details were explained, Mark said goodnight, wishing Babu and Bibi a wonderful sleep.

'What time would you like me to pick you up in the morning?' Mark asked as he walked towards the door.

'Don't come before 10am,' Babu said. 'We want many hours to enjoy the shower!'

Mark laughed to himself and left them to it, knowing that as soon as he closed the door, Babu and Bibi would be jumping into the most appreciated shower in the history of showers. What a joy it was for him to see an everyday experience through new eyes and gain a deeper appreciation himself each time he turned a tap, and hot water magically came out.

Chapter 24

Biscuits

"Generosity. Bring all you have.
It's ok to be brave and afraid at the same time."
—BRENÉ BROWN

The next morning, after Babu and Bibi had plenty of time to shower, I sat in our lounge room, biting my fingernails as I waited in anticipation. The last time Shay, Charlie and Jabari had seen their grandparents, just before we brought them home, the children had become distressed, clinging to us and crying. Although Babu and Bibi had visited the baby home regularly, the twins didn't know them well. Jabari had lived in their care until a week before he came home to us, but despite their obvious love for him, they were unable to earn enough to meet his needs. Four months had passed since they'd seen each other, and I had no idea what to expect today.

I had been preparing the kids as well as I could—showing them pictures of Babu and Bibi and telling them they were coming to visit today, and that then Babu and Bibi would go home, but they would stay. It's hard to know how much children this young were taking in. I told them in words (in English and in my best Swahili), I showed them in photos, I drew it in pictures, we played it out with toys, and I even did a puppet show. Blank faces stared back at me no matter how I told them. If they were worried, they weren't showing it. They weren't showing anything.

I sat and waited as Mark picked up Babu and Bibi from the hotel down the road. Once he arrived, I propped the screen door open for the procession of children to follow me onto the porch. I picked up Jabari in my arms and carried him out while Shay crawled through the door, slapping the cool concrete floor with her hands, Charlie held onto the walls for support as he wobbled his way along, attempting to walk before falling down and crawling the rest of the way, Jemima bounced and skipped and sang to herself, and Jackson carefully stepped over babies trying to find a spot to stand. We waited together on the porch as the car parked in the gravel area in front of our house. Mark, Babu and Bibi climbed out of the car and approached the gate.

CHAPTER 24

When they came into view, Jabari immediately tensed in my arms and started screaming. He screeched a panicked, terrified scream, like a person being murdered. For a child that barely ever made a sound at all, it was a shock. He scratched and kicked and tried to get down. The other children stood still, unsure what was happening. I left Mark with the rest of the children and took Jabari inside. I walked him through the living room, down the hall and into his bedroom. His little body shook; he couldn't hear my voice or look at my face. He teetered between screaming and suddenly falling silent and staring at the door. If I took a step closer, he screamed again. I sat with him and told him over and over, 'It's okay, you're safe here, you're staying with us,' but I could see none of it went in. He was completely gripped by fear.

I listened as the kids greeted Babu and Bibi in the Swahili greetings we had taught them. They chatted at the door for a little while and then came inside. Mark invited Babu and Bibi to sit at the dining table where we had morning tea waiting. We'd prepared some classic Tanzanian snack foods—*chapati* (flat bread), *mandazi* (Tanzanian donuts), *samosas* (savoury pastry triangles) and some cakes and biscuits. Mark poured tea and coffee and the other kids took a snack and wandered off to play in the adjoining toy room.

I looked at Jabari in my arms and said, 'Jabari, *chakula*? Mmmmm… yummy cakes. *Chakula*?' I knew Jabari loved eating and if any word was going to reach him at this moment, it was *chakula,* Swahili for *food.* He looked at my face. I took a step towards the door, and he squeezed me tight, but didn't cry. I slowly walked him towards the table and sat down with him on my lap. He gripped me so tight I would later find bruises around my arm and shoulder. He silently turned his body and stared at Babu. Each time Babu and Bibi tried to interact with him, he would scream. He just wanted to sit and stare. They listened, backed off, and waited patiently for Jabari to settle. Their restraint was beautiful. I was deeply aware of how difficult this must have been for them—to love a child so deeply and yet see him respond in fear. As always, they put him first. As the adults chatted, he sat, staring, for a long time—maybe half an hour—and then he moved.

Jabari pushed himself forward and reached across the table for a biscuit. He held it tightly in his grip and then slid himself onto the ground. I thought he was taking a snack and running away, but he didn't. He walked on his wobbly little legs, supporting himself by holding the edge of the table, and made his way around to the other side of the table. He came right up next to Babu and held the biscuit up to Babu's mouth. Babu smiled at us, then opened his mouth and Jabari shoved the whole biscuit right in. We watched in amazement.

As soon as the biscuit was in Babu's mouth, Jabari came back to me, climbed up again, took a second biscuit and returned to Babu. He held up the second one, and Babu, who was still chewing the first biscuit, laughed a muffled laugh, and let Jabari try to jam a second biscuit in. Jabari came back and sat on my lap, straight-faced, and watched Babu intently. He didn't take his eyes off him. Each time Babu finished eating, Jabari grabbed another snack, slid down and pushed it into Babu's mouth. The gravity of what Jabari was doing was apparent to all of us. He was feeding Babu. He knew Babu had been hungry. He knew how it felt to be hungry, and he was showing Babu, '*We have food here.*' It was an astounding picture of love and care, from a terrified toddler to the man who saved his life.

By contrast, Jabari paid no attention at all to Bibi. He didn't look at her, acknowledge her at all, but kept his eyes planted on Babu. Bibi, who we discovered has a great sense of humour, started to joke about it. 'Jabari,' she said. 'What about me? Have you got one for me?' Jabari didn't even look at her but just kept his focus on Babu. We all laughed as this continued—a snack for Babu, a plea from Bibi, and tunnel vision from Jabari. Mark and I served Bibi a big plate of snacks and she giggled as she told Jabari, 'Don't worry about me, Jabari, I'm just fine!'

There are moments when the trauma of our children's past is so visible. It's right there for us to see and feel, and it cuts our hearts. The pain of what Jabari had lived through was laid bare before us that day. The reality of starvation. The clarity of his expression of it. The complicated nature of a relationship that held both deep love and unavoidable neglect. The meeting of a past life and a new present. I was learning Jabari was an astounding kid. He was a fighter. He was surviving. He was defying the odds and the countless predictions that he wouldn't make it. He was going to make it, alright. He was going to make it in his own way, in his own time, and with determination like I'd never seen.

Babu and Bibi's visit was a wonderful success, despite the rocky start. We shared four days together playing with the kids, showing them around Moshi and spending precious time together as a family. For the first time, Babu and Bibi were able to just be grandparents. On a bus ride home at the end of a visit to a local waterfall, Charlie sat snugly on Bibi's lap and I watched his eyelids droop lower and lower as the gentle bounce of the bus on the dirt road lulled him to sleep in her arms. As I watched them, I hoped this was everything Babu and Bibi had dreamed and prayed for. Shay, Charlie and Jabari were healthy, growing, happy and together in one family. These three little ones had brought the most unlikely of families together, and we were now very much a family.

Mark, Jackson, Jemima and me at Tarangire Safari Lodge shortly after arrival in Tanzania, 2010.

Our view of Mt Kilimanjaro from our backyard in Moshi, Tanzania.

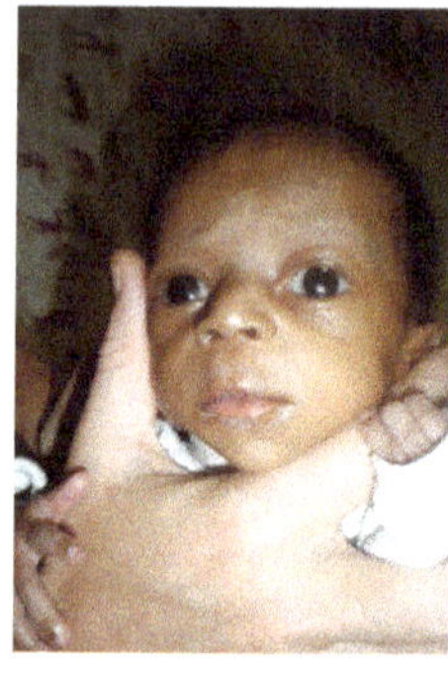

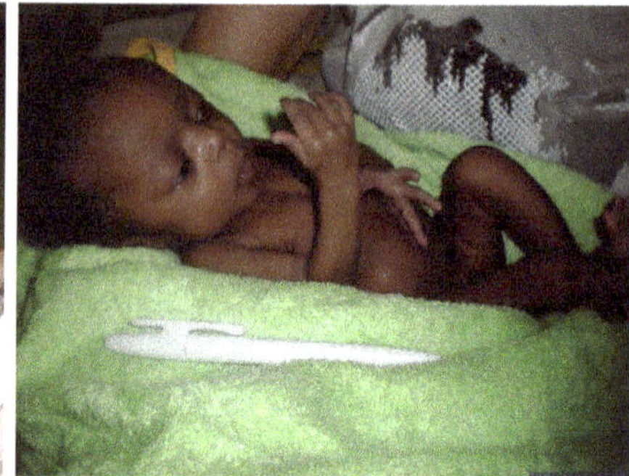

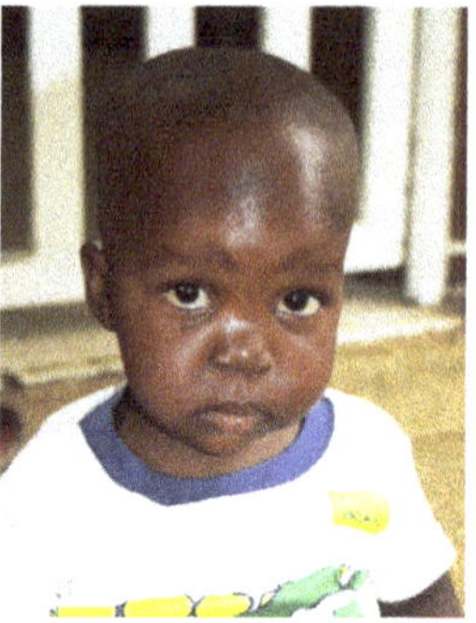

Charlie (left), Shay next to a pen for size comparison (Centre), and Jabari (right) on arrival at Forever Angels Baby Home.

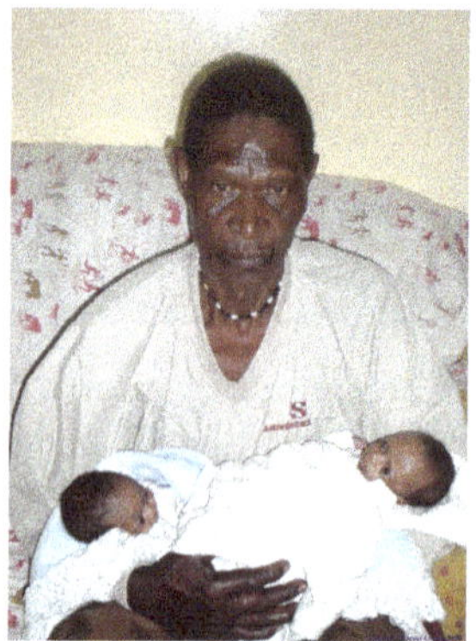

Babu bringing the twins to Forever Angels, October 2009.

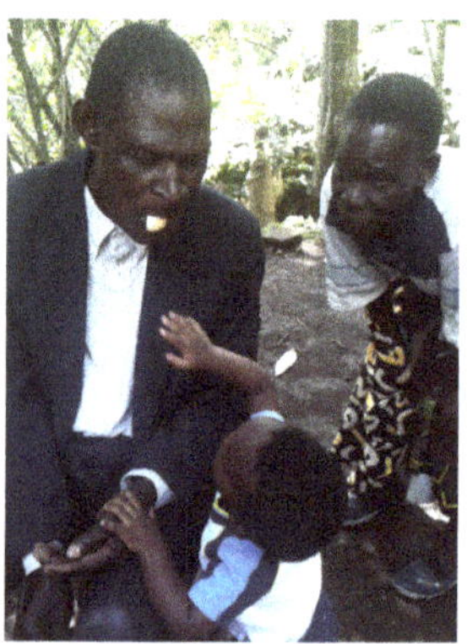

Jabari feeding Babu, 2011.

Our first family picture, December 2010.

How we tried to get around with four one-year-olds and one four-year-old.

Jabari (left) next to Jemima, who is younger, but was almost twice his height and weight at this time. December 2010.

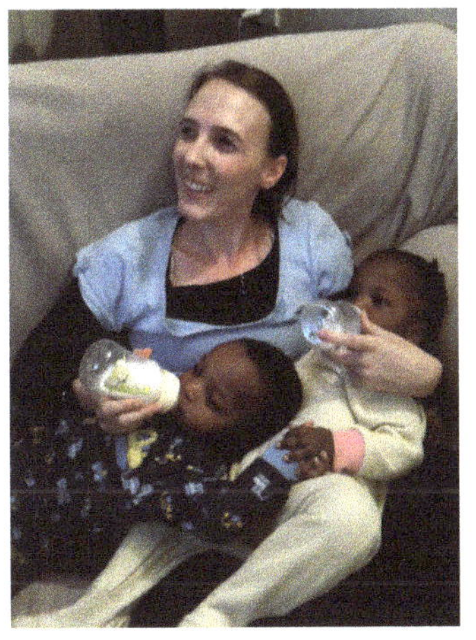

Sweet hand-holding twins, 2011.

Jackson and Jabari, 2011

Lunch time in our garden, 2012

Bath time fun, 2011

Jabari, Shay and Charlie, all dressed up for Court.

Babu and Bibi with Charlie, Jabari and Shay at the High Court of Tanzania in Moshi, June 2013.

Adoption finalised and time to celebrate.

Climbing Mt Kilimanjaro. August 2013.

On the summit of Mt Kilimanjaro. August 2013.

Jackson, Jabari, Charlie, Shay and Jemima with Mt Kilimanjaro in the background at Amboseli National Park, September 2013.

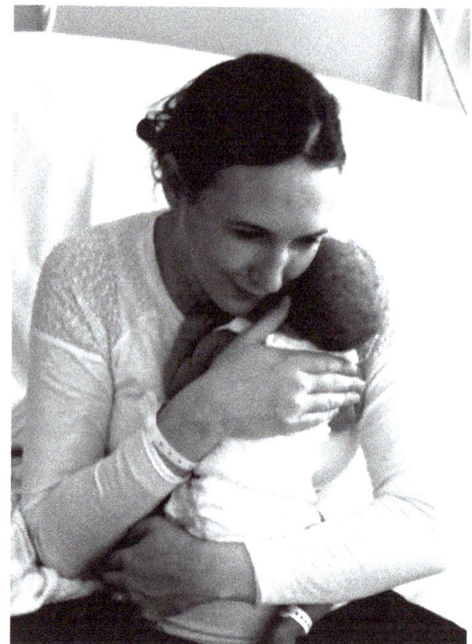

Me, with baby Max.

Max meeting the fam, September 2014.

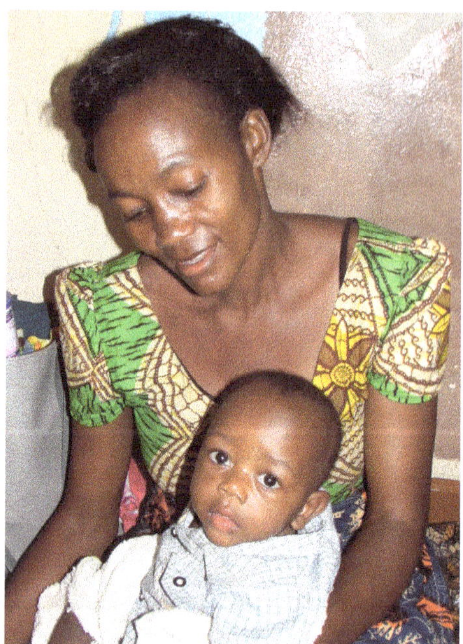

Shakuru, with baby Joseph.

Shakuru at her sewing business.

"I had already lost hope for my son. I was living in a challenging environment. Now I work from home. I can cook for my kids. There is such a huge difference. I walk proudly on the road. I live a life where I can relax."-Shakuru

Amy Hathaway and all the children at Forever Angels Baby home, shortly before we took Shay, Charlie and Jabari home in 2010. 50 babies lovingly cared for, but without a family to belong to.

How the picture has changed! Every baby in this photo is in their mother or family members arms, instead of being abandoned in a baby home. These are just some of the 2,100 women who have been through this program. Thanks to the short term support funded by Forever Projects, these women have a business, they have hope for their future and they have their babies - home, forever.

Shay, Jabari, Charlie and Jemima each holding a baby at Forever Angels, July 2019.

Our family today - Jemima, Charlie, Jackson, Shay, Max, Mark, Jabari and me. Wollongong, Australia.

Chapter 25

Maize

"Time moves slowly, but passes quickly."
—ALICE WALKER, *THE COLOR PURPLE*

We were in a holding pattern. We had our children home, but we had not been in Tanzania long enough to apply for their adoption, and we had no solid information about the changes that were to come. Often, it felt like time was standing still, and it was unsettling. It wasn't until we had been in Tanzania for a year that I could identify this feeling and locate its cause. It was the seasons. Or rather, the lack of seasons. We have four very distinct seasons in Australia, each with their own characteristics. Our lifestyle changes with the seasons. We wear different clothes, socialise differently, play differently, and use our homes differently depending on the time of year. But Tanzania is like an endless summer. The only change is the rainy season when, for a few weeks, the skies open and dump incredible amounts of much-needed rain on the dusty earth, turning everything to mud. Apart from the rain, the rest of the year stays the same. It's warm. I love warm weather, so I wasn't complaining at all. But the lack of seasonal change created this feeling of being stuck in time.

When I realised this, I began to look around for the things that did change, and it was the maize crops that became my new markers of time passing. Maize crops lined the streets around Moshi and the surrounding areas and followed a year-long progression. Clear fields of brown earth were planted with seed from which tiny seedlings emerged, growing into tall green straggly plants that climbed six feet in the air. After a few months of intense sunshine, the plants turned a pale gold colour, swaying in the warm breeze, before harvest time when the stalks were slashed to their bases, and the fields were cleared for the process to begin again. I began to watch the maize closely, appreciating its beauty and allowing it to be my marker of time. The maize grew, and so did we.

Our second year at school got off to a much better start. We felt like it took a full year to learn this place, to feel its rhythms, and relax into them. The second time round we knew a little more about what to expect.

New boarders arrived in my boarding house, and sweet, familiar faces returned. I had missed my girls over the long break, and we spent the first few weeks catching up and hearing tales from their trips home or overseas. Some had loving families that missed them during their terms at school and were making massive sacrifices for their children's education. Others felt they were sent to boarding school because their parents didn't want them around. Holidays were hard for these girls, and returning to school was like coming home. For most of my girls, school *was* home, and they were each other's families. Their bonds were unbreakable, and although I would regularly break up epic fights, the truth was they would do anything for each other.

I'd spent time over the holidays reading and learning about how to improve in my role as a boarding parent. It still felt new, and unfamiliar. There were days I felt I was doing alright—building connections with my girls and starting to understand their world—and others where I was sure I was making their lives worse.

My boarders often wanted to talk about our family. Living so closely together, there was nowhere to hide, and it was clear that we were not the kind of family these girls were used to. Gender roles in Tanzanian families are firmly established. Women are primarily responsible for raising children and looking after the home, and men don't involve themselves in these tasks. Mark and I functioned differently to what they knew, and we regularly looked around the dining hall to see hundreds of surprised eyeballs staring at Mark as he fed our kids, wiped their messy faces, and cleaned up dinner plates.

One afternoon, Mark and I were washing up in our kitchen and looked out the window in front to see a group of six girls staring, stopped dead in their tracks. They scurried away when we saw them. At first, we had no idea what was so fascinating about our life, but as they grew more comfortable, the girls started talking. Curious questions fired from their mouths in quick succession.

'Was he helping you wash up?'

'Did you make him do that?'

'Does he do stuff like that all the time?'

'I've never seen my dad wash a thing!'

'How come he helps you with those babies? I saw him carry three of them!'

'Well, I saw him take all five of them babies to the swings and you wasn't even there!'

Their fascination became clear. The previous boarding parent had been an older, single woman who had no children living at home. I sat with the girls, fielding their questions and told them that this was totally normal in our culture.

In most Australian families, parents raised their children together, sharing both the duties and the joys of parenting.

'No way,' one commented, 'He's just doing that to mess with us. It won't last. I never heard of no man who does housework!'

One evening I sat on the porch with one of the older students, chatting about life and boarding and her studies. Mark walked past in the distance and waved to us, and we waved back. She grew quiet for a few minutes.

'You okay?' I asked. She tucked her knees up under her chin and kept staring out into the quiet darkness, then said, 'How come you're so quiet when he beats you?' I turned to look at her face in the dim light.

'What?' I asked, not sure I'd heard her correctly.

'We never hear you screaming or even crying. None of us have. How come you're so quiet?'

'I'm not quiet,' I said gently, 'he just doesn't beat me.'

She turned to face me, scanning my eyes for signs of deception. It was so hard for her to believe. I held her gaze honestly.

'You know,' I began, 'there are so many beautiful things about your country and your culture. The rest of the world could learn a lot from Tanzania—like how to value community, how to slow down and take time to see each other and be together, how to be content with little, how to normalise grief and support each other.' I paused. 'But how women are treated here is not my favourite.' I smiled at her and put my arm around her shoulder. 'It doesn't have to be this way. You don't have to accept that violence will be a part of your family one day.'

'What about that time last week when you guys were talking and he'd been to town, and you were sassy with him and you said, 'How could you possibly spend three hours in town and come back with nothing?"

'Oh my word,' I laughed. 'Do you guys hear everything?'

'Pretty much!' she said. 'He didn't even beat you for talking sassy to him?'

'Even then,' I said, 'we argue, we don't always agree, we hurt each other with our words sometimes, but I promise you, he never beats me. And I never beat him.'

She rested her head back against the couch with a deep sigh.

'Come on,' I said, pulling us both up off the couch. 'It's curfew. And you've got a kind future husband to start dreaming about.'

I walked her to her room and said goodnight, did my rounds, tucked in my other girls, and walked back through the adjoining door to our home. I felt a huge weight of responsibility—not just knowing these girls were watching and listening to our whole life, but realising how drastically different it was from everything they knew. Part of me wanted to install soundproofing between our home and the boarding house to give us some privacy, but there was something beautiful about sharing our life with these girls. It felt intensely vulnerable, opening our home, our marriage, our parenting, and our faith for all of them to see. I was so painfully aware of our failures, the times we were less than admirable in our speech or our behaviour, but it was certainly an honest, warts-and-all existence, and it went both ways. I saw the best and the worst of my girls, and they saw the best and the worst of us.

Chapter 26

Disaster Moments

"Africa changes you forever, like nowhere on earth.
Once you have been there, you will never be the same.
But how do you begin to describe its magic to someone who has never felt it? How can you explain the fascination of the vast, dusty continent, whose oldest roads are elephant paths?"
—BRIAN JACKMAN

I hated being alone on campus with the kids during the holidays. Another term had come to an end, and I hugged my boarders goodbye for the holidays and waved them off as the campus emptied of staff and students once again. Mark could barely believe his luck as he packed his bags to take a group of students on a school ski trip to Switzerland. Ten days of snowboarding in powdery snow, incredible views and breakfast pastries awaited him once he handed the students into the care of the ski instructors. Lucky for him, but I was home with the kids, and the school was empty.

It was eerily quiet. The school generator was not in use during the holidays, so if the town power went off, we could be left without electricity (and eventually without water as it was pumped by an electric pump) for days on end. Solving the everyday logistical problems was more difficult without Mark there to help, so I was especially glad to hear that our friend, Hannah, was coming to stay for a whole month. Hannah's family were dear friends of my family over many generations, and she'd been on her own adventure in Malawi.

Picking her up from the airport, I could see immediately that Hannah wasn't herself. Her usual gentle, joyful expression was replaced with a pale tone and a pained expression that she tried valiantly to override as she greeted me. Poor Hannah had picked up a stomach bug of some kind in Malawi that was determined to stay with her. Instead of a busy schedule of sightseeing, we spent many lazy days at home with the kids, playing with them, reading and watching movies.

Our "babies" were quickly becoming busy toddlers—all of them now walking, running, jumping, climbing and, most of all, dancing. Shay had insisted on learning to dance before she could walk, pulling herself up on unstable feet before shaking her little butt and waving her arms to the music with a huge grin. Learning to walk was really just a sidenote to broadening her repertoire of dance steps. There was a natural rhythm and swagger in them all, and we had music playing non-stop, mostly because I loved watching them groove.

Jabari's little legs had grown stronger and more stable, but his feet still pointed out to the sides like a ballet dancer, and the tendons at the back of his legs were too short because he had spent so long sitting, so he walked on his toes without his heels touching the ground. Over many months of daily physio exercises, we stretched and stretched his tendons to improve his walk and were thrilled when his heels finally reached the ground and he managed to avoid surgery. His walk was a little odd, but thanks to his turn-out and tippy toes, he danced like a ballerina. He felt music in a deep part of his soul, and Hannah and I had fun swapping suddenly between different styles of music and watching his interpretation of it.

Having three new children join our family while living so far away was a bit like bringing triplets home from the hospital and not being allowed to have friends and family visit, so I loved having friends stay, and I loved being able to share our day-to-day life with them. The changes in us were also most palpable when visitors from home came. Small changes over time that were imperceptible to us became obvious when we were with those we had known forever. A slight change in our accent, a difference in our opinions, a growing confidence, a lack of concern over small things, and a casual acceptance of the crazy happening around us.

I left the house as infrequently as possible when it was holidays and Mark was away, to avoid dealing with the inevitable problems. I didn't have anyone to call for backup, and there were always problems. Our new car had been mostly reliable, but now it was having an issue with the fuel pump. The spare part required to fix it wasn't available, but we had worked out a way to restart the car ourselves when it failed, so it wasn't a major issue.

One afternoon, Hannah and I drove into town for some groceries and stopped by a fruit stall on the side of the road. We filled our arms with succulent mangoes, avocados, tomatoes and bananas, enough to last a few days, and piled them into the back seat, the car filling with the sweet scent of ripe fruit. I went to restart the car and it failed. I tried again, and still nothing. I knew this was the fuel pump playing up again. The empty *clink clink clink* from the engine was now a familiar sound.

'It's okay, I know how to fix this,' I said to Hannah, before popping the hood of the car.

I went around the front of the car, lifted the bonnet, and climbed over the engine. I pulled off the black rubbery tube that brought the fuel up from the tank and sucked it until the bitter fuel reached my mouth. I quickly reconnected the pipe and spat the fuel onto the dusty earth beside the car. I wiped my mouth with the back of my hand, unknowingly leaving a smear of dirt and grease across my face. I pumped the fuel pump manually a few times, knowing the fuel had now been syphoned up the pipe, and then jumped down, closed the hood with a dusty thud, and climbed back into the car. I turned the key, and like magic, the car started.

I looked over at Hannah, relieved to have started the car again, to see her looking back at me in shock. 'What's happened to you?' she asked, looking half-horrified and half-amused. I caught a glimpse of myself in the rear-view mirror and both of us burst out laughing. 'Since when do you suck petrol out of a car, spit on the side of the road, and not notice that your face is covered in grease?' she giggled.

'I guess things have changed a little,' I said, putting the car into gear and taking off towards the safety of home. I hated the constant problems and dreaded the arrival of the next one to come, but there was something deeply satisfying about learning to manage, becoming resourceful, and testing my strength. And there was comfort in the company of friends from home.

There were other changes that our visitors from home noted too. We were softer and more relaxed about the small things—we let our kids take more risks, we weren't phased by inconveniences, changing plans, or people being late. But we were harder too. We stood our ground if we were being ripped off, taken advantage of, or treated poorly. As they pointed this out, I knew exactly what they meant. Our experience here was shaping us into different versions of ourselves.

Not long after Hannah left, another Hannah arrived. My friend Jo had been pregnant when we left for Tanzania and now, walking through the arrivals' doors in Moshi, she had a toddler in her arms—baby Hannah. Jo is a natural beauty, with soft blonde curls and eyelashes for days, but it's her kindness that makes her exceptional. Friendship with Jo is pure sunshine, and seeing her walk through those airport doors and stand on the dusty earth that was now my home made me a mess of tears and excitement.

I took Jo and Hannah to all of our usual favourite spots. It was the rainy season, and the roads were terribly muddy and slippery. I hated driving in the worst affected areas during the rainy season, as it was so difficult to maintain control of the car. The mud was so thick and slippery on many roads that any car driving along would be sliding sideways, the rear of the car swinging around towards the front before the driver regained control and straightened up again. It was actually quite fun at times, if I was the only car in sight and the road was safe, then the slipping and sliding made both the kids and me giggle and bounce around. If it was a road I knew quite well, I could relax enough to enjoy it. Driving further from home was more daunting, but I was well practised by now at getting myself out if I became bogged and finding the firmest roads to take. Having guests in the car was no time for sliding around, and I drove slowly and carefully with my friends on board.

Jo and I set off for a visit to Tarangire National Park, our favourite of all the national parks we had visited, with little Hannah strapped snugly into one of the kids' car seats in the back. We watched the afternoon sun paint a soft glow over the vast stretches of land either side of the road as we drove across the plains. Every so often, we saw a herd of cows being tended to by a small Maasai child, dressed in bright reds and purples, wielding a long stick. Some of these children looked no more than six or seven, yet they were far from anywhere and responsible for a large herd, and they skilfully managed their task.

Every hour or so, the road took us through a bustling village market, where timber-framed stalls held large mounds of brightly coloured fruit and vegetables, stacked in perfect pyramids, and mamas sold produce with their babies strapped snugly to their backs or crouching in the dust at their feet. Men pulled timber wagons with single rickety wheels, their loads piled perilously high, and we drove on slowly to avoid a collision with the donkeys, bicycles and motorbikes we shared the road with. There was so much to see—such vibrant colour, unusual sights and impressive innovation. A full-sized bed on the back of a motorbike was no problem. A mini-bus overflowing with people, three or four gripping on to the outside, laden high with sacks of grain or vegetables, and a man riding on top was a common sight.

As we pressed on along the road that was now so familiar to me, I told Jo the many tales of wrong turns here, getting lost up there, breaking down in that town, puncturing a tyre near that tree, all the while hoping and praying for an uneventful trip with her!

We reached Tarangire Safari Lodge, parked the car, and walked in to see the breathtaking view. The lodge is nestled on a ridge overlooking the plains, with a gentle slope leading down to the river below. The open foyer frames a panoramic display of elephants shading themselves under acacia trees, zebra and waterbuck drinking in the river, or giraffes walking gracefully across by the baobab trees.

We set down our bags.

'Wow,' Jo breathed, mesmerised by the view.

We stood motionless, taking it all in. Down in the river, a family of warthogs drank and played before a wayward wildebeest charged through and sent the warthogs running off in a splash.

After checking in, we opted for the takeaway "lunch box" option, an assortment of finger foods prepared by the chef, rather than eating at the lodge, so we could make the most of every minute. We jumped back into our trusty 4WD and set off for a closer look. I knew the roads of the park inside out by now and set off to find as many exciting animals as possible to show my dear friend. Every safari is different—an exciting game of hide and seek, and I wanted to track down lions, cheetahs, elephants, giraffes, waterbuck, warthogs, meerkats—everything! I wanted to show her everything.

The animals were playing their part very well, and in the first hour of driving around, we had seen a lot already. I was cautious in the wet, muddy areas, preferring to stay on the gravelly roads to be safe. We came down to a river crossing which I had passed across many times without any trouble. We drove carefully down to the short, steep gravel road leading down to the river. The river was fuller than I had seen it before, the water was running past more quickly, and I paused at the river edge to consider what to do. I was reluctant to cross in case it was too deep this time. I thought about it for a few minutes. I could see tyre tracks coming up the other side that looked reasonably fresh, which meant other cars were passing across, but I was still reluctant. The water was moving quickly. I wasn't sure of the depth.

'I think we should just drive around the other way instead,' I said to Jo. 'There's another crossing further along that will be safer, so let's drive up there.'

'Sure,' she replied, trusting my judgement.

I checked behind me and put the car into reverse to go back up the hill where I had come from, but the road was too steep, and I couldn't make it up backwards. Beside the road, there was a flat area that looked dry and stable, so I decided to turn the car around there and drive back up the hill forwards. This was no problem. I was used to driving off-road. But then, as I turned the car and drove off the gravel path, the ground that had looked dry and stable gave way. We sank into deep mud. My heart sank with it. Despite my attempts to drive on, our wheels spun uselessly, unable to grip anything to help us out. I rested my head on the steering wheel in hopelessness.

The challenge of being stuck on safari, of course, is that you can't just get out of your car and dig yourself out. Without a gun on hand to protect ourselves from animals, we couldn't leave our car. Our visibility around the car was quite low, since we were in a small valley beside the river, with trees and bushes around, and I couldn't be sure we would be safe to dig ourselves out.

We had to stay put. In these situations, it's best to call the lodge and ask for a ranger to come and help get you out. So, I picked up my phone and—no reception. I climbed through the window and up onto the roof, while Jo watched for lions, and held my good old Nokia phone high in the air, hoping for those beautiful little bars of reception to return. No luck. I climbed back through the window into the car and looked at Jo.

'Well,' I said, 'still no reception.' I looked apologetically at her, the feeling of doom growing in my stomach. I hated these moments so intensely—although we were used to constant problems and nothing going to plan, it felt worse when I was responsible for a friend and her baby.

'I'm so sorry!' I said. 'Things like this happen all the time, but I was hoping we'd have a really problem-free trip this time! I'm sure someone will drive past soon and see us, and we can send for help.'

'It's totally fine,' Jo assured me, with a genuine smile on her face. 'We're okay here, Hannah's happy, and we have food and water and everything we need. We can just wait!' This was classic Jo. Nothing was an inconvenience for her. There was nothing you could ask of her that was too much—she was generous to a fault, calm under pressure, and she seemed quite happy to just sit in the car and wait for someone to come by.

So we sat. Every half hour or so I would try and get reception again, to no avail, and we would sit and wait some more. The afternoon was wearing on, and we stayed firmly in the mud. Jo and I were never short of conversation, and we chatted the hours away. Hannah slept in her car seat, her long dark lashes and rosy cheeks making her look like a perfect doll, and then she woke and played happily. Jo remained calm, as if we were hanging out in our lounge room at home, but as time went on, I was becoming more concerned. *Shouldn't someone have driven past by now? Why aren't there more cars around?* I wondered to myself silently, biting my bottom lip.

As I checked for reception again from the roof, I looked up the river and noticed some large elephant prints by the river edge. I wished I had seen those prints before I drove into the mud. The depth of their imprints showed how soft the mud really was. The prints concerned me though, as I wondered if the elephants would return for another drink. Inside our car we were quite safe—even if a pride of lions came, they might investigate the car and even climb on it, but they couldn't get in. However, our car was no match for an elephant in a bad mood. Knowing we couldn't drive away was an awful feeling. I told myself there was very little chance of anything going wrong—even if a herd of elephants came, they would likely show no interest in our car.

As the sun disappeared behind the trees, and the warm orange glow gave way to soft grey shadows, it became clear that we might in fact be waiting for a rescue that wouldn't come.

'I'm so sorry, Joey,' I started apologising again, 'I really thought someone would have driven past by now.'

'It's fine,' Jo insisted, 'Really, we're fine! There's nothing else we can do anyway. Someone will find us eventually!'

I loved her so much for her capacity to be calm in this moment.

'It's getting dark,' I said, pointing out the obvious. 'I think most of the safari guests will have returned to their lodges for dinner, so I'm not sure there's much hope for a car this late.' I paused, 'We might have to sleep here.'

'Yeah, I know,' she said. 'But that's fine. We have everything we need right here in the car. And it'd be a pretty cool story!'

'Yes, that's true,' I laughed. 'But your husband is going to kill me!'

I kept my concerns about the elephants to myself, deciding there was no point giving Jo something else to worry about. I wondered if our lodge would check if all their guests had returned, or notice we weren't at dinner. I wondered if Mark had been trying to call, and if he would call the lodge when he couldn't get through to us, and they might then send a car out to find us. I knew the park was enormous, so I doubted they would have success even if they tried.

Then, as we resigned ourselves to the idea of a car sleepover, some headlights appeared on the other side of the river. The driver had driven down to the water's edge and then, like me, had decided to turn around. On that side of the river, the road was wider and the driver had managed to turn around without any trouble. I envied him! In the dim light, he had not seen our car, so we shouted out the windows and beeped the horn, worried he was not going to stop. He heard us, turned, and came back to the river's edge.

'Can you help us?' I shouted across the water. 'We're stuck and can't get out.'

The driver looked at the river carefully, considering his capacity to cross over and help us.

'I don't think my car will make it across, but I'll call the ranger on my radio phone and ask him to send a stronger car to pull you out.'

'Thank you so much!' I yelled. 'Thank you very, very much!' If it weren't for the threat of wild animals, I would have swum across the river to hug him.

He turned his car around and drove off. The relief was immense, and we waited once again, this time with the very real hope that help was on its way. We kept the headlights on so the ranger would see us more easily and waited. Another hour passed, and again I worried we might not be found, but there was certainly more hope.

Then, a huge, khaki-coloured 4WD appeared over the ridge on the other side of the river and came down the hill, gliding through the water as if it was barely there. It drove in front of our car. The rangers got out, gun and flashlight at the ready, and hooked a cable to our front bumper bar. They asked Jo, Hannah and me to get out of the car with one of the rangers in case the car tipped, so we stood in the mud of the riverbank with our new friend beside us as our car lurched forward, tipped steeply to the right, balancing on two wheels, then landed with a thud on all four wheels again. We cheered and clapped, thanked the rangers profusely, tipped them generously, and drove ourselves back to the safety of the lodge. We arrived at the lodge well past dinner time and assumed we had missed dinner.

'Welcome back,' one of the staff greeted us as we came in. 'We hear you've had quite the day! We've kept dinner for you in the dining room.'

Back in our tent after dinner, tucked safely in bed with Hannah sleeping soundly in her cot, we could finally laugh at our adventure.

'What are we going to tell Williams?' I asked, giggling. Jo's husband was also named Mark, so we referred to him by his surname, Williams. 'He's going to kill me! He's never going to let me take you anywhere ever again!'

'He'll be fine!' she lied with a grin, knowing we would never live this down.

The rest of our safari was, thankfully, much less eventful. But before Jo was safely on a plane home, there was a second incident—a seemingly harmless coffee farm tour that took a turn for the worse (thanks once again to the wet season mud!) and had us slip-sliding down a steep mountain, losing complete control of the car, the back end repeatedly drifting out as the wheels spun and we hurtled perilously close to the steep embankment beside us, again and again, as we descended the mountain. I white-knuckled my way down, begging God not to let us die, and berated myself for letting us get into another dangerous situation. We made it down, and I vowed to never let another visitor come in the wet season!

Jo and Hannah went home, and as always when visitors left, it hurt my heart once again. Distance was hard. Really hard.

I always felt a strange mix of emotions when friends from home left. I wanted their visits to be smooth and wondrous and easy, and dreaded the inevitable problem-solving when things didn't go to plan, but after it was all over, I was also grateful that the disaster moments gave our friends a real feel for what life was like for us now. An easy, problem-free visit would have left them with a misrepresentation of our life. It was never easy, and disaster moments were shaping us. Disaster moments were the birthplaces of courage and ingenuity, of determination and deepening faith. They felt terrifying, but then exhilarating. Intensely vulnerable, but then empowering. We were being chiselled and carved and shaped, one disaster moment at a time.

Chapter 27

The Dutchies

"The secret, dear Alice, is to surround yourself with people who make your heart smile. It is then, only then, that you will find Wonderland."
—LEWIS CARROLL, *ALICE IN WONDERLAND*

A new family had arrived in Moshi from Holland, and the news of their arrival quickly found its way to us, in particular, because they had even more children than we did. Before long, we were seeing new blonde-haired, blue-eyed faces around the school and knew these must be the Van Zwetselaars. News of our family must also have reached them, as it wasn't long before we were invited to their home for dinner. Marieke, a paediatric neurologist, and Marco, an IT guru, had moved to Moshi for Marieke to work at KCMC, the local teaching hospital. Their children, Ida (11), Willem (9), Doris (8), Hugo (6), Stephen (4) and Vicki (1) welcomed our five kids into their home and took them off to play.

We followed Marieke into the kitchen, chatting about their arrival. Marieke was a tiny bundle of buzzing energy—darting around the kitchen as she spoke with bright eyes and a huge grin. As we talked, she found an empty four-litre juice bottle and began filling it with water. Then she screwed the plastic lid back on and placed it on the kitchen bench. She took out a huge kitchen knife, raised it high with two hands and stabbed it loudly into the top of the plastic lid, turning it firmly to create a large hole. I watched with interest, wondering what she was doing as she chatted on, never missing a beat. She took out 11 straws, put them into the hole, and placed the bottle on the floor of the kitchen.

'Kids,' she yelled, 'there's water here for you!'

I liked her immediately. She was a whirlwind pocket-rocket. She could be baking bread, finding someone's shoe, starting a load of washing, stirring a pot of *mchicha*, reading a child's homework, and telling you about her latest research all at the same time. She was exhausting to watch and energising to be around.

There were many meals like this one—their home became one of our favourite off-campus escapes, and Marieke, Marco, Mark and I would often marvel at how there could be 11 children roaming the property somewhere, and yet we could have an uninterrupted conversation for hours.

We spent many afternoons with them in our backyard, watching the children bounce on the trampoline or wet each other with the garden hose as we sat and shared stories of the latest craziness from around Moshi.

They had a fabulously clunky old 4WD, with bench seats in the back and home-made seat belts fashioned from harnesses that looped around the chest. We would pile both of our families into it, packed like sardines, and drive off to dinner together. If we weren't going far, the big kids would ride on the roof. It was not uncommon to see the horde of kids push-starting the car, reminiscent of *Little Miss Sunshine*. Our car, on the other hand, had five child seats that met Australian safety standards and were fitted with five-point harnesses. We often laughed at the contrast and placed our full faith in Marieke to come to the rescue if anything went awry. Having a doctor on hand was incredibly comforting in a place like Tanzania.

I walked out the back gate of the school one afternoon in the hot afternoon sun, down the dusty dirt road that led into the village, and dropped by Marco and Marieke's house to find Marco had removed and dismantled the entire engine of the 4WD and laid each piece out across the yard.

'What are you doing?' I asked with a grin.

'Well, it broke down, so I figure if I take it apart, I might work out what's wrong with it,' he replied, without the certainty you might expect from someone with car parts covering their yard.

'Do you know how to rebuild that?' I asked.

'No,' he replied nonchalantly, 'but it can't be that hard, can it?'

I guess it wasn't for Marco, as before long he had it back together and working again.

A few months after the 4WD engine, Marco did the same thing with the CAT scan machine at the hospital. It had been donated to the hospital and took pride of place in its own purpose-built room, but after a while sat broken and unused for many years as no one knew how to fix it. Marco found a copy of the manuals, which were as thick as several telephone books glued together, studied them, took the enormous machine apart, and found a way to fix it.

Life in Tanzania suited the Van Zwetselaars perfectly, and their friendship suited us perfectly. Sharing life with the many friends we adored made all the highs and lows of life in Tanzania bearable. They were there to bear witness to the insane, share the extraordinary thrills, and pick us up when it all became too much. We were there to do the same for them. Everyone we knew in Tanzania was living their own wild adventure, and travelling along with others was a privilege.

Mark was thrilled to have an opportunity to help Dusty with a family he was assisting in a remote village. After all the times Dusty came to our rescue, Mark jumped at the chance to return the favour. Dusty was overseas on a trip home, and received word that a young Maasai girl in a family he worked with had been attacked by an elephant as she collected water from a river. The elephant's tusk had pierced through her leg and although she survived the attack, her injuries would need significant medical attention. Mark was eager to help and agreed to collect the girl and take her to the hospital, but he realised our car was at the *fundi* (mechanic) for a service. One of our colleagues had left their car with us, parked in front of our house, while away on a trip, so Mark grabbed the keys to that car and raced off, thinking they wouldn't mind for such an emergency. Turns out, they would mind.

Mark collected a Maasai man who waited alongside the road for him to show the way to the young girl. Thank goodness for this guide, as there was no way Mark would have found her without his directions. They drove deep into a vast rural area without defined roads, signposts or landmarks of note. Dry, dusty plains stretched for miles and the pair travelled over the bumpy earth, turning left at a large boulder, right at a bent tree and onward in this manner to find a stoic young lady with a horrific wound. Retracing their path, they drove her to the hospital where her wound was treated. She would need numerous ongoing appointments and treatments over the next few months, but she was going to survive the attack.

Mark drove her home to be cared for by her family, and his guide travelled back with him again, showing him the way home. When they approached Moshi, smoke started floating out from under the bonnet of our colleague's car. Mark felt sick. It wasn't our car.

He pulled over, and since they were almost at the guide's drop-off point, Mark explained to his guide that he would need to seek assistance for the car, which would likely take a long time, and that he was free to leave Mark to sort it out and go on his way. The Maasai guide would not leave Mark's side. The usual crowd began to gather, some offering assistance, some watching out of curiosity. Mark was wary. Last time he was pulled over after a run-in with a huge hole in the road, a group had gathered to assist, which they did, but as he drove away, Mark realised his iPod was gone. We'd also had our fuel tank syphoned, radiator lid swiped, and various other bits and pieces disappear when a crowd gathered to help. Mark's Maasai guide was a shield of protection, and no nonsense was going down while he stood guard. Mark called Gabriel, the *fundi,* whose number was on speed dial, and asked for help.

An hour or two later, Gabriel arrived, driving our car, to rescue Mark once again. Mark bid farewell to his wonderful Maasai guide and sat in the front seat of his own car while towing our colleague's car back to Moshi. We paid for it to be fixed, replaced a deteriorated clutch while we were at it, and when our colleague returned, Mark handed over the keys and regaled the tale of how this car came to the rescue of a young Maasai girl who was once impaled on an elephant tusk. Our colleague wasn't impressed. A car is only really safe in a car park, after all. It wasn't left in our care again, and probably for the best.

Chapter 28

Acclimatising

"The best way to treat obstacles is to use them as stepping stones. Laugh at them, tread on them and let them lead you to something better."
—ENID BLYTON

Whenever Mark went up a mountain, things happened. Our adoption process often felt like an endless world of delays and waiting. But inevitably, when Mark was up a mountain, things happened. Sometimes, they were great things, like Babu and Bibi deciding they wanted to meet us. Other times, it was bad news, a setback, a delay, a change that would rattle us. It was silly to imagine the timing had anything to do with the mountain, but like clockwork, when he climbed, things happened. I came to half dread, half dare to dream, when Mark was going up a mountain.

Mark had signed up to take students to the summit of Mount Kilimanjaro. But they wouldn't get there in one push. The program put students through training to work up to the summit, taught them skills, and ran trials that would eventually culminate in attempting the summit of Mount Kilimanjaro. They had to take it bit by bit over time, climbing a little then coming back down. Then climbing a little higher and coming down again. Each climb pushed them a little further, into higher altitude, forcing their bodies to adjust to the conditions, before finally attempting the peak.

Mark had climbed part way up Mount Meru with the group on a past trip, before having to turn back with an unwell student. This time he was climbing part way up Kilimanjaro. The group wasn't aiming to reach the summit this trip but attempting to reach a higher altitude than past trips and to increase the students' chances of succeeding on a summit trip later in the year.

The trip went well, and the group climbed to Kibo Hut, 4,720 metres above sea level and the "base camp" for summit attempts on the Rongai route. I was "watching" from home—knowing I couldn't see him but staring up at the beautiful mountain nonetheless, praying he was safe and happy, and bracing myself for a phone call.

Sure enough, a call came. I saw Mama Uriah's name appear on the screen of my phone as it rang, and I could tell right away it wasn't good news. She called to tell me there was a host of new Social Welfare policies coming, to be applied to all current adoption processes, including ours. The policies were in response to the new law, which we already knew about, which required potential adoptive parents to stay in the country for three years before going through Court to finalise the adoptions. The old law only required a one-year stay. The change was intended to make it more challenging for foreigners to adopt 'on a whim' or come and volunteer on a short-term basis and adopt a child. We thought the law change was excellent. Requiring families to live in the country for three years rather than one year would give those families (like ours) a much fuller and deeper experience of the country, its language and its culture.

The law change was one thing, but in addition, there would then be the changes made by Social Welfare to their own processes in response to the law change. These new processes weren't law, but you couldn't get an adoption through Court without the support of Social Welfare. So essentially, whatever changes they brought in, we would have to follow. We wanted to tick every box and make sure we were squeaky clean, so whatever they said, we would have to do.

Mama Uriah could not tell us exactly how this would affect our adoption. But I could hear concern in her voice. She was worried for us. It was a warning call, although she didn't know exactly what to warn us of. It wasn't disastrous news, as we didn't yet know what those changes were, but it was a caution of challenges that lay ahead. It was providing us a smaller hill to climb, to test our strength and acclimatise us in preparation for a higher summit. We barely knew anything about the new law or its application then. But in the next few years, it would change our lives.

When uncertainty swirled, the best thing for me to do was concentrate on the kids. They were growing so quickly, and raising them was an ongoing mix of joy, learning and challenges. Climbing, acclimatising, climbing again. Them and us, both. It was certainly easy to be distracted by our five little people. They were enthralling. I could sit and just watch them for hours and be in constant fits of laughter. A good few minutes lying on the sunken trampoline, surrounded by toddlers bouncing each other over, could fix all the problems of the world. I was in awe of them.

We were not short of parenting challenges, by any means, and the ongoing impact of their early life was very much a daily reality for Shay, Charlie and Jabari. It was hard. We were learning, and failing, and sometimes succeeding, then failing again, but bit by bit we were all making progress. Pushing higher.

In our ongoing attempts at developing attachment in Shay, Charlie and Jabari, we had given them a soft toy each to sleep with in their cots. Jackson had a collection of soft toys that he liked to call "bed friends", and felt it was important that Shay, Charlie and Jabari had their own bed friends. Jo had shopped for us in Australia. When we first brought the kids home, she sent over a cream-coloured teddy bear with a purple bow around its neck for Shay, a fluffy green, stuffed frog for Charlie and a soft, floppy grey elephant for Jabari.

Each night we'd tuck them in, say goodnight, and Jackson would give each their bed friend. They were immediately rejected and thrown out of the cots like missiles, one after the other, like unwanted pests. But night after night, Jackson persisted. We played with the bed friends during the day, carried them around so they smelled like family, and tucked them in again each night. For months, the toy missiles flew like clockwork, as soon as they were tucked in. But after a while, the toys were tolerated briefly before being launched. Then they were kept a little longer but found on the floor in the morning. Finally, after a year or so, they became beloved treasures, the thing that was their very own rather than shared toys, and flying missiles no more.

The toys came in the car on a trip to town one day with us as I ran some errands and picked up a few things. I stopped at the bakery for some bread. I came here every week or two, and there was an old man who hovered on the street out the front. His ripped shirt was held together by a single button and revealed his emaciated chest. His one visible tooth poked outwards, and his bare feet were dusty and covered in small wounds. He knew our car, as I bought him a loaf of bread each time I was here, and he usually appeared soon after I pulled in. But this day, he was nowhere to be seen. I bought a spare loaf regardless, hoping to find him, and I sat back in the car looking around.

'Hmm,' I said aloud to myself, 'I wonder where my bread friend is?' I waited a little, not wanting him to miss his loaf, and kept looking around. He appeared from further down the street and came hobbling quickly towards the car.

'*Asante Mama, Asante sana*. Thank you, Mama, thank you very much,' he called as he approached.

'*Karibu Bwana*. You're welcome, Sir,' I replied. '*Uko salama?* Are you okay?'

'*Ndiyo Mama, asante tena*. Yes Mama, thank you again.' He took his bread and hobbled away. I watched him cross the road safely, the familiar ache of witnessing overwhelming need rising in me once more. I started the car to drive us back home. A small, concerned voice emerged from the back seat.

'Mumma,' Jackson said, tentatively.

'Yes, buddy,' I replied, looking over at him to see a serious face looking back at me.

'Is that man your bed friend?' he asked.

'No, no, no!' I nearly choked laughing. 'I said "bread" friend, not "bed" friend!'

'Oh,' he replied, laughing with relief, 'that's good, Mumma. I don't think Dad would like that man being your bed friend!'

'I agree!' I said.

'This my bed friend!' chimed in Shay, trying to join the conversation and holding up her bear proudly. 'Is mine! Is Shay Shay's bed friend!'

'Yes, sweet girl,' I replied. 'That's your bed friend. It's all yours!'

The bed friends turned out to be a hit in the long run. Our bread friend, on the other hand, had a sadder ending. On a trip to town a few months later, I was parked across the road waiting for Mark and saw the old man collect a loaf from another shopper at the bakery. At first, I was thrilled to see others providing for him. But after that car drove away, I watched the man hobble further up the street with the loaf, where a group of young men sat in a circle on empty milk crates playing cards. The old man gave them the loaf, and I watched as they took it from him roughly and added it to a pile of loaves mounding up behind them. They hurled sharp words at the man, rushing him to return to the shop to collect more, as they continued their card game. My heart broke. Some things we never acclimatised to.

Chapter 29

"Scooter Dombkins"

"Africa—You can see a sunset and believe you have witnessed the hand of God. You watch the slow lope of a lioness and forget to breathe. You marvel at the tripod of a giraffe bent to water. In Africa, there are iridescent blues on the wings of birds that you do not see anywhere else in nature. In Africa, in the midday heat, you can see blisters in the atmosphere. When you are in Africa, you feel primordial, rocked in the cradle of the world."

—JODI PICOULT

The school had a monkey problem. A large troop had taken up residence on the school campus, and valiant attempts by the ground staff to remove them had so far failed. Monkeys are quite a serious concern as they carry rabies, and a scratch from a monkey can transfer disease that can quickly kill. Word on the street was that the only way to move the monkeys on was to kill one and string it up dead in a visible place as an example to the others. Needless to say, the school deemed this was probably not appropriate in an educational setting. So the monkeys stayed. They loved sneaking into the school kids' lunch boxes, looking for fruit. The long line-up of bags on hooks outside classrooms was irresistible to a hungry monkey!

One cheeky monkey came straight into our house one morning and grabbed a banana from the dining table. I stood on the lounge, stretched high to make myself as tall as possible, and yelled loudly at the monkey. It ignored me completely, finished its banana, left the peel in a mess on the table, and strolled back out the door, closing the screen door behind itself on the way out. Cheeky bugger.

Our attempts at monkey management at home so far consisted of warning the children about the dangers of monkeys so they didn't see them as playmates in the garden and practising how to quickly come inside if and when they came along. It was a little like a reverse fire drill, and was applicable to monkeys, snakes, and any other dangerous creatures that may appear in the garden. Jackson, who we joked had been born an 80-year-old man, was very serious about safety, and would often, of his own volition, call a "staff meeting" for our other children. He would line them up in a row, sit them down, and talk to them about safety before conducting another safety drill. I'm sure they had no idea what he was talking about, but they sat and listened nonetheless, and when he gave the call, they ran inside on cue.

Snakes were another major concern. Black and green mambas were common in the area, as well as less venomous snake varieties that could just as effectively scare the hell out of us. A snake in the dorm during study hall was a recipe for 30 boarders standing on their desks screaming at the supersonic pitch reserved exclusively for terrified teenage girls. As a boarding parent, the responsibility for snake removal fell squarely on me, and this was certainly not in the brochure when we signed up.

A solution to our unwanted pest predicament arrived in unexpected form on one of our regular weekends at Dusty and Marlaina's house. These weekends continued to be a joy and a refuge from the intensity of living on campus. We enjoyed long lazy weekends playing cards, watching TV (a novelty for us as we didn't have one!), sharing meals, and telling stories of the latest crazy from each of our lives. Best of all, there were no knocks on the door at all hours, followed by, 'Miss Annnnnaaaaa! I need you!' When I was off campus, I couldn't be reached, no matter the drama, no matter the unwanted pest, and it was pure bliss to do nothing important, and to do it without interruption.

Not long after the school year started, Dusty and Marlaina's cat gave birth to kittens while we were visiting. This delighted Jemima to no end, as she was quite fond of dragging their poor cat around, tucked under her little arm as she toddled around the yard. The kittens also happened to be born on Jemima's birthday, and as we watched them wobble around sleepily with eyes still closed, it dawned on us that a little ball of fluff like this may be the very thing we needed.

The idea of a family cat was especially appealing to me, not least because I'd been a cat-lover my entire life. It was certain to be of excellent use around our house with the endless stream of strange and wonderful creatures that made their way in uninvited.

And so, a few weeks later, this tiny kitten born on Jemima's birthday came home with us. She was quickly named "Scooter Dombkins" by Jackson, who happened to be riding his scooter around the house as we were discussing cat names. Scooter Dombkins was a short-haired tabby with striking green eyes, and she was the perfect mix of chilled-out with the kids, but vicious with unwanted backyard predators.

Scooter was, of course, also required at staff meetings where Jackson would first try to sit her in line with the other children, then give up and hold her dangling from his arms while he instructed the cat, along with the children, on her role during an emergency. Another drill would follow, where thankfully Scoots played her part well, as her job was to remain in the yard and kill or scare away the predator.

The safety drills served their purpose well, as sure enough there were many occasions where the kids' outside playtime would be disrupted by an uninvited guest. Jackson would give the call and within a few seconds, the children were safely inside, and Scooter Dombkins was chasing away the pest. Our system—created, implemented and managed by a four-year-old—was as effective as it was unconventional.

In the boarding house, Scooter Dombkins and I became a perfect snake removal team. When the tell-tale screech came from the dorm, indicating a slithery friend had entered, I'd throw Scoots in there. Quick as a flash, she would race around, pounce on the snake and drag it out the front gate. My trusty blunt-end shovel and I would then chop off its head while Scoots kept the snake pinned down, and the crisis was over. How I loved Scooter Dombkins.

Chapter 30

The Matriarchs

"Oh I can't wait to see you again
It's only a matter of time"
—LIN MANUEL MIRANDA, *WHO LIVES WHO DIES WHO TELLS YOUR STORY*

We received a devastating phone call from home one afternoon. Mark's mum, Barbara (or Babs, as she was affectionately known), had been diagnosed with cancer once again. Babs had been fighting and winning her battle with breast cancer since she was first diagnosed in 1991, with Mark's dad, Greg, always by her side, but after seven years of remission, the cancer had returned. This time it had travelled to her bones. The sadness of that diagnosis struck us deeply, and the distance across the Indian Ocean that stretched between us and them had never felt further.

Immediately after her diagnosis, Greg and Barbara booked flights to come and meet their new grandchildren. Knowing that once Babs started chemo, it wouldn't be safe for her to travel to Africa, they planned to squeeze in a quick visit to us before returning home for the next stage of her treatment. We were overwhelmingly thankful that we would be able to see them, and they would be able to meet the kids. We were thrilled to hear Mark's sister Kate was able to come along as well.

Mark's family is all things wonderful. Greg, Barbara, Mark and Kate—each remarkable in their own way—formed an A-team of superhumans that I loved dearly. Their visit was an intense mix of sadness over the diagnosis, relief to be together, and joy in watching the kids meet more of their family.

We took them to all our favourite places, showed them around Moshi, enjoyed a safari together, but mostly we just spent valuable time together with the kids. Greg and Babs had always delighted in their grandchildren—and there was no shortage of grandchildren now! They spent the mornings waking babies, feeding babies, changing babies, playing in the toy room covered in crawling babies, or sitting outside in fits of laughter watching the kids play with a hose, three of them trying to squirt water in their mouths at the same time in an epic battle to be hose champion of the Dombkins family.

By 10am, it was sleep time and I took the babies off to their rooms, changed a line-up of nappies, and tucked them into bed. Returning to the lounge room, I found Greg, Babs and Kate all lying fast asleep on the lounges. A morning of entertaining five busy children had wiped them out, and Mark and I had a good giggle watching them exhausted by four hours in our home.

We took them on safari and enjoyed all the wonderful sights, sounds, smells and experiences, including (of course) a car breakdown. Our new car was trusty and reliable most of the time, but on this trip, something was going awry. When we reached a certain speed, the motor cut out. Far away from home, we returned to a small-village *fundi* (mechanic) to try to have the problem fixed. He thought he knew the problem but needed to make some alterations and test out his progress. This would involve driving the car at speed to see what happened when we reached 100 kilometres per hour. We had Greg and Babs jump out to make space for the *fundi,* and they sat on a concrete wall in front of a small *duka* (shop) to wait.

The *fundi* fiddled with a loose connection, closed the hood, jumped back in the car still containing the rest of us, and took off down the road at 100 kilometres per hour. We zoomed past Greg and Babs sitting on the wall, and I cringed wondering what on earth they were thinking. It was a remarkably accurate visual representation of our relationship—us zipping past in a crazed whirlwind, and Greg and Babs calmly watching on in support. The car cut out again, the *fundi* pulled over, fiddled again, and we zoomed back. We zoomed back and forth, and back and forth in front of Greg and Babs sitting on that wall numerous times before the *fundi* got it right and the car was fixed. It took many hours and many attempts, but it was finally fixed. We picked up Greg and Babs once more, bracing ourselves for their understandable questions about the state of our life. They were incredibly good-humoured and mostly commented on their astonishment that the kids were still sitting happily in the back of the car. This, perhaps, was less an indication of excellent behaviour and more an indication of their familiarity with car disasters!

We were also blessed to have my family visit. My mum, Rhonda, dad Rod, and brother Tony and his wife Meg, were all able to come, in bits and pieces, and I dearly loved introducing them to our new kids and our new life. My dad was in and out semi-regularly as he travelled for work, my brother arrived as a special surprise treat, and my mum was able to come on a few visits—my favourite was to celebrate her 60th birthday and my 30th, which both fell in the same month. My mum was clever, wise, kind and strong. She had an excellent sense of humour and wriggled her nose like Samantha from *Bewitched* when she had an idea or thought something was especially wonderful. She was a no-nonsense, roll-your-sleeves-up, get-things-done kind of woman, and she taught me a thousand lessons in servant-hearted love, hard work, efficiency and getting on with life no matter the challenges. Her belief in me was unwavering—there was nothing she thought I couldn't do, and her stable confidence in me was a precious gift.

Somehow, mercifully, Mum's visits were quite smooth and disaster-free. The cars behaved, the wild animals behaved, and she enjoyed getting to know our world. Although we were disaster-free, she did get to witness the craziness of normal life, and one day she watched on as we dealt with a broken freezer.

Our fridge was operating well when the power was on, but the top section (the freezer) had stopped working. I'd let Pembe (the head maintenance guy) know, and he had agreed to come and take a look. After waiting a few days, Pembe came back with Darius, another maintenance worker, to look at it. They decided he needed to take it to town to have it fixed and would bring a temporary replacement for us to use in the meantime. Mum and I emptied out the fridge while he went to get what he needed. Emptying the fridge wasn't a huge job, as we were so used to power outages that we didn't keep too much in there anyway.

Darius and Pembe came back, and they took the fridge out, leaving it on the front porch. They disappeared for a while and came back with fridge 2. Only they couldn't get fridge 2 in the door because fridge 1 was in the way. They didn't move fridge 1, deciding instead to manoeuvre fridge 2 past fridge 1 by laying it down in the garden, squashing the plants. This hurt my heart a little, as I loved my garden, but I wasn't about to complain to two men who were valiantly trying to get me a fridge that worked.

They got fridge 2 into the house, took it to the kitchen doorway, and realised it didn't work. The power was off, so I wasn't sure how they realised it didn't work, or why they only realised this once it was in the house, but nonetheless, it didn't work. They left fridge 2 in the house and went off to get another fridge.

They returned with fridge 3. The same problem occurred at the front door. They couldn't get it past fridge 1, which was still on the front porch. Instead of moving fridge 1 out of the way, they repeated the garden squash option. Once in the house, fridge 2 was blocking the way, so they spent 45 minutes manoeuvring one past the other in the hallway. Once in the kitchen, they decided fridge 3 was too small. All our food (mostly 9 litres of milk for the day) wouldn't fit in there, so fridge 3 had to go. Only they didn't take it—they left it there while they got fridge 4.

By this time, they were running out of spare fridges on campus, so they took the fridge from the boarding house, since it was holidays and the boarders weren't there. They brought fridge 4 in the back door that connected our home to the boarding house. Of course, fridge 2 and fridge 3 were still in the hall. An hour and a half of moving them around in the most ridiculous ways later, and fridge 4 was finally in the kitchen (fridge 2 and fridge 3 were still in the hall). They had not yet considered removing any of the fridges out of the house.

With fridge 4 now in the kitchen, they attempted to plug it in. However, the power cord for fridge 4 was too short. It couldn't plug in. They asked for a power board, and Grace brought them the one from our washing machine. Only it had the wrong plug on the end. There are two types commonly used in Tanzania, and this one had the wrong end. They ripped that off, wired the other kind onto the end, and plugged in fridge 4.

There was still no power, so they couldn't test it. But they were happy with their work, so they went about removing fridge 2 and fridge 3. Fridge 3 had to go out the back door to the dorm, and fridge 2 out the front door. But they were the wrong way around, so with another half hour of manoeuvring, they swapped them around and took them out. They left fridge 1 on the porch. Mum and I looked at it, confused. Wasn't the whole point that fridge 1 was going to town to be fixed?

Later in the evening, the power came back on. But the fridge didn't. I waited a few hours in case it was just slow, but still nothing. I turned it on and off, tried everything I could think of to get it to work, but still nothing. Fridge 4 didn't work after all.

By now it was 8pm on a Friday and we still had no freezer, but now we also had no fridge, no washing machine (because they changed the plug and I didn't have another extension cord) and a ruined garden. Fridge 1 was still on the front porch, and as it was the weekend, no maintenance guys would be returning until at least Monday.

Mum and I sat on the couch and had a good laugh. It wasn't a disaster, but she certainly was getting a good glimpse into daily life. I loved showing it all to her, watching her nose twitch at the hilarity, seeing her delight as she got to know the kids, and collecting the nuggets of wisdom she casually dropped into conversation, treasuring them in my heart.

Our kids were incredibly blessed to have three amazing grandmothers—Bibi, Babs and Rhonda—each with their own strength, beauty, wisdom and courage. They profoundly influenced their grandchildren's lives. They loved them deeply. Their fingerprints were all over each one.

In the coming years, we would lose all three of these remarkable women. All of them would lose their lives to cancer. One by one, we would say goodbye and grieve their loss. Their losses were unbearable; their impact on our lives, incredible; their legacy, immeasurable. Each of these women climbed and conquered their own mountains, showing us the way and leaving us with their wisdom and example—their grace, compassion and resilience became a compass to guide our path.

Chapter 31

The Second Attempt

"Mountains know secrets we need to learn. That it might take time, it might be hard, but if you just hold on long enough you will find the strength to rise up."
—TYLER KNOTT

The time had come for Mark's second attempt at climbing Mount Kilimanjaro. This time he would aim for the summit. It's no easy feat for anyone to summit Mount Kilimanjaro, but Mark had the additional challenge of bringing a large group of students with him.

The preparation and previous trips had gone well, and while he was filled with excitement and hope for a successful climb, we were both nervously anticipating what may occur while he was up there. Once again, it seemed silly to expect something significant to happen just because Mark was up a mountain, but it had happened so predictably that I was once again bracing myself.

The school "lorry"—a huge, yellow, open-sided passenger truck that resembled an oversized, open-air safari vehicle—was loaded up with climbing gear, packs, students and teachers. The kids and I cheered them off from the school car park, blowing kisses and running behind the truck yelling, 'Go Daddy!' and waving as they set off to begin the climb.

They were taking the Marangu Route—a five-day trek up the east side of the mountain and returning down the same route. As usual, I watched the mountain from the backyard at home. The first few days looked like great climbing weather—clear skies and moderate temperatures. But on the third day, the weather began to change. A dense, dark cloud descended over the mountain. My heart sank watching it come over. The mountain made its own weather systems, and no forecast could predict what the mountain may do.

From home, all I could see was the thick grey curtain of clouds that separated the world below from mysteries above. High on the mountain, Mark and his students were hit by a blizzard. They walked as far as they could through snow, ice, and high winds before reaching the base camp at Kibo Hut to try and wait out the storm. But the storm didn't pass. A snowstorm at 4,700 metres was no small issue. It set in and raged on, and the group had to begin the difficult discussion about their next steps. It didn't seem possible to go on, and yet no one wanted to give up on the hope of reaching the summit.

While Mark wrestled with the hopes and dreams of a dozen teenagers high on the mountain, I got another phone call. Mama Uriah was calling to confirm that the new changes in Social Welfare policy would, in some ways we were yet to understand, be applied to our case. I couldn't understand what this would mean for us. We already had the children with us, according to policy as it was at the time. I understood they were changing how this would operate for future cases, but I didn't understand what this had to do with us. We were years into fostering the kids and should be soon approaching our time to proceed through Court and finalise the adoptions. Instead, we were facing new hurdles, and they were completely unknown. Our own storm clouds were gathering, that much I knew for sure.

Up on the mountain, discussions reached the only logical conclusion. It just wasn't safe to continue higher into a turbulent storm with no end in sight. With immense disappointment, they turned back and began their descent. They retraced their path, enduring a gruelling 30-kilometre trek down the mountain through the same snow, ice and cold that had thwarted their hopes for success. Walking up a mountain in ice and snow in the hope of reaching the summit is one thing, but walking back down is entirely different. It was gruelling and demoralising.

As they returned home, the curtain lifted and revealed the spectacular mountain peak once more. It was particularly beautiful, with the late afternoon sun causing the mass of fresh snow to sparkle with pink and orange hues. It looked calm and magical. The only remaining sign of the fierce storm that engulfed it just moments ago was stunning beauty. The storm passed and the beauty remained.

Chapter 32

Struggling

"If you want to fly, you have to give up the things that weigh you down."
—TONI MORRISON

'NO, NO, NO!' I screamed in a furious, out-of-control rage as I stormed out of the house and into the garden, slamming the screen door loudly behind me and waving a tea towel in the air frantically. '*ACHA! ACHA SASA HIVI!* STOP! STOP RIGHT NOW!' The volume of my voice and the uncontained fury flowing completely unchecked from my pounding heart, through my veins and out my mouth stunned me, but I couldn't stop.

'*NENDA MBALI. SASA. NA USIRUDI TENA HAPA.* GO AWAY. NOW. AND NEVER COME BACK HERE.' I finished screaming, as the vein in my forehead threatened to burst. The stunned Tanzanian man standing in my garden, on the receiving end of my temper, froze in shock.

I closed my eyes, clenching a damp tea towel in my hands tightly, and breathed in deeply, willing myself to calm down. *How did I get to this point?* I wondered. The loss of control terrified me. This feeling was completely foreign. I was always calm, cool as a cucumber, even in a crisis. On the outside, at least.

I wondered if it was just the continual build-up of stress. The challenges of day-to-day life, raising five little people, trying to get through an adoption process, and attending to our jobs and responsibilities were constant, and although there were ebbs and flows in how much it took out of us, it was definitely taking its toll over time.

We lived on a heightened level of alert, always anticipating the next problem to solve, always trying to stay a step ahead of the next disaster. I noticed after a while that the old familiar feeling of losing track of time while driving, suddenly arriving at my destination with little memory of the journey, no longer occurred for me. It almost seemed laughable to recall driving along without a care in the world.

We had been warned on arrival in Moshi that if we were ever to inadvertently cause an accident and run someone over, we should not stop, or we would be killed. I laughed the first time we were told this, assuming it was a joke, but it was absolutely not a joke. We were told to drive directly to the Police station and bring a policeman back to the scene with us. Our friends knew someone who had experienced this exact situation. She hit a pedestrian and instinctively pulled over and got out to help. She was run down by a crowd that gathered, and only escaped by fleeing through a field of tall maize plants and hiding. Driving around these areas was like dodgem cars at times, with pedestrians wandering where they pleased, donkeys using the road, motorbikes weaving in and out of traffic, and unroadworthy vehicles everywhere. Hitting a pedestrian was not unlikely. An accident of some kind, at some stage, seemed inevitable.

The level of stress we were under was certainly beginning to take its toll. Most of the time, we functioned well and pushed through one frustration after the next, debriefing at the end of each day, but there were also times we weren't coping so well.

Our "not-coping" moments sometimes appeared in the ways we might expect and other times in the most unlikely of places. Our most stressful moments often required us to keep our cool, not respond, and suppress our emotions. Unfortunately, this sometimes meant that emotion was misdirected towards unsuspecting randoms. For me, it was the lawnmower guy. He was one of the school gardening staff, and his job was to mow the lawns of the school grounds. The grounds were quite extensive, and our yard was a part of his mowing territory. It was also a gateway to the yard behind the boarding house, which was also his territory. He was hardworking, thorough and quietly went about his work.

I had put a lot of time, money and effort into beautifying our garden and growing the lawn, largely because the grass growing thickly over the dirt below reduced the amount of mud that my children tracked through my house daily. I hated the mud, and especially in the wet season, grass was a game-changer. I would lovingly tend to my grass, carefully encouraging runners to extend over dirt patches and before long, I had achieved a pleasing result. Then the lawnmower guy came. He had the mower prepared on a setting so low it not only cut the grass, it decimated it. Any slightly raised areas of lawn became bare earth once again as the blades chopped away my beautiful grass, roots and all. I was intensely frustrated. *It's not his fault,* I told myself, *he doesn't know you're trying to grow the lawn. Just talk to him. I'm sure he'll help you grow it if he knows what you're trying to achieve.*

So I talked to the lawnmower guy and explained the situation. I asked him to put his mower on a higher setting, so it didn't destroy the lawn. He looked at me as if I was the stupidest foreigner he'd met yet, but agreed. I went back to tending my lawn.

A month or so later, I'd made some progress, and then the lawnmower guy returned. He decimated my lawn once again. This time, something snapped in me, and all my pent-up rage came hurtling straight at him.

So here we stood, the lawnmower guy and I. He, frozen in shock, and I, clutching my tea towel, willing myself to calm the heck down. I brought the fury down a few notches only to find I'd swapped it for condescension. In an attempt to explain myself, I pointed out the grass he had killed, I showed him once again how to adjust his mower to a higher setting, in an intensely patronising way, as if he didn't already know, and then I banned him from mowing our lawn. It wasn't actually even our lawn—it was the school's property, and he worked for the school. I had no place to ban him, and my behaviour was disgraceful. I was losing my mind, and I knew it. I found him later and apologised. But I still asked him to refrain from mowing our lawn.

I confessed my shameful behaviour to Mark later that day, and he had one comment. 'Mumma,' he said with a grin, 'you are struuuuuugling!' He was right. I was struggling, and I needed to get myself together before any more unsuspecting grounds staff found themselves on the receiving end of my displaced anger.

The lawnmower guy did stop mowing our lawn, I'm sure out of fear of the crazy lady living inside. Instead, he just passed through the yard on his way to the boarding house with the mower on a high enough setting to not reach the grass. One day, I came home, and he'd mowed straight over my new garden hose, ripping it to shreds. *Touché,* I thought. *I deserved that.*

These were the kinds of stories that sounded crazy when we shared them with family and friends back home. We never wanted to worry anyone, so we kept some of the wilder moments to ourselves, knowing they just wouldn't translate well, and there was no way to normalise these things for people not living here with us. It was when friends visited that they saw the realities of it all, and we could share the warts and all stories in full.

If anyone was ready for the warts-and-all version of our life, it was my dear friend Jess, who stepped off the plane at Kilimanjaro Airport on a still, sticky evening and into the warm Tanzanian air. Jess grinned as she dragged her suitcase along the bumpy path. I squealed as she came into view, and pulled her into a hug, squeezing her tight and rocking her side to side.

Jess and I had shared a long friendship through many seasons of life. She is bubbly but relaxed, with sparkly, laughing eyes and a great sense of humour. She's insightful, clever and impossibly stylish, but totally ready to jump into adventure. She was a part of a small group of precious friends who meant the world to me. Jess and I, along with Jo (who survived her visit with us and her baby daughter Hannah and lived to tell the tale), and two other dear friends, Katie and Michelle, had been meeting together and praying for each other every week for many years. Even after we moved to Tanzania, I would Skype in while they met—midday for me and evening for them. They are the kind of friends every woman in the world should have—the laugh till you cry, call you on your crap, talk till 2am, love you with their life kind of friends. Without them, I'd be lost somewhere in the wilderness of my mind, aimlessly wandering, I'm sure.

Jess and I had an exciting trip planned—in addition to travelling around the local safari parks, showing her our life in Moshi and spending time with the kids, we were also going to Rwanda, to visit the genocide memorial and venture into the beautiful Virunga Mountains. It was my first visit to Rwanda too, and it was fun to be tourists together. Rwanda was strikingly different to Tanzania, despite being neighbours. It's appropriately known as "The Land of a Thousand Hills" with its volcanic mountains covered with lush tropical forests that meander down to clear blue lakes. But it was the stories of forgiveness and healing told at the genocide memorial that left an indelible imprint on me.

I was stunned by the capacity of the nation to forge ahead through unimaginable pain and devastation and keep moving forward. Walking the streets you would never know what happened here less than 20 years prior. Somehow, the people of Rwanda were finding a way to live with their pain, anger, guilt and fear. Somehow, they offered forgiveness to former friends and neighbours who had brutally killed their children, partners or parents with machetes. Somehow, they received forgiveness for unspeakable atrocities and returned to living alongside one another in communities. The best and worst of humanity are on display right alongside each other in that place. It moved and challenged me deeply.

Following our trip to Rwanda, we were going to visit some rural communities with Dusty to see some of his microfinance projects in action. We enjoyed a surprisingly smooth trip, with no breakdowns or major disasters, but enough exposure to the realities of life that Jess had a good sense of what life was like for us now. Perhaps my favourite moment was driving off-road, at speed, across vast barren plains in Dusty's truck, which had windows that were wound down and currently couldn't wind back up.

On arrival, we were completely covered in a film of orange-brown dust, which had been blown into every orifice imaginable by the billowy clouds of dirt flying straight in our faces. Jess' usually well-mascaraed, dark lashes were now a pale tan colour, dotted with tiny bits of village dust. As we exited the car, we were greeted by a woman who immediately noticed our condition, took out a cloth and started beating Jess down with it, to remove the dust. It was an unconventional welcome that took Jess by surprise until she realised the purpose of the cloth beating.

We stood on smooth dirt, immaculately swept with brooms made from twigs, and surrounded by small, round, mud-brick homes with thatched roofs. We held chickens that flapped in our faces, ate homemade bread with honey that attracted a swarm of bees as we sat frozen still, hoping not to be stung as we pretended the swarm was totally normal, and watched a demonstration of the water well that Dusty's team had helped the village to install. We sat on upturned buckets and drank milky, sweet tea from tin mugs as we listened to incredible stories from the people of this village.

Jess took it all in her stride with curiosity and humour, enjoying each adventure, eager to find out more at every step. She had asked me a few times about how we were going, and I'd given my best attempt at explaining how life was for us. But over dinner one night, as she and I looked out over the plains at Tarangire, she gently but firmly asked me the hard questions... How was I really going? Was I looking after myself? Was I eating? Was I sleeping? How was I coping in the hardest moments?

I loved her for knowing me deeply but cringed at my less-than-adequate answers. My initial attempts at, "it gets pretty stressful at times, but it's okay really," fell flat, and the tears in her eyes told me she was serious. I had never been good at self-awareness—at knowing my capacity or realising when I was beyond it. I was a soldier-on, whatever the cost, it'll be fine, kind of girl. Truthfully though, I wasn't always coping so well. This was evidently obvious to Jess. Her wise words and careful questions were like a flashlight revealing the cracks in my armour. I hated those cracks, but I knew they were there, and I loved her for gently pointing this out to me.

There were times when Mark and I had excellent practices for self-care, discipline to do the things we knew were good for us, and motivation to work hard on well-being. Other times we struggled, reverting to old habits, numbing stress and pain, and getting by however we could.

In honesty, we were very ordinary people, living an extraordinary experience. There were no superhero capes or magicians' wands—just the two of us, in all our humanity, bumbling our way through as best we could, climbing our mountain. The struggle moments were revealing to us both that something had to change. As bad as things were, we didn't know they were about to get so much worse.

Chapter 33

Send Them Back

"Winds in the east, mist coming in,
like something is brewing and about to begin."
—MARY POPPINS

Mark sat in the dimly lit waiting room for an hour or so, watching the slow movements of the people around him. Others waited with him, their own pressing needs drawing them here in hope of answers. A cleaner passed through with a dustpan, and half-heartedly flicked a cigarette butt into it. He missed, and didn't bother trying again. The pace of life was excruciatingly slow. Efficiency as we knew it was a foreign concept, and although we were accustomed to it now, it was intensely frustrating when we were on a clock.

Mrs Nazari, the Deputy Commissioner for Social Welfare, called for Mark. He entered her dark, stuffy office and greeted her. Mark's many late nights learning Swahili served him well—his Swahili was fluent now and he was able to talk with Mrs Nazari in her native tongue. Getting down to business, Mark enquired about the status of our application, noting that as we had now lived in Tanzania for close to three years, we would soon be ready to submit our application for a Court date.

Mrs Nazari looked at our file in front of her, then closed it and shifted in her chair.

'There's been a change,' she began. 'Things were different three years ago when you began your adoption, and the time has come for us to review our procedures.'

'I see,' said Mark, immediately sensing danger. 'What does that mean for us?'

'We want all of our cases to follow one process, to streamline everything, so each is the same. Your case began a long time ago, and your process has been different. The time has come for your case to fall into line with our new system.'

'What would you like us to do exactly?' Mark asked, concern growing rapidly within him.

'I want you to start again, from the beginning, so that your case has all the new paperwork.'

'Start again?' Mark said. 'You mean start the paperwork again?'

'No, it will not be that simple. I mean start the whole process again. First, you must apply to foster, then you can select a baby home, and then you can select children from that baby home.'

'But we already have the children with us—they've been with us for over two years already!'

'Yes. So you must send them back and begin again,' Mrs Nazari said firmly.

'We can't just send them back!' Mark replied, matching her firmness. 'They're children! They almost died where they were, that's why we have them! We can't just return them; it would devastate them.' Mark felt his pulse racing.

'It would only be for a year or so, while you submitted new paperwork, then you can choose them again, if you like, and they can return to you,' Mrs Nazari pushed.

'This is unbelievable,' Mark responded. 'If you want the file to look the same, then just fix the paperwork to match, but don't make the children suffer for your change in procedure. Besides, our file already looks different anyway—you can't undo what has already been done.'

'No,' Mrs Nazari interrupted. 'Your file will be destroyed. There will be no record of the children coming to you at all yet.'

'I can't believe what I'm hearing,' Mark said, struggling to keep his temper. 'Your file will be a lie if it doesn't record the truth for these children. What's done is done, and it was completed perfectly within your process at the time. You can't undo it and pretend it never happened. We have done nothing wrong. All you need to do is apply your new process to cases that start now and allow a period of time for old files to phase out.'

'Mark, it is not your place to inform the practices of Social Welfare. If you want to adopt these children, you will follow the new procedures. Try your luck in Court if you dare, but you will not succeed. It will only be a few more years to do it our new way. Send them back and start again,' she finished.

Mark's blood was boiling as he tried to take in all he was hearing. He was furious. But he knew this world inside out now, and he was well practised at controlling his emotions. There was nothing more he could say at this point. He had to keep his cool and leave the meeting before it unravelled and our application was further damaged. He steeled himself, thanked Mrs Nazari, and left the meeting.

Holding himself together until he left the building, he walked a few metres down the street and then slumped against the wall, panic taking over his body. He pulled out his phone and called my number.

'How'd it go?' I asked as soon as the call connected.

'Send them back,' Mark struggled to even say it out loud. 'She said we have to send them back.'

Chapter 34

A Faraway Land

"You can't go back and change the beginning but you can start where you are and change the ending."
—C.S. LEWIS

Mark returned to Moshi, and we were grateful to be together again. The ups and downs of this journey were torturous, and we were each other's support. Following our phone call, Mark had made one last attempt at sorting through the issue with Social Welfare in Dar es Salaam. He went over Mrs Nazari's head and was granted a short meeting with her boss, the Commissioner himself. The meeting was cordial enough—the Commissioner heard Mark out and sympathised with our perspective. He said he thought it was a bit extreme to return the children. But he didn't step in to act. He ultimately pushed it back to Mrs Nazari's desk, and we were no closer to a solution.

We weren't sure what our next move should be. It struck us that throughout the entire process so far, nothing had ever been achieved or moved forward without us pushing it. We wondered if Mrs Nazari intended to act on her claim that we must return the children—if she would be bothered, if she would, for the first time, do something. It was hard to imagine. And yet, if she did, the prospects for our children were unthinkable.

We decided to go and see our lawyer in Moshi. We had our own copies of the Tanzanian adoption law, and we knew it inside and out, but we wanted to talk it through with her and find out exactly what powers Mrs Nazari had, and what we could do legally to contest her decision if she did try to remove them.

Our lawyer, Patricia, was exceptional. She was professional, punctual, and hard-working. We had every trust in her, and she always followed through for us. We made an appointment as soon as we could on Monday.

Patricia's office was in downtown Moshi. Visiting her was like stepping into a world where efficiency came to life. Outside in the sleepy streets, Moshi life meandered on, but up the stairs and into this office, work was done. Patricia dressed as professionally as she worked, and just sitting down with her made us at least feel like we were achieving something.

We talked Patricia through the latest, laying out our concerns and asking her advice for how to move forward. What she said stopped me in my tracks.

'I don't think you need to worry about the Commissioner,' she said. 'You've been here almost three years, so it's time we can submit to Court. If they come to take the children, we will have to deal with that then, but there is no legal reason for that to happen. I don't see how they can legally take them. Everything that you have done is according to the law, so let's get your submission ready and proceed to Court.'

'What?' I replied. I could barely let myself believe her words. 'We can really do that?'

'Yes, we can,' she said. 'There are still some documents you will need, but we can start work on that, and soon we will be ready to begin your Court process.'

'But what about approval from the Commissioner?' Mark asked.

'I can see here that we are required to notify the Commissioner when we intend to submit to Court,' Patricia explained, 'but we don't require a response.'

'Mrs Nazari did say we could try our luck in Court,' Mark said. 'But she also said we were sure to fail.'

'There's no reason for this case to fail,' Patricia replied firmly. 'Listen, we don't know what Mrs Nazari will do next. If she comes for the children or not, we don't know. We can't worry about her. We will worry about the things we *can* do. And what we can do is prepare this case for Court.'

Mark and I left the building, stunned. "Going through Court" had always been a faraway land where other adoptive families lived, but not us. An hour ago, we felt we were about to jump back three years and start the whole process again, and now we had reached the promised land. We were "going through Court". It was our turn. We checked with each other and checked again, making sure we hadn't imagined what Patricia had said. But it was true. We were going to submit our Application for Adoption to the High Court of Tanzania.

Chapter 35

The Letter

"When you reach the end of your rope, tie a knot in it and hang on."
—FRANKLIN D. ROOSEVELT

We spent the next two months preparing paperwork and organising everything we would need to submit our application to the High Court. There was a long list of requirements, with each document representing an important part of the process. We needed to prove our suitability as parents and meet each requirement of Tanzanian Law. We knew this law inside and out. Since the moment we settled on Tanzania as our new home, I had read and re-read that law. Over and over, checking and double-checking, to ensure I wasn't missing anything that would ultimately disqualify us.

All the documents we could prepare in advance had been ready and waiting for the past three years. I had every document ready. I had spare copies of every document ready. There were a few things we needed current copies of, such as updated Police checks for Mark and me, from both the Australian government and the Tanzanian government. Wheels were in motion to get these organised and finalise all our paperwork.

We hadn't heard anything at all from the Commissioner since Mark's meeting and hoped this meant that no action was being taken, that no news was good news, that all would be well if we just stayed away and stayed quiet.

Then one day in April, a letter arrived for us in the mail. It was from the Department of Social Welfare. This was a surprise. We had never had any contact at all unless it was initiated by us. Chills ran down Mark's spine as he held the letter in his hand. His mind rushed back to his meeting with Mrs Nazari, where she had told Mark to begin the process again.

He opened the letter and began to read, his heart immediately racing. Written in formal Swahili, the letter took him a few minutes to understand. Panic took over Mark's body as he read and re-read the unfamiliar words, beads of sweat forming on his forehead. Wanting to double-check, he raced the letter to a Tanzanian colleague. He was correct. This was the letter we had feared.

Mark rushed home, and I could see from his pale face that something wasn't right. He pulled me into our bedroom, shut the door and took out the letter. We read it together. The Commissioner was writing to inform us that he was directing our social worker (Mama Uriah) to remove our children and return them to Mwanza. There it was in black and white—the worst possible letter we could receive. I crumbled forward, head in my hands, and began to silently sob. Mark wrapped his arms around me and we sat together, devastated.

The letter indicated that three copies of the letter had been sent. One had come to us, one was being sent to Mama Uriah, and a third was being sent to Mama Manessa, the social worker in Mwanza. We continued to sit, staring at the letter in disbelief. Throughout this whole process, we had tried to maintain an understanding of the perspective of others around us. We were the foreigners—we were the new ones, coming into a culture that wasn't our own, and trying to navigate a system regulated by the beliefs and values of Tanzanian people.

Often, we could understand their perspective, albeit different to our own, and accept that we needed to patiently follow along. But this time was different. We just couldn't find a common understanding. We couldn't view this from any angle that made sense. Sure, we understood that the Social Welfare departments had a new system and wanted to implement it consistently, but we couldn't see how that need for every file to look the same could come above the best interests of the children. We knew the trauma our children had already endured—to lose their birth parents, to lose their grandparents, to be without parents at all, and to finally move to a new family. We couldn't imagine what it would do to them to be taken again. It was unbelievable to us that anyone could think this made sense.

The adoption rollercoaster was in fine form. From the high of beginning our application for Court to the low of this letter. It was taking its toll on us both. Quiet tears continued to roll down my face as we held that letter. We hugged each other tight and prayed our little hearts out, pleading for a solution. It was terrifying. These three little people we loved so dearly were in danger of being removed, and we didn't know if or how we could stop it. The feeling of someone else having control of our children was intensely painful, and we longed to be free from it. We felt we were so close, and yet here was another mammoth obstacle.

Once the shock wore off, we started to discuss our options. What could we possibly do? We felt like it really couldn't be legal for the Commissioner to do this. We knew the children were in our care legally, at the request of Babu and Bibi, following every regulation at the time, and that there was no good reason to remove them. No one had any concerns for the children in our care—they were happy and settled and growing, and we had glowing reports from our social worker's visits. Should we fight this somehow? Call the Commissioner and argue again for him to change his mind? We felt like that was a futile mission. Could we take legal action to appeal the Commissioner's decision? We knew how long any legal process would take in Tanzania, and the children would be removed months before we could get any progress made on that.

After discussing any and all options we could think of, we decided our best course of action might be to wait. The letter didn't actually direct us to do anything ourselves. This felt like the last thing we wanted to do—we wanted to fight, or kick and scream, and take some kind of action that would make us feel at least as though we had some control. It took all the restraint we had to decide to wait and see what happened next.

We began an excruciating period of time, where we waited for the phone to ring, or Mama Uriah to turn up at our door, ready to take the kids. It was sickening. Living on a school campus, with a boarding house attached to our home, there was always someone knocking at the door. There were constant phone calls and messages. And every time, every single time, it could have been someone coming to take the kids. We looked and felt like death warmed up. Our nerves were shot, and we could barely stand the suspense of wondering what was ahead. We felt like we were walking into an ambush that could appear at any moment.

A few days passed, and we heard nothing. We talked constantly about what might happen. We knew there were two more copies of our letter out there. We knew Mama Uriah believed the kids should be with us. She had watched Jabari transform from a deathly baby into a giggling toddler in our home. We also knew she was an honourable woman. She would do her job exactly as directed, and although she would hate to have to remove our kids, she would do as she was told. We respected Mama Uriah so much, and we would never want her job to be at risk. As more days passed and we still heard nothing, we wondered what was happening. Maybe Mama Uriah was talking with the Commissioner herself. Maybe she was convincing him to change his mind. But we felt if that was the case, she would still call us and let us know that's what she was doing.

The third letter was in Mwanza—addressed to Mama Manessa. She didn't need to act on the letter but would expect that at some stage the children would arrive back in her region. Would she call Mama Uriah to discuss? Would she call us to talk about it? We had no idea. She was a complete unknown.

We continued to wait. After another week passed, with no action, the suspense became intolerable. We were barely sleeping. We were jumpy and anxious. Just looking at the kids, knowing they could be taken any day, any minute, made me weepy. I didn't want to let them out of my sight. We decided Mark should book a meeting with Mama Uriah and try to find out what he could. He made an appointment for the next day.

Entering her office, he proceeded through the usual Swahili greetings before chatting further.

'*Habari za nyumbani?* How is everything at home?' Mama Uriah asked.

'*Safi.* Fine.' Mark replied and waited for her to comment further.

'*Haya. Habari za watoto?* Okay. How are the children?' she asked.

'*Nzuri tu.* All well,' Mark replied, and waited again. The waiting became awkward as Mama Uriah wondered why Mark was there, and Mark wondered if she was going to mention the letter. But Mama Uriah didn't mention the letter.

'*Habari za kazi?* How is your work?' Mark asked, fishing again.

'*Eh, sawa tu, lakini kazi nyingi kwa sasa.* It's okay, but I have a lot of work to do at the moment,' she replied, without elaborating further. Mark tossed around whether or not to say anything himself, and eventually, the awkward silence got the better of him.

'*Umesikia habari yoyote kutoka Dar es Salaam hivi karibuni?* Have you heard any news from Dar es Salaam lately?' he asked, as casually as possible.

Mama Uriah scoffed a little. '*Sijasikia chochote kutoka Dar es Salaam kwa miezi kadhaa.* I haven't heard anything from Dar es Salaam in months! I never seem to hear anything anymore,' she replied, clearly frustrated by the lack of communication. Mark blinked a few times. She hadn't received the letter. Unsure whether to mention it or not, he decided to stay quiet for the moment.

'*Hiya. Pole kwa kazi. Tutaonana badaaye Mama Uriah.* Oh, I'm sorry to hear. See you another time soon, Mama Uriah.' Mark wrapped up the meeting and returned home.

It was wonderful news to us that Mama Uriah didn't have the letter. We knew the letter may still arrive—maybe her copy had been sent later than ours, maybe it had just been delayed in the post. But we also knew the Tanzanian postal system was notorious for losing mail. We prayed and hoped that this awful letter had disappeared, like socks in the dryer, with the millions of others that never make it to their final destination.

The pressure lifted a little, but there was still the third letter. What were the chances that it was lost too? One call from Mama Manessa to Mama Uriah, and we were in trouble again. We battled on, still on edge, but with a little more hope than before.

In the meantime, we continued to prepare for Court. We knew that ultimately, a Judge would decide where the children should be, and all we could do was proceed as quickly as possible with our Court process. This process usually took 12 months to complete from start to finish, but there was a lot of variation. By the beginning of May, we made our first submission to Court. Our lawyer had been working hard on this for us and submitted our preliminary paperwork.

Most cases in our local Court had been on hold. There was a rotation of Judges in process, and the previous two Judges had left. The Courts always close over Christmas and then start the new year with the criminal cases first. The first few months of the year are busy with these cases, and other issues, such as adoption cases, are attended to later. One of the new Judges had arrived, and another was yet to arrive. Our lawyer had prepared us that it may be quite some time before one of the new Judges picked up our case. And then there was an anxious wait to find out whether the new Judges felt positively about adoption. There were a lot of variables flying around, and we continued on, one step after another, hoping for the best.

Towards the end of May, we were stunned by a call from Patricia to say our case had been picked up by the new Judge, and we had been given a date for our Mention in Court. It was in only four days' time! This was unheard of.

An adoption case in Tanzania requires three visits to Court. The first is the Mention, where the case is literally just mentioned in Court, the second is the Hearing, where the whole case is presented along with all documentation, and the third is the Verdict, where the Judge gives the final decision. Sometimes, this can be a bit of an endless cycle, as it is common for a case to be scheduled for a date, but then not actually be heard on that date. If an applicant has a successful Mention, but then the Hearing falls through, that applicant then has to start again with another Mention.

Some friends of ours, who were also adopting, were given the same date as us, but this was their seventh Court date, and they were yet to have a successful Mention. We tried to restrain our excitement, as we knew it was unlikely it would be successful. It might take six months or more to achieve a successful Mention.

Even so, we had a Court date! And yet, we had a letter saying our kids would be taken away. The conflicting emotions within us were almost unbearable. We had a beautiful beacon of hope emerging before us, and yet the threat of disaster was right there in the background. Still, we prayed and stayed as positive as possible.

One of our biggest challenges was carrying on in normal life with a storm raging around us. We both had jobs, and most importantly, our five little scallywags. They were now aged seven, four, four, three and three. We didn't want them to be affected by the ups and downs of this process, and so we worked hard each day to protect them from the stress of it all. They were a beautiful distraction, in truth, and spending the days in the garden surrounded by their giggles and frivolity was pure joy. I sat in our garden under the Jacaranda tree and listened to Jackson conduct a staff meeting with the kids gathered in a huddle.

'What we have here, kids, is a tarantula hawk wasp. It has stung this spider to paralyse it, and now it will lay its eggs in the spider's belly.' The kids watched the spider/wasp pair with fascination, as the wasp dragged the spider across the grass. Jackson continued to explain while trying to block Scooter Dombkins from eating said spider.

'Soon, the eggs will hatch inside the spider and eat her alive from the inside out,' he told them, to the astonishment of four wide-eyed little faces. I'd never heard of a tarantula hawk wasp before, but knew better by now than to doubt him.

'Where did you learn about that?' I asked.

'From this book,' he said, before opening a bag he carried around most of the time, which he called his "future bag". In it was, of course, things you may need in the future—a compass, first aid supplies, binoculars, a small Swiss Army knife, tissues, and a small pocketbook titled *Wildlife of East Africa*.

My heart was so full, and in the garden with the kids, it was easier to push all thoughts of pending doom out of my mind and just be present with my family in this crazy, wonderful season of life.

Chapter 36

The Mention

"After climbing a great hill, one only finds that there are many more hills to climb."
—NELSON MANDELA

Our Mention was in four days, and we didn't have much time to plan. Mark was scheduled to attend a week-long hike up Mount Kilimanjaro. His group's last attempt had come so close, and he was excited to have another chance at the summit. Climbing Kilimanjaro is challenging enough for anyone, let alone climbing with a group of teenagers to look after. Thankfully, our Mention was scheduled for first thing in the morning. The school agreed to let Mark attend Court in the morning and then catch up to the group of climbers later in the day.

In the bright morning light, we lined up outside the Court with all the other hopeful souls attending that day. Also in line with us were our friends, waiting for the seventh time. It felt greedy to hope our own Mention would succeed on the first try, while sitting alongside someone waiting on their seventh attempt.

After an hour of waiting, our case was called. It happened so quickly we barely knew what was happening. We didn't even enter the room—Patricia went in on our behalf, and as quick as she was in, she was out. *That can't be good,* I thought, as she returned to us so quickly. But her smile told a different story. She grinned at us and told us that the Mention was successful, and more than that, we had been given our next Court date—for the following week!

We wished our friends the very best for their Mention and raced off to drive Mark to the base of the mountain. In the car, we screamed and danced and grinned in celebration. What was happening? How was this possible? We had a successful Mention, our Hearing was scheduled for the following week, and the Verdict was always soon after the Hearing. If our Hearing was successful and the Judge ruled in our favour, we could legally adopt our children in a matter of weeks! We could barely believe it. It wasn't certain—the Hearing might fall through, which would mean we would have to go back again and start with another Mention. And there was still that pesky letter floating around. But everything was happening in such an extraordinary way that we really started to believe this must be a miracle unfolding before us.

As we drove towards the mountain, we were acutely aware once again of the significance of the mountain in our story. Somehow, big things always happened when Mark was up a mountain. Looking up at the snow-covered summit, Mark said, 'I'm going to summit this time, I just know it. I'm going to summit, and when I get back, we're going to have a successful Hearing. It's all finally coming together.' It was almost too much to believe.

Mark changed out of his suit and into his hiking gear in the car, and as we pulled up to the meeting area, his group of students were ready to go. He spun me around, kissed me and ran off to join his group, grinning from ear to ear.

I drove home, picked the kids up from school, and scooped them all up in a big hug. 'We've almost done it,' I whispered to them, 'Almost!'

We spent the afternoon lying in the sun on the trampoline, looking up at the mountain, where in the distance Mark was climbing. It was an incredible day.

Our poor friends, on the other hand, had another unsuccessful day in Court. Not only did they not get a Mention, but they were allocated to a different Judge—one that was not even in town yet. They would now have to wait for their eighth Court date, and it would likely be a long wait. We felt for them deeply.

Mark practically skipped up the first day of the climb up Kilimanjaro. Energised by our positive day in Court, he took delight in attempting once more to climb the great mountain. Mark so badly wanted to summit, but it was not just up to him. He could be feeling fine and climbing well but end up having to turn back for the sake of an unwell student. They could come across poor climbing conditions for a second time that could force them to turn back. There were many barriers between Mark and the summit, but he wanted it so badly.

The climb was going to plan for the first few days—students and staff both coping well and the weather was cooperating. But as the days went on, some of the students began to tire or suffer the effects of altitude sickness. Some of the staff were also struggling and happily turned back with those who couldn't go on. Mark was feeling well and continued on with the remaining climbers.

By the fourth night, summit night, there was a small group of nine tired but excited souls who had made it this far and dreamed of the summit. Crawling out of their tents at 11pm after a few short hours of breathless sleep, they clipped on their backpacks and set out for the final push to the summit. Snaking their way up the steep zigzag paths ("switchbacks") lit by the head torches of climbers ahead, they started off well, but it wasn't long before a few students started fading. The air became thinner and thinner as they ascended, exacerbated by the icy chill and stinging wind.

Mark started to notice one student, Lucia, lagging behind. She wore a bright striped beanie that made her easy to spot below. With each switchback, she was a little lower than the group. Lucia was a determined young woman with a thousand-watt smile and a glint of mischief living permanently in her eye. She was a boarder in my boarding house, and Mark and I both knew and loved her dearly. Each time the group stopped, Mark waited for Lucia to catch up, cheering her on. Her usual smile was replaced with pained determination. She was a fighter, and Mark had every confidence she could make it. But each time they started again, Lucia would find herself behind the group.

Some other students were struggling too, and although the summit was only a few more hours away, they decided they couldn't go on. This group, along with a guide and one of the other teachers, had to turn back at this point and return to base camp. Lucia was one of them. She didn't like it, but she wasn't going to make the summit in time, and both the teacher and guide insisted she descend to base camp with them.

Mark continued on with one remaining colleague and the final remaining students. It was getting late now, and they needed to pick up their pace to make the summit in time. The early hours of the morning present the best opportunity to summit, as the weather tends to be calmer. As the wind picks up and the day's weather comes in, the summit becomes more dangerous. It was now 7am and the sun was well and truly up and shining. The group was still hours away. They needed to pick up speed urgently. Mark helped his group push on, encouraging them to fight that little bit harder.

A few more hours of climbing passed, and Mark and the remaining students were coping well and travelling at a good pace. Stopping for a quick drink break and not wanting to sit or take their packs off, they leant against some large rocks for support. The sun was now much higher in the sky, warning them of the ticking clock. As they rested briefly, Mark looked down the mountain, surprised to see more climbers below them still hoping to make the summit. Trailing at the end of the group, four or five switchbacks below, was a familiar figure in a bright striped beanie. Mark's heart sank.

'Lucia?!' he yelled. It couldn't be her. She had gone back with the other group. Lucia didn't even look up. She raised one hand to wave at Mark to identify herself, and kept on walking. Mark stood in shock, unsure of what to do next. Lucia was at least 40 minutes behind the group and travelling slowly. He couldn't leave her walking with just a porter, nor could he leave the group he was with now. If he went back for her, the whole group risked not making the summit. He was in an absolute pickle. The school policy required each group of students to have a teacher present. Leaving students with mountain guides, no matter how capable, was against policy. And yet here was Lucia—without a teacher, on the world's highest freestanding mountain. She was the most vulnerable student here now, and he couldn't pretend he hadn't seen her. Mark had no choice but to wait for her.

Mark asked the guide with his group to continue ahead with the students in that group while he waited for Lucia.

'I'll try to catch her up to us as quickly as I can,' he said to the guide. 'But you carry on with these students, and don't let a single one out of your sight. If I don't catch up, take them to the summit and straight back to me.'

Mark felt sick with worry. He was in a no-win situation. If he let all these students miss out on the summit because of Lucia, he knew they would be furious. Mark's heart sank as he waited for Lucia. He knew he may be walking away from his last attempt to summit. Of course, the students came first, but there was no small amount of disappointment having come so far.

'What are you doing here?' he asked in frustration as Lucia approached. 'You were supposed to go back with the other group!'

'I can make it,' Lucia puffed, not stopping for the discussion and putting one foot in front of the other with intense determination. Mark had a few seconds to assess the situation. She wasn't injured or sick, she was just slow.

'Lillian, listen to me,' Mark said sternly, making her stop and turn towards him. 'I know you can make it. You're strong and determined, and if that alone could take you to the top, you'd be fine. But we're running out of time.'

'I can make it,' she insisted fiercely. Mark held her gaze. He wanted her to make it. He wanted to make it himself. He had an idea.

'Alright,' he said, 'if we have any chance of making it, we have to catch up to the other group. They're 40 minutes ahead and gaining. I want this summit as much as you do, but we're going to have to work together.'

Lucia nodded, hopefully.

'You walk in front of me,' Mark said, 'and I'm going to push your pack from behind. It'll give you some support and momentum, and you just keep going, one step up at a time.'

They set off again and managed to find a good groove—Mark pushing Lucia up from behind, increasing her speed and bearing some of the weight of her pack, and Lucia steadily and trustingly placing one foot in front of the other. Their pace increased, and a glimmer of hope returned. They began to gain on the group ahead.

As he pushed Lucia up the mountain, he was clinging on to the hope of reaching the summit and contemplating our adoption rollercoaster. The events of the past few days and weeks were never far from Mark's mind as he kept praying earnestly that a successful Hearing was coming, just days after he would return home. Summiting Kilimanjaro was, of course, far down the priority list compared with completing the adoption of our children. But somehow his journey on this mountain had paralleled the ups and downs of our experience, and he spent much of the climb beseeching God for a smooth ending to this process. As he pushed Lucia onwards, an image came to him. The image was of the same scene before him, but it was Mark in Lucia's place, struggling onwards, exhausted but determined to conquer the mountain that was our adoption process, and it was God pushing him onwards, supporting him, lending his strength to Mark to help him carry on. The image brought immense comfort and joy to Mark.

Mark and Lucia continued climbing, making up ground and approaching the rim of the mountain. The rest of the group had continued on with the guide, and Mark was thrilled to see them coming back down from the summit as he and Lucia made their way around the rim to the very peak. The rest of the group had made it safely to the summit with their guide, rejoiced in their success and began their descent. They proceeded to descend a little further to an agreed-upon stop where they would then wait for Mark and Lucia.

They walked together around the rim, the midday sun now high in the sky, and they were both thankful the conditions were so perfect in allowing them to summit so late. Every other climber on the mountain had either reached the summit already or turned back along the way. They walked their final steps towards the famous sign at the very top:

CONGRATULATIONS

YOU ARE NOW AT

UHURU PEAK, TANZANIA, 5895M

Lucia tapped the sign with her hand, turned around and walked straight down. Mark let her go, knowing the other guide was ahead, and took a few moments to enjoy the summit.

He stood alone on the peak of Mount Kilimanjaro, the highest freestanding mountain in the world, and the highest point on the African continent.

Surrounded by breathtakingly beautiful, almost otherworldly sights—enormous glistening glaciers and a deep volcanic crater—far above the clouds.

He was aware of how unique this experience was. How many people in the world get to stand on this peak alone? It struck him that there were times in the journey we were on where being alone and feeling isolated felt like agony. In this moment, however, being alone felt like being filled with belief and hope. From his vantage point atop the mountain, he could see Mt Meru far in the distance, a thick carpet of cloud between them, but nothing else in sight. He recalled being on that other mountain and getting the call that Babu and Bibi wanted to meet. It struck him that Mt Meru looked tiny from where he was, almost like a stepping stone from that place to the place he stood now. How much had happened since then.

His thoughts drifted back to the Mention just a few days earlier. Standing on the peak of this mountain now, he felt sure that the timing was right. A final push for the end, and we would make the summit.

Chapter 37

The Report

"Laughter through tears is my favourite emotion."
—TRUVY, *STEEL MAGNOLIAS*

Our Hearing was scheduled for June 6th, and it was approaching fast. We had expected to wait another year for this moment, and suddenly we had only a week to prepare. I was giddy with excitement, my thoughts racing, butterflies backflipping in my belly, a mile-long to-do list, and barely a minute to spare. I darted around preparing paperwork, preparing myself, and preparing the kids.

Charlie's hair had grown long and fluffy, which I loved because it suited his personality, but this was not the Tanzanian way. He needed a neat haircut for Court. The kids also needed special clothing to wear to Court, and second-hand clothes from the market weren't going to cut it this time. I found a little shop in town that sold fancy, shiny suits that all the Tanzanian men wore for special occasions, and ordered one each for Jabari and Charlie, complete with ties and waistcoats. Dressed in their tiny suits like miniature old men, they stood tall and proud, momentarily captivated by each other before bursting into laughter and rolling on the ground. For Shay, I found a beautiful blue and white dress, just as shiny as the boys' suits, that spun when she twirled. And oh, how she twirled.

They all looked gorgeous. The challenge for them, however, would be sitting still and quiet for the duration of the case—which would be hours. In Tanzania, this was important and expected. Unruly behaviour in Court would be frowned upon. Sitting respectfully and quietly would indicate we were raising them to respect Tanzanian culture. I was just hoping they wouldn't roll on the floor or twirl.

Our other big task to complete before Court was to bring Babu and Bibi to Moshi. They would accompany us to Court and give their testimony that they were unable to care for the children, and that it was their wish for the children to be adopted into our family. Given the last attempt to bring Babu and Bibi to Moshi was so fraught with difficulties, we decided to fly Mark to Mwanza to bring Babu and Bibi to Moshi himself. We knew the flight would be difficult for them to navigate, having never flown before, and we wanted to care for them as much as we could through each step of the process. They were excited to come, and we wanted to make sure we didn't lose them again.

Mark flew off to Mwanza to collect Babu and Bibi and bring them back to Moshi himself. Just minutes after his flight departed, I received a concerning call from Mama Uriah. She called to say that she was preparing her report for the Court but had realised that she needed Mama Manessa (the social worker in Mwanza) to contribute to part of the report. Straight away I knew this was going to be a problem. Mama Uriah and I talked for a while about what she needed and why, and although it didn't make sense to me, she was sure that she needed assistance from Mama Manessa, since the children originally came from her region.

We had so much respect for the work Mama Uriah did, despite the difficulties. She was preparing a report for Court, and yet she didn't have any resources. Her office didn't have a computer, a printer, or even stamps to send off her paperwork. She purchased the stationery she needed out of her own pocket in order to complete her work. She was up against it, and she was a hard-working woman. We always tried to support her in any way we could.

I told Mama Uriah that Mark was on his way to Mwanza, and he could go and see Mama Manessa and ask for whatever she needed. But I knew there he was bound to run into problems. I called Mark, and he knew it too.

The biggest issue was, of course, the letter.

Mama Manessa had the third copy of the letter. It seemed unlikely that she would be willing to help us. Nevertheless, Mark went to Mama Manessa's office to do his best to get what Mama Uriah wanted. Poor Mark had set off for a quick visit to Mwanza, where he would have a nice dinner with Amy and the baby home staff, pick up Babu and Bibi, and return to Moshi. Now, he had less than 24 hours to solve this problem and arrive back in Moshi with Babu and Bibi.

Mark called Mama Manessa's office—it was closed for the afternoon. He was given an appointment the following morning, but there was another issue. Mama Manessa wasn't there. She was away on leave and wouldn't be back for a few days. At first, Mark thought this may be a blessing in disguise, as the junior social worker in her place, Gloria, might be more helpful.

Mark sat down and began to explain what he needed, hoping Gloria might be able to help. The information Mama Uriah needed was right there in the file. All Gloria needed to do was photocopy it and hand it to Mark.

She got out our file and opened it, looking through it for the necessary information and found it. Mark happily told her that was it, and asked if she could just photocopy the page and give it to him to take to Mama Uriah. Gloria picked up the paper, but then put it back down. She said she should probably call Mama Manessa first to check. Mark's heart sank.

Gloria made the call. Mark watched and listened as she explained our request, and waited as Gloria listened to Mama Manessa's reply. Gloria flicked through our file again as Mama Manessa continued to talk. After a few minutes, she set the phone back down and turned back to Mark.

'Mama Manessa says that you can have the paperwork, as long as you first write a letter to the Commissioner requesting the paperwork. He will write you a letter of reply, and then he will write a letter to Mama Manessa instructing her to photocopy the paperwork, and then we will send you the paperwork in the mail.' Gloria finished her explanation and looked up at Mark. The process she described—writing letters and waiting on replies and sending paperwork via the post—would take around six months. It was Tuesday, Mama Uriah's report was due to the High Court on Wednesday, and our Hearing was set for Thursday. We didn't have six months to wait—we didn't even have six hours to wait. Mark started to feel himself unravel.

'And there's another thing,' Gloria began, and she turned the pages of the file to reveal the letter. There it was. The third copy of the letter from the Commissioner. 'There is a letter here indicating that the children should be returned to Mwanza. Mama Uriah is listed here as a recipient of a copy of this letter, so she should have seen this.' Gloria picked up the letter and placed it on the table in front of Mark.

'Gloria,' Mark began, 'I've met with the Commissioner many times about our adoption. We know it began under the old system, and the system has changed, but we can't just send our children back—there's nowhere for them to go. The Commissioner himself told me we could try our luck in Court, and that's what we are going to do. I believe the Judge will agree that it's best for these children to remain with us. But Gloria, I don't have time to wait for months for this report. Our Court date is this Thursday, and Mama Uriah is ready to write our report today. She has been visiting us with the children for three years now—she knows they're happy in our home. She just needs that paperwork to add to her report.'

'Yes, Mark, but we cannot ever send paperwork by hand. Many adoptive parents like you come in and ask to carry the paperwork by hand to save time. They want to fly the reports across the country themselves, but we do not allow it. All paperwork must travel through the post,' Gloria explained.

Mark knew Gloria was just doing as she was directed, and he felt for her, but he could feel our chance at getting to Court slipping away, and he began to break down. For the first time in this whole, crazy process, Mark began to cry. Trying to keep himself together enough to continue the discussion, he wiped his face and cleared his throat, but the hot tears kept coming.

'Gloria, please, make an exception in this case,' he begged. 'I know your policies are there for good reasons, but there must be times where an exception could be made. We've sent all our paperwork by mail for the past three years, but we don't have time to wait now,' Mark continued, wiping away tears. 'Gloria, please understand, we must get to Court this week. Back in Australia, my mum is very unwell. She has cancer in her bones, and the very first thing she did when she was diagnosed was to fly here and meet these children. She loves them as her own, but she hasn't been able to see them in over two years. I just want to get home. I just want to look after my mum. I just want to finish this adoption and go home.' Mark's voice was breaking as he tried to explain the depths of his concern and the importance of this one piece of paper.

Gloria was unmoved. She wasn't cold or harsh towards Mark, but she didn't soften in response to him, and she certainly didn't change her mind. 'I'm very sorry to hear about your mum,' she said, 'but there is nothing I can do to help. You must be willing to wait and follow the process for sending paperwork by mail.' Mark lay his head in his hands on the desk in front of him in despair, unable to see a way forward. He could see Gloria wasn't going to change her mind. She didn't have the authority to.

'Now, Mark,' Gloria said, as he raised his head, 'I think it's important that Mama Uriah see this letter.' Mark lifted his head and saw Gloria holding the letter from the Commissioner in her hand. She copied the letter, as Mark's mind raced with what she might say next. The stress of it all was unbearable. We were hovering precariously between finishing our adoption in three days, and having our children sent away. One path was unimaginable joy, the other was unimaginable pain.

'Take this letter to Mama Uriah,' Gloria said, and she passed the copy to Mark. Stunned, Mark took the letter. He paused for a moment, wondering if Gloria might realise her oversight. After all the discussion of only sending paperwork through the post, she had put this letter right in his hand. She could call Mama Uriah herself or send the letter by post, but instead, she had left this job with Mark. Mark slid the letter into his bag and stood to leave. While he didn't have the paperwork he came for, he did have the third letter. If Gloria decided to call Mama Uriah to discuss the letter, we would still be facing the removal of the kids. But as she decided to send the letter with Mark, it seemed less likely.

CHAPTER 37

Leaving the office, Mark called me to explain. It was a lot to take in—we didn't have the report, which meant Mama Uriah wouldn't write her report, which meant our Court date would be wasted. But we had the third letter. It was a feeling of incredibly conflicting emotions. There was intense relief to have the letter in our hands, but there was such frustration that we couldn't get what we needed to get to Court. Maybe the Commissioner was right—we could try our luck in Court, but we wouldn't get through.

We discussed our options from here. We had flights already booked for Babu and Bibi, and although it was now unlikely we would be proceeding in Court, we could at least bring them to Moshi for a visit with the kids. We decided to proceed as planned, bring Babu and Bibi to Moshi and meet with Mama Uriah together in the afternoon, and hope for another miracle.

Babu and Bibi had never been on a plane or imagined they would ever have the opportunity to do so, and this was a terrifying and wonderful experience for them. They marvelled at the propellers out the window and the buttons and gadgets around their seats. It was a welcome distraction for Mark to watch the experience through their eyes. It was a familiar feeling for him—a crisis brewing in the background, but life marched on.

Babu and Bibi white-knuckled their way through the flight. It took them over the vast plains of the Serengeti, the extraordinary Ngorongoro Crater, and past the summit of Mount Kilimanjaro, which is an incredible, imposing thing to see out the window of a plane—towering as high as the plane flew. These classic Tanzanian landmarks were known to Babu and Bibi in their imaginations only before this flight—known through stories passed down from those fortunate enough to have travelled beyond Mwanza. But today they came to life as the small plane carried them above the beautiful, vast landscape. Their eyes captivated by their own stunning country, they sat in quiet awe, faces pressed to the window, as Tanzania unveiled herself in a dazzling dance just for them.

Touching down on the tarmac jolted Mark back to reality. It was early afternoon, and we had only a few hours to turn this situation around. Mark took Babu and Bibi straight to their hotel, knowing how much they were looking forward to their warm shower, and left them there to settle in. Then he raced home to pick me up, and off we went to Mama Uriah's office.

Mark held little hope for the meeting, as he had already spoken to Mama Uriah on the phone, and she was firm in her position that she was unable to write the report. But we couldn't just sit by and let our Court date go to waste, and we wanted to at least talk in person all together.

Mama Uriah welcomed us in and expressed her deep condolences that we were unable to bring home the paperwork from Mama Manessa. She spoke again about how she was unable to proceed and how it was such a shame since everything had been proceeding so well. I asked her to go over with us, once more, her understanding of why she could not write this report. She spoke about how the children had come from Mwanza, which is not her area, and as such, she was not the authority on how and why the children came into our care to begin with. She had met us and the children once we had brought them home to Moshi and had been visiting us in our home regularly for the past three years, so she could only attest to that.

Hearing her out, I said to her, 'Mama Uriah, why don't you just start your report there—from the time you met us—and include all the parts that you *can* attest to? You are right that you can't comment on the children coming into our care—so leave those parts out and just include the parts that you *can* speak to.'

Mama Uriah paused. For once, maybe for the first time, it was a good pause. Her face was changing—softening slightly. I continued, 'Mama Uriah, Babu and Bibi will be in Court themselves, and they can testify in person about how the children came into our care. It was their request to begin with that a family be found for the children, remember? That part of the story can be told to the Judge by Babu and Bibi themselves. Your part of the story starts after that, and your report can include everything you have seen since the day we came into your region.'

Mama Uriah considered my words carefully. 'Well,' she said, 'yes, I think you're right. The Judge can request a further report if she needs one from Mama Manessa, but I can at least submit my part of it, I suppose.' I turned around to Mark, who was standing behind me, and gave him an enormous grin, barely able to believe what I was hearing.

'But,' said Mama Uriah, her tone becoming concerned, 'I think we have now run out of time. It's 5pm. I haven't even started the report. I don't have a computer to work on, or a printer, and the report is due to be at the Courthouse at 8am tomorrow.'

'Mama Uriah,' Mark said, 'we could help you. Please, we have to try. We have a computer at our house and a printer in the school. Let's go to our house together. We'll get some chicken and chips on the way home for dinner, and we'll get the report finished and printed tonight.'

Mama Uriah grinned. 'Chicken and chips? Oh yes, I am hungry. That sounds good. We'll go together and we'll get this report done!'

Back in our car, with Mama Uriah following us home in hers, Mark and I could barely believe we had found a way forward. I tried to contain my excitement and hope, screaming into my hands while Mark, exhausted from the stress, wiped away tears. The ups and downs of the day had been so intense and stressful, but here we were, back on track.

'I can't believe that just happened,' said Mark. 'She's really going to write it!'

'I can't handle much more of this,' I said, wiping tears from my cheeks. 'It's just too much.' Mark took my hand in his and kissed it.

'Me too,' he said, pausing for a minute. 'This has been the craziest day ever!' I looked at his exhausted, bewildered face, and we both burst into laughter. An overwhelming mix of depletion, desperation, hope and joy came tumbling out in a messy mix of tears and laughter as we drove down the Jacaranda-lined streets of Shanty Town back to our home.

We set the table for dinner, and I put the kids to bed while Mama Uriah got started on the report. I tucked each little one in with a kiss and prayer, and an extra-long hug.

It struck us once again how difficult it was for Mama Uriah to get her work done without many of the resources she needed to do it. We were thrilled to be able to help her after all she was doing for us.

Hearing what Mama Uriah wanted to say in her report was just beautiful. It reminded us again of the path we had walked these past few years, and the incredible change in the children. She spoke about seeing Jabari for the first time and how she wondered if he would survive at all. She spoke about watching him come to life over her visits—how he transformed from a starving, sickly child into a giggling, bouncy toddler. She spoke about her joy in watching our two families merge into one, and how impressed she was with the way Jackson and Jemima welcomed and loved their new siblings. 'I've been watching those two closely, you know,' she said of Jackson and Jemima, 'because children don't hide their feelings for one another. If it wasn't working, I would see it in the children first. But here, there was genuine love from the start.'

More tears flowed from my leaky eyes as I heard these words. We knew our kids were great friends, but it was so affirming to hear Mama Uriah's observations, and even more lovely to know that tomorrow, our Judge would read these words and begin to form her own ideas about our family.

By 9pm, our report was written, printed and safely in Mama Uriah's hands, ready to submit to Court at 8am tomorrow. Mark and Mama Uriah had a long chat by the door as she left, once again in Swahili. Mark's language had developed so far in the past few years, and they could now converse freely and quickly with sophisticated language. As she went to leave, Mama Uriah stopped to once again comment on Mark's Swahili progress.

'Mark,' she began, 'your Swahili! You are struuuuuggling!' she finished, emphatically.

There it was once again. I could see Mark deflate, as if wondering if he would ever reach a level of fluency that would satisfy her.

'Mama Uriah,' he responded with both exasperation and amusement. 'I've tried so hard to impress you with my Swahili. Where am I going wrong?'

'Oh yes,' she replied, 'your Swahili is exceptional, and you're always improving even more. You are struuuugling, Mark!'

He took a moment to try to reconcile her seemingly opposite statements. 'Mama Uriah, in Australia when we say "struggling", it means you're not doing well.'

'Oh no,' Mama Uriah interrupted, 'when we say "struggling", we mean you are putting in great effort and succeeding. It's a great compliment in our culture to struggle. It takes courage and persistence to overcome something challenging. It means you refuse to give in and are persisting until you succeed.'

Mark and I erupted into laughter.

'All this time, we have thought you were criticising him!' I said. 'We've been trying so hard to impress you!'

Mama Uriah threw her head back and laughed. 'No, Mark,' she said, 'you are not *Australian struggling*, you are *African struggling*!'

It was a hell of a day, but we had found our new favourite family expression. African struggling stuck with us from that moment. I loved Mama Uriah's view of struggle. To honour and respect the effort and determination required to push through challenges resonated with me so deeply.

Chapter 38

Wednesday

"Hoping for the best, prepared for the worst and unsurprised by anything in between."
—MAYA ANGELOU, *I KNOW WHY THE CAGED BIRD SINGS*

Babu and Bibi, fresh out of the shower and smelling like coconut oil, sat in our backyard in the warm morning sun. It was Wednesday, the day before our Hearing was scheduled in Court. Mama Uriah's report had been safely delivered to the Courthouse for the Judge to read before the Hearing, and we sat in a semi-circle of camping chairs in our garden, watching the children play on the trampoline. Mark and I were still reeling from the day before, trying to emotionally catch our breath.

'Babu, Babu,' Shay called between jumps, eliciting a grin from Babu at the sound of her using his name.

'Look at me!' she bounced from her feet onto her bottom proudly before rolling to the side, laughing.

'*Alisema Nianglie!* She said, "Look at me!' I translated for him.

'*Hiya. Nzuri sana, Nzuri sana.* Oh, very good, very good,' he responded, grinning. Babu and Bibi marvelled at their growth and the changes in their development, but it was the strengthened connection to them, the comfort in their presence, the way the kids took their hands and dragged them off to play, or climbed into their lap with a book, that kept a grin plastered on Babu and Bibi's faces.

After a lazy morning in the garden, we took Babu and Bibi into town to meet with our lawyer, Patricia. We met at her office to go through everything one last time before Court in the morning. We had so much faith in Patricia, and as expected, she was thoroughly prepared. Patricia talked Babu and Bibi through everything that would happen in Court, and I greatly appreciated the care she took with them. Leaning forward in her chair, forearms resting on her desk, she listened intently to their story, hearing it for the first time from Babu and Bibi's perspective. She dabbed small tears with a tissue as they shared how their heartache had turned into joy, watching the children run, play and laugh freely. Then she checked one last time that they were sure they wanted to relinquish the children. This must have been a huge moment for Babu and Bibi—although it had been almost three years since they originally asked us to take the children, tomorrow would be the moment they would officially and permanently relinquish their rights to care for them. We knew this was what Babu and Bibi wanted, but we also knew they must feel a gamut of emotions as they carried it through.

Patricia went through all the paperwork in our submission, double- and triple-checking we had everything we needed. The submission was huge. The checklist of paperwork we needed seemed a mile long and with good reason. It was an incredibly thorough process to adopt a child, as you'd hope it would be.

As Patricia flicked through all our supporting documents, she stopped, looking closely at one of the pages. 'Oh,' she said, 'I've just noticed that I have a photocopy of your marriage certificate, rather than the original. You will definitely need the original for Court tomorrow—a photocopy won't be acceptable. Can you bring the original with you in the morning, and I'll swap them over?'

'Yes, of course,' I said. 'That's strange. I wonder why we would have given you a photocopy instead of the original.' It was puzzling. Enough to make my stomach drop and the warm spread of adrenaline shoot outwards to my hands and feet, but I was sure the original was safely in our file at home and we must have just picked up the wrong one. I assured myself of that as I slow-breathed my heart rate back to a normal pace.

We finished the meeting and took Babu and Bibi home. We spent the afternoon together, swimming with the kids and relaxing. I loved watching Babu and Bibi as they watched the kids swim. They had never seen children who could swim before, and every time Jackson would dive under the water, they would gasp, grab each other and stare at the water until he emerged. We assured them a thousand times that he could swim and was perfectly safe, but they couldn't take their eyes off him. It was hilarious. The younger children wore inflatable armbands that kept them above the water, but even these didn't put Babu and Bibi's minds to rest. Each time one of them put their head in the water, Babu and Bibi would shriek and laugh and point, and each time their little heads popped back up, Babu and Bibi would sigh with relief and marvel at how they managed not to drown. It was like a magic trick that never got old.

Later in the evening, once Babu and Bibi were back in the warm shower at their hotel, and the kids were tucked into bed, trying to sleep through their excitement for the next day, Mark went to get the marriage certificate from our file. Only, it wasn't there. The section of the file where we kept the marriage certificate was there, and it contained a number of photocopies, but no original. This was odd. We were so careful with all our documents—knowing the importance of each one in the Court process. We couldn't understand why it wasn't there, or where else we would have put it.

Assuming it was just put away somewhere else, Mark and I started checking the obvious places where we thought it could have been accidentally filed away. But it wasn't in any of the obvious places. I started to get more concerned and intensified our search, looking through files and drawers and any places that held paper. No sign of the original certificate. By about midnight, and still without the certificate, we resorted to searching through the entire house, inch by inch. It was only a small house, and we didn't own a huge amount since we had moved internationally, but nevertheless, it took us a few hours to search through every single nook and cranny. It wasn't there.

It was 2am, and our Court Hearing was starting in a few hours. After all the work we had done to get ready for this date, how could we possibly be missing a document? Sure, the Court date had come a lot sooner than expected, and we had a week to prepare rather than the year we were expecting, but even so, we'd had this certificate ready since we flew into the country. A horrible mix of anger with myself, exhaustion and fear overwhelmed me, and I just wanted to crawl up in a ball and rock in the corner.

Once we were sure it was not in the house, and with no idea where else to look, we went to bed. I don't think I slept a wink. I was turning over all the possibilities for what might happen in the morning. Would the Hearing even be able to go ahead? If not, we would have to start again with another Mention. But would this be a good thing? It would give us time to find the original marriage certificate, but it might also mean a long string of unsuccessful Mentions, and that delay might leave time for the Commissioner to follow through and have the kids taken away. But if the Hearing does go ahead without the original marriage certificate, what will happen? Will the Judge throw out the case? Will she allow us to continue the Hearing and submit the certificate before she makes her Verdict? Would we be able to find the original certificate before then? Where could it be? I prayed and prayed in my mind, *God, please, I know you know where that certificate is! Help us find it. Just one more miracle!*

Chapter 39

Thursday

"When the Lord closes a door, somewhere he opens a window."
—MARIA VON TRAPP, *THE SOUND OF MUSIC*

The next morning, we got up early and searched again, although we both knew the marriage certificate wasn't in the house. We talked through our options and agreed to just continue as if we had it and wait and see what happened. We couldn't bring ourselves to cancel the Hearing, we just had to hope for a possible solution.

I got the kids up to get ready for the day. Jackson and Jemima were off to school as usual, and Shay, Charlie and Jabari needed to get their fancy Court clothing on. While I was sorting the kids, Mark was going to meet Patricia to finalise the submission and give her the marriage certificate that we didn't have. I would then bring the kids, pick up Babu and Bibi, and catch up to them.

Mark stopped by the school office on his way out of the compound to pick up a copy of our work contracts, which were kept in our files at school. There had been some contention at a recent staff meeting over whether staff were allowed to have access to their school files. The issue was still being debated, but as it stood, we were not. It was no big deal to Mark and me whether or not we could access our file, since it only contained copies of documents we had given the school ourselves, but some staff felt uncomfortable about being denied access to their own files. Knowing this, Mark went into the office and asked Bob, our school headmaster, to have someone retrieve our contracts for him.

It was early, and the office staff weren't at work yet. Bob kindly went to grab the contracts himself. He was in a rush, and instead of looking for the contracts, Bob simply pulled out our files and handed them to Mark. One file for each of us, containing all our school paperwork. Mark thanked him and jumped in the car, amused that he had just been given this file that was being so hotly debated.

At Patricia's office, Mark sat in the waiting room, nervous and anticipating her reaction to the news about the missing original marriage certificate. As he waited, he flicked through his school file to find his work contract. He rifled through reams of paperwork and found the contract. As he lifted it out of the file, he caught a glimpse of the edge of one of the papers further back in the file. He opened the page to find our original marriage certificate. There it was, sitting in front of him.

He blinked a few times, double-checked it was indeed the original, and pumped his fist in the air in celebration. Waves of relief flooded over him. It all made sense now. We had given our original marriage certificate to the school office three years ago, as they needed a copy of it for our work permits, and instead of copying it and returning the original, they had mistakenly filed the original and returned a copy to us.

Back home, I was on my way in the car with three beautifully dressed children in the back, still anxious about how the day would proceed. I picked up Babu and Bibi, who were looking their best and grinning with pride. My phone rang, and it was Mark.

'We've got it!' he said. 'We've got the original marriage certificate!'

'What?' I exclaimed. 'Where was it?!'

'It was in the school file! Bob was in a rush and gave me my whole file instead of just the work contract, and inside the file was the original marriage certificate!'

'Oh my goodness!'

'We've got it all, hon, everything we need. The Hearing is going to go ahead; I can just feel it. We're going to get this finished!'

I hung up the phone and danced in the car, more tears of relief streaming down my face. I took a deep breath and closed my eyes. *Are you for real?* I prayed quietly. *I mean, seriously, how do you keep doing that! Thank you, thank you, thank you!*

I met Mark in the Court car park, and the look on his face was pure joy. We were all here—Mama Uriah, Patricia, Babu and Bibi, Mark and I, and, of course, the kids. We quickly asked around and found out that our Judge, Aisha Nyerere, was here too. That was all of us. The Hearing would proceed!

Judge Nyerere, we discovered, was the daughter-in-law of Tanzania's revered former president Julius Nyerere, who was known as the 'Father of the Nation' for his commitment to his people, his devotion to social justice and equality, and for successfully leading Tanzania to become the peaceful, stable East-African nation it is today. To have our case presided over by his daughter-in-law was an honour we treasured.

Our case was called a few minutes after we arrived, and we entered the Courtroom, bowing in respect to the Judge, which we had been advised was the custom. She sat at the front of the room and smiled as we entered. I liked her right away. She wore her glasses down low on her nose and lifted her eyes above the rim to see us. I wondered if she would interact with the children—it had been difficult to know what to prepare them for, and it was a lovely surprise to see her call them forward. They looked at me, and after a quick nod to show them it was okay, they walked forward and met the woman who would decide their future.

The kids greeted her with a traditional Swahili greeting, and she was impressed. She conversed with them briefly and sweetly, making them feel comfortable, and asked them their names. They answered, Shay twirled just a little, and no-one rolled on the floor. Their short conversation was a success, and now we seated the kids in a row of timber chairs towards the back of the room. They would have to sit here for the next few hours, silent unless spoken to. No easy feat for three three-year-olds!

The case began, and the mood was serious. Patricia was well prepared and presented our case confidently. She began presenting our documents, one by one, admitting each one as items to the Court. As each document was tabled, it was like a flashback through the past three years of our life. Every single document had its own story, its own tale of battle and triumph, and only Mark and I really knew the blood, sweat, and tears behind each stack of papers. It was a pure joy to watch them passed to the Judge.

Judge Nyerere was extremely thorough and carefully viewed and checked every item. She was writing notes as we went. In fact, she was transcribing every word spoken, by hand. It was long and tedious, but the upside was that everyone spoke nice and slowly, and this helped my understanding of their Swahili.

Babu and Bibi were called to testify. They stood and began to tell the Judge their story. They spoke passionately and relayed the tale of the day they were left with the children. Judge Nyerere was captivated by them. There was such pain in their story—being abandoned by their son, whose duty it was to care for his elderly parents, and then being further burdened by the responsibility for three infants who were near death. They spoke of the deep heartache they felt, combined with such love for these babies.

Despite their pain, there was so much hope. They spoke of their dreams for the children—that they would live, and more than that, have a family to call their own. That they would have parents who would live long enough to raise them, and that they might recover from the devastating start to life they had experienced. Their courage moved me to tears. This was a world away from their home—they had flown on a plane, across the country to be here for this moment—to tell this story to the Judge themselves. They must have felt incredibly intimidated in her presence, but if they did, it didn't show.

Judge Nyerere sympathised with their plight and praised their goodness in seeking first the best interests of the children. She asked questions relating to how often they had seen the children since they came to our home, and their impressions of how we care for them. Babu and Bibi came alive again, telling tales of seeing Jabari's face form a smile, hearing him laugh, seeing him walk and run, and watching them all learn to swim. They were such proud grandparents. There was such genuine delight in seeing their hopes for the children come to life before them.

Judge Nyerere moved on to a more serious line of questioning. Had we given them any money in exchange for the children? Had we given them property or goods of great value? Had we persuaded them or pressured them in any way in order to influence their decision? Babu and Bibi were firm in their response. They explained to the Judge that they had approached Social Welfare to ask for a family for the children before ever meeting us, and that they had been praying that God would send a family that would be willing to adopt all three children to keep them together.

They also explained that Amy had, in fact, tried to persuade them not to seek adoption for the children, including her offer of a home and an easy cleaning job that would allow them to both keep the children and be cared for in their final years. And they explained once again the reason they made their remarkable decision—they wanted a long-term family for their three grandchildren. Judge Nyerere listened intently and responded, 'You are quite extraordinary people. I'm sure your grandchildren will always know the sacrifice you have made for them.'

By this time, about two hours had passed, and the children had been doing amazingly well. They had been sitting quietly on their hard wooden chairs, with barely a sound, for two hours. Only now they were getting tired, and all three were starting to slump in their chairs, falling asleep. Jabari was not the quietest sleeper in the world, and pretty soon his loud breathing, verging on a snore, was audible throughout the Courtroom. Mark and I were trying not to giggle, and we were unsure of what to do. Was this disrespectful? Should we wake him up and have him sit up and pay attention? We felt like it was slightly unreasonable to expect them to keep still after so long.

After a few minutes, the sound of Jabari's snores reached the ears of Judge Nyerere at the front of the Courtroom and she looked up to check in on the kids.

She herself had a good giggle, looking at the three of them slumped over each other, asleep.

'Let's take a short break,' she said, 'and you can take the children home now and return.'

Relief flooded my mind. I appreciated her kindness.

I woke up the kids, packed them back into the car and dropped them home to Grace as quickly as I could. I tucked them into bed for an afternoon nap and kissed their little foreheads. 'It's going really well, I think,' I whispered to them. 'I like this Judge. I think she'll make you all ours forever.'

I dashed back to the car, spinning Grace in a hug on my way past.

'*Inaendelea vizuri sana*. It's going very well,' I called back to her. She broke into a celebratory song and dance, whooping, clapping and jumping in a circle as I climbed back into the car.

I raced back to the Courtroom, where the case continued. In all, it lasted four hours in total. Throughout the proceedings, there was not a single moment that concerned me. All the paperwork was there, every question the Judge had was answered well, and her mood set a lovely, positive tone.

When the Hearing was over, we left quickly and met with Patricia to find out her feelings towards the case. 'It was very good,' she said. 'I'm certain she will rule in favour of the adoption. If she had any concerns, she would have raised them for discussion. We would know if there was going to be a problem. What she will do now is read over all the documents submitted today, check they are all in order, and prepare for the Verdict.'

Intense joy and hope. That was the feeling that afternoon. We were so used to the constant hiccups that we weren't fully celebrating yet—we wouldn't really believe it until we heard the Verdict. But it was all looking so positive that it was really hard not to get ahead of ourselves and celebrate. The Verdict was booked for June 21st—two weeks later. Two more weeks of holding our breath, daring to hope, but bracing for setbacks, just in case.

Chapter 40

The Verdict

"I do think families are the most beautiful things in all the world!"
—LOUISA MAY ALCOTT, *LITTLE WOMEN*

We sat in the Courtroom with nervous, hopeful anticipation. Judge Nyerere entered, and we stood and bowed in respect. She took her seat and began reading her Verdict, carefully summarising the case and her response. She granted the adoption order with confidence.

She called each child forward, with friendly formality, and ceremoniously spoke their new names over them:

'Henceforth, you shall be Charles Ashley Omari Dombkins.'

'Henceforth, you shall be Shalom Amani Kate Dombkins.'

'Henceforth, you shall be Jabari David Douglas Dombkins.'

I stood and cried silent streams as each child stood before her to receive their new name. Each child's name was made up of their original name, which we wanted to preserve, a Swahili name, and a family name of significance, along with their new Dombkins family surname. Each name was a beautiful blend of their heritage and their new family. They would always belong to both.

Judge Nyerere then took some time to speak further about the case. Her words were incredibly moving and affirming. It means the world to us, after all the struggle, to sit before this exceptional woman and receive her vote of confidence. For someone of her background and stature in Tanzania to bless this moment was incredible. It was a stamp of approval from this beautiful country allowing us to raise three of its children.

At the completion of the ceremony, we were ready to celebrate! This was the moment we had dreamed about. Officially finished. No more possible hurdles, no more last-minute disasters, no more terrifying hiccups. It was over. We had completed the adoptions.

We had one task to do at the Courthouse before we could return home. We needed to pay the adoption fee. Adoption around the world can be incredibly expensive. The Australian process we had begun all those years ago was going to total around $20,000. Other countries have similar fees. We went to the office at the Courthouse to pay the Tanzanian adoption fee. It was the equivalent of three Australian dollars to cover the fancy paper the certificates would be printed on. That was it. We paid it with joy. It was one of the reasons we had confidence in the integrity of this system—no money changed hands. The baby home didn't charge fees, Social Welfare didn't charge fees, there was no financial gain anywhere here that might lead to exploitation.

We returned home feeling an incredible lightness, a sense of joy and liberation that exceeded our expectations, like we didn't realise the weight of what we were carrying until we set down the burden and walked freely. We took photos with the kids to commemorate the moment, bought them ice cream and cake (because Court was boring for three-year-olds and they didn't really understand, but ice cream and cake was something to celebrate), and called home. We Skyped friends and family and rejoiced with them as we shared the news. It was a special moment for Mark's family, as his sister Kate got engaged the same day. Kate's fiancé James was loved by all of us, and now we were celebrating another new family member.

A lot had happened in one day, and we collapsed on the lounge at the end of it all, invited the Dutchies and another friend, Raph, over for dinner, ordered takeaway Indian food, and sat there reeling. Extreme joy overwhelmed me. I closed my eyes, smiling to myself in a room surrounded by people I loved, and breathed in deeply. I exhaled a long, slow breath, pushing out all the intense emotion within me, trying to capture every remaining skerrick of doubt, fear, foreboding, frustration and dread, and expel it from my body. I took these deep breaths over and over, my gentle tears slowly leaving, and my heart filling itself up instead with gratitude, hope and joy.

Chapter 41

A Visit from Mama Uriah

"Everybody can be great, because everybody can serve. You don't have to have a college degree to serve. You don't have to make your subject and your verb agree to serve. You only need a heart full of grace, a soul generated by love."

—DR MARTIN LUTHER KING JR.

Mark flew out the next morning to Argentina, where he enjoyed a holiday with Kate and James, and earned the name "Dead-weight Dombkins" for his inability to make any decisions, have any preference, or give any input into their plans. He happily followed Kate and James wherever they went, like a puppy, eating, drinking and relaxing. He felt as though he was almost in a state of shock following the past few crazy months, and Kate and James often laughed at his extreme incapacity to make any decisions. He was blissfully happy in their presence and revelled in the feeling of not having a care in the world.

Back in Moshi, my phone rang one morning during the holidays, and it was Mama Uriah. I felt overjoyed to hear her jovial voice and chat with her again. She was trying to set up an email address and asked if she could come over for some help. I was thrilled to invite her over. Mama Uriah was very special to us, and it was nice to be able to help her out.

She arrived and we began setting up her account. We chatted about her son, her family, and the challenges of her work at the moment. Mama Uriah stopped abruptly and said, 'Oh, I mustn't forget to tell you about the letter!'

'What letter is that?' I asked, fearing that I knew the answer.

'Well, you know how I mentioned that I haven't been receiving any mail at all, and I had been wondering what was going on? Well, it turns out, the Commissioner had forgotten to pay the rental fee for my P.O. Box, so all my mail was being collected at the Post Office but not sent on to me!'

'Really?' I asked.

'Yes,' she said, 'and the day after we finished your case in Court, the account was paid, and all the mail from the past three months came to me in one pile!'

'Oh, Mama Uriah!' I said.

'Yes, but wait. You won't believe one of the letters that was in my pile,' she went on. 'There was a letter in there, from the Commissioner himself, instructing me to come and take your children back.'

My heart was skipping beats. Of course, I knew the letter she was talking about. What I didn't know was what, if anything, she wanted to do about it. Her mood was so light and happy that I couldn't think she was about to tell me any bad news. She was regaling this tale as if it was the funniest she had ever told.

'Can you believe it?' she asked, 'The Commissioner asks me to take the children, and then stops the letter from reaching me himself, by not paying the fees!'

'Mama Uriah,' I questioned, 'There's no way he could make any problems for us now, is there?'

'Oh, no! Your adoption is final in the High Court! There's nothing he can do now.'

'Mama Uriah,' I asked curiously, 'if that letter had reached you before we went through Court, what would you have done?'

'Well, I would have had no choice but to take the children back to Mwanza,' she explained. 'It would have broken my heart, but I would have had to do it.'

We looked at each other with intense relief. We had both dodged an unthinkable situation.

'How long did you say the Post Box was closed for?' I asked.

'From February until June,' Mama Uriah replied.

Chills went up my spine once more. 'That's the exact time that we were going through Court,' I said. Mama Uriah threw back her head and laughed and laughed. She slapped the table and stamped her feet a little.

'You know,' she said when she regained her composure, 'God is good. God is so very good.'

Chapter 42

Climbing Boots

"George didn't say a word. He felt quite trembly.
He knew something tremendous had taken place that morning.
For a few brief moments he had touched with
the very tips of his fingers the edge of a magic world."
—ROALD DAHL, *GEORGE'S MARVELLOUS MEDICINE*

I enjoyed the rest of the holidays with the kids at home—not even the power staying off or the usual string of logistical problems could burst my bubble. They almost became amusing once I knew we only had a few more months here, and I wondered if we would miss them. I lay on the trampoline with the kids for hours, staring up at the jacaranda above, watching monkeys swinging in the trees beyond, and feeling grateful for all the crazy parts of our adventure.

Following our Verdict, Mark and I had rushed around with a long list of tasks, the top of which was resigning from our jobs. Our head of school celebrated with us, as he had known our journey well, and accepted our resignations, which would be effective from the end of the year. We knew it would take a few months to organise visas, but we hoped to return home for Christmas. We booked our flights home for December, in faith we would have everything needed by then. With the admin done, I lazed on the trampoline dreaming about going home.

Kilimanjaro broke through the clouds and towered above our backyard again. I savoured every glimpse I could get, knowing it wouldn't be my backyard view forever. It was extra special now, as Mark had stood all the way up there, on the very top. I knew I wouldn't have the opportunity to climb—I was working on boarding duty every second weekend, and the cost to climb it independently was a lot for us, and not a priority. I wasn't disappointed, although I would have loved to climb. It was enough for me to just look at it as often as possible.

One day after the holidays, Mark surprised me.

'You're climbing Kili!' he said gleefully.

'Whaaaaat?!' I screamed, 'Are you serious?! How? When? What do you mean?'

He knew how I loved the mountain, and he wanted to give me the chance to climb. He put his mind to work and created an epic gift for me. I couldn't even get my head around it. I really had been satisfied to not climb it, but suddenly having the opportunity, I realised just how thrilling the idea was.

Mark had another surprise up his sleeve. He told me only that I was going to climb and when, but he wouldn't tell me who I was climbing with. This was kind of an important piece of information, since I would be spending a week with this person and attempting a pretty daunting and challenging feat. But he wouldn't tell.

I was confident that I could work it out as Mark is a terrible secret keeper. He loves to plan a surprise, but I always work it out before the day. He's a talker, he just can't help himself.

A few years prior, he had planned a surprise weekend away to celebrate our wedding anniversary, and as we set off in the car to our mystery location, we stopped for petrol. I used the ladies' room while Mark paid for the petrol, and in that time, Mark managed to tell the man at the counter all about our trip, forgetting to mention it was a surprise. Mark returned to the car, and as I came past the counter to exit, the man called out his best wishes for our lovely trip, revealing the surprise location as he did so. I got back in the car laughing. 'You just can't help yourself, can you?' I said.

I was quietly confident I would crack him. There weren't really that many people it could be—we were a fairly tight-knit community, and I had a good idea of who had climbed already, who was climbing with the school, and who didn't want to climb. It had to be someone on staff, I figured, or maybe another parent, someone fit and healthy, someone whose company I enjoyed (hopefully).

A few days before we were set to leave, I was in the laundry, tending to the never-ending pile of dirt-covered clothes, when I heard a familiar voice floating in from outside.

'Did someone order a mountain climber?'

I stopped in my tracks, dropped the clothes in my hands and ran to the door. It was the unmistakable voice of my big brother, Tony. I flung my arms around his neck. Following shortly after me came the kids.

'Uncle Tony! Uncle Tony!' they yelled and ran to join us on the porch. Tony is tall and thin, with short, dark, wavy hair and wears a daily uniform of jeans, a black T-shirt and outlandish Nike joggers. He has a broad, cheeky grin and a glint of mischief always in his eye. He's a niece and nephew's dream—full of crazy stories, encouraging silliness and agreeing to everything Mum says no to. The kids broke into their Uncle Tony dance, chanting 'Unkie like a Monkey! Unkie like a Monkey!' in deep voices while jumping side to side and making monkey movements, their arms swinging by their sides and scratching their armpits.

I could not have been more shocked to discover the identity of my mountain climbing buddy. It had not even entered my mind to think beyond the people living in our town. I never would have imagined it would be someone flying across the world. I was thrilled. Mark was thrilled too, as he had managed to successfully keep a secret for the first time in his life.

We had a day or two to get organised before we left. We met with our guides, who would be taking us up the mountain. They were full of helpful information, sharing their years of experience guiding climbers up Kilimanjaro.

Our guides carefully took us through the risks. It's an easy climb in the sense that no mountain-climbing technique is required and no previous experience is needed. It's essentially walking slowly up a very high hill. Nevertheless, around 10 people a year die on Kilimanjaro (quite a small percentage, since around 30,000 attempt the climb each year), but still, people die. And the effects of high altitude can be very serious.

In the three years we had been living so close to the mountain, we had known many who attempted the climb. Some we thought were never going to make it—they seemed ill-prepared and not what you might consider fit and healthy. However, the altitude had minimal effect on them, and although extremely difficult, they made the summit. Others we had known were super-fit, athletic, and thoroughly prepared. However, the altitude made them terribly ill. Some still made the summit, enduring great pain to do so, while others weren't able to continue. There seemed to be no predicting who would or would not suffer the effects of altitude sickness. Neither Tony nor I had ever been at high altitude before, so it was anyone's guess how we would fare once we ascended above the clouds.

As we sat and listened to our guides, we were asked if we would like vegetarian food as we climbed or not. I answered quickly that yes, vegetarian would be great. Knowing that any meat carried up the mountain would not be refrigerated and also knowing where it was likely to be sourced from, I knew there was no way we wanted to be eating meat. Tony requested the non-vegetarian menu. I quickly and quietly told him to trust me and change his mind, but there was no swaying him.

We were given lots of great advice, such as how we should walk at a slow, steady pace, and that we should wear shoes that were a size or two larger than normal, as coming down the mountain our toes would hurt from running into the end of our shoes. We went over our packing lists and ensured we would have everything we needed. Then we ordered take-away from a local restaurant called El Rancho, which ironically served Indian food, and we sat back and enjoyed our last evening at home before braving the wilderness.

The morning we began the climb, I could barely contain my excitement. We set off in 4WDs provided by our guides and drove up to the starting point. Along the way, we needed to make one quick stop-off, we were told. About 15 minutes into our journey, the 4WD pulled over to the side of the bumpy dirt road. I looked out the window and grinned.

'Hey, Tone,' I said. 'Ready to see your meat?' He looked across, and there on the side of the road was a small, open-walled butcher shop. It had a large cow carcass hanging from the timber roof by a thick rope, swaying gently in the sun, with flies busily swarming around. The colour drained from Tony's face. 'Are you kidding me?' he said. I laughed just watching him.

Our guide chatted with the store owner, who then took a large knife and hacked a thick piece of meat from the carcass. He brought the meat over to a wooden block, waved the flies from the pools of blood dotting the surface of the wood, cut the meat into smaller pieces, wrapped it in newspaper and passed it to our guide.

'How long has that meat been hanging there? Why is it in the sun? Where is he going to keep it now?' The questions fired out of Tony's mouth.

'In his bag, for the next five days, I presume,' I answered. I couldn't help myself, 'I told you to go with the vegetarian menu!' I giggled. He shook his head in disbelief.

The first day of our climb took us through thick, lush rainforest on the lower slopes of Kilimanjaro. It sprinkled with rain a little, and we were shaded nicely by the canopy above. The walking was quite easy—step by step up a sloping path, well worn by previous climbers. Our guide, Dennis, was a knowledgeable and experienced Tanzanian climber who spoke English fluently and had led many climbers to the summit before. His advice on day one was to follow his pace. 'Climbing Kili is a slow walk uphill,' he told us. 'You can't race to the top. Your body must acclimatise. Just follow my pace and take it slowly.'

It was thrilling for me just to be out of our school complex, walking around freely. Back in Moshi, it wasn't safe for me to walk alone in many places. I could go into town and walk through the shops or to the clothing market alone. But I would never have walked out the front gate of the school by myself and set off for a walk. A number of times, we had known of friends or students being mugged along our street. Most often, potential muggers were hiding in the large drains beside the road. They would jump up, chop a woman's handbag strap with a machete and steal the bag. So, it had been a long time since I'd been free to walk like this. I ran for fitness every morning, but I went around in circles on the school pitch, not out into the streets.

Needless to say, I was walking on sunshine as we went up that mountain. As the days passed, the initial excitement wore off for Tony and he became increasingly grumpy. He was committed to the climb, and was even thinking of attempting Everest one day, but the slow walking was monotonous to him, and clearly not his favourite part of summiting a mountain. I'm sure I was the most annoying climbing partner in the world for him at this point, since I was enjoying it so much. My giddy enthusiasm wouldn't wear off, and it must have driven him crazy. The last thing you want when you're in a bad mood is a smiling sidekick.

'It's just so beautiful,' I gushed for the thousandth time.

'It's rocks and trees,' Tony growled back. 'It's the same rocks and trees we've been staring at all day.'

'I know, but isn't it just so wonderful to be up here? It really is beautiful! Look how high we're getting! I just love this!' I was annoyingly positive, but I couldn't rein it in. I felt a glorious freedom on this mountain. There was no bursting my bubble.

It struck me how this climb so far resembled our experience in Africa. Everything was so new, exciting and energising at first, and although it was challenging, our energy was high and we enjoyed the journey. The way to climb this mountain was one foot in front of the other, slowly, a million times until you reached the summit. Feeling energised or not, enjoying it or not, terrified or not, the only way to summit was one foot in front of the other. I might not feel like skipping the whole way up this mountain, but I was well-practised at putting one foot in front of the other.

A team of porters climbed along with us—seven of them in total! They were incredible humans. Each one carried 20 kilograms of supplies on their heads, as well as their own gear in a backpack. Tony and I carried a small pack, weighing seven or eight kilograms. Our porters walked at lightning speed, their experience on the mountain proving invaluable, and arrived at our next camp hours before we did, where they set up our tents and cooked our dinner.

Each afternoon, we would reach camp, exhausted from the day of climbing, and sing the praises of our guides who had prepared camp for us. We would dump our packs in our tents and enter the dining tent—a special tent set up for us to eat our meals. Dinner time was a highlight each day, especially for Tony, who hated the walking. The meals we were served were pretty amazing, given the circumstances. We were served hot soup to start with, which was exactly what we wanted. The temperature dropped lower as we climbed higher, and the delicious hot soup warmed our cold hands and bodies. The main course, for me, was a vegetarian dish and rice.

For Tony, he was greeted each night with his special piece of meat. The first few nights, he ate it, which I thought was quite impressive. But as the days passed, and he thought more about the origins of that meat, and how long it had been in someone's bag, he couldn't stomach it any longer. Looking enviously at my delicious beans and rice, he had to work out what to do with his meat. He didn't want to offend, but he wasn't going to eat it!

When we were kids, Tony and I were world-class experts at hiding food. Unwanted vegetables disappeared from our dining table without a trace, and not into our mouths. Mum and Dad would leave us at the table to finish after we sat there for long enough, and once they were gone, we got to work. We buried broccoli in pot plants, flung zucchini into the air to land on high windowsills, fed Brussels sprouts to the dog, filled our pockets with cauliflower and flushed anything we couldn't hide down the toilet. Our overweight cat was walking evidence of our squirrelled-away food.

So Tony was well-prepared for the situation he now faced. He smuggled that meat out of the tent, disposing of it in the bushes or digging it into a hole. Luckily for him, I shared my rice and beans, and there was more food than either of us could eat.

With each day, as we ascended higher, the vegetation changed. The tall trees and cheeky colobus monkeys of the rainforest zone gave way to the small shrubs and bushes of the low alpine zone, where the ground beneath our feet became rocky and unstable, and the temperature started to drop below zero. When we opened our tents on day three, we looked out and realised we were above the clouds. What a view!

By day four, the terrain felt more like a foreign planet. The high alpine zone was like walking on the moon, with strange cactus-like trees called Giant Groundsels reaching up out of the ground here and there. It was barren and eerie, like something out of *The NeverEnding Story*. We walked on, using hiking poles for stability, higher and higher up Kilimanjaro. Turning around to look below, it was stunning to see how high we were. Turning to face the mountain, the peak of Kilimanjaro towering above, it was apparent how much higher we still had to climb.

By this time, all talk of Everest had ceased. Tony's body was beginning to show signs of wear and tear. He was driven, determined and wanted to reach the peak, but he wasn't enjoying the process at all. Day four was punishing. By the end of the day, all around us was grey rock and dust, a barren wasteland, and a relentless incline. We walked into camp and collapsed into our tents, thankful once again for the porters who came before us. Our schedule now was to have an early dinner and then try to get a few hours' sleep before waking at 11pm to get ready for our attempt to climb to the summit.

Camp four is at an elevation of 4,600 metres, and sleeping at this altitude without much acclimatisation is difficult. Each in our own tents, we tossed and turned, trying to keep warm, trying to get comfortable, trying to stop the excitement of the final summit from keeping us awake. We dozed at best, but didn't sleep.

At 11pm, Dennis woke us up to climb. The zippers on our tents were frozen shut, and a thin sheet of ice covered the canvas. It was freezing. I'm one of those people who feel the cold, and I intensely hate being cold. I find it hard to think about anything else except getting warm. But I didn't want the cold to ruin this experience for me—I wanted to enjoy every minute. So, I put on all the clothes I had with me. I wore long-sleeve thermal tops, two warm hiking jackets, a fleece jumper, a down jacket, a rain jacket, a pair of thermal pants, tracksuit pants, snow pants, three pairs of socks, toe warmers, two pairs of gloves, a balaclava, a beanie, a crazy furry hat, a scarf and a neck warmer. I felt like a walking marshmallow, but I was warm.

We drank a cup of warm tea and filled our camelback water packs. We would only be carrying a small daypack to the summit, with just our water and a few lollies for energy, and we would wear our head torches and use our walking poles. It was so exciting—pitch-black darkness all around, a clear night above the clouds, and a hum of activity around us as all the climbers prepared to climb.

Before long, we could see a trail of lights ahead. The climbers who had departed before us were snaking their way up the mountain. At this point, the mountain is so steep that climbers walk back and forth along zig-zagging switchbacks, climbing a little higher with each pass. The glimmering headlamps of those ahead of us revealed the path we were about to follow.

We set off before midnight. Up the path we went, following the zigzags steeply upwards. At this altitude, it's much more difficult to breathe, so even walking slowly feels like running at speed.

Tony and I were both feeling good in terms of the altitude. We weren't suffering headaches or feeling unwell at all. We passed many climbers as we went who were throwing up at the side of the path. It was fascinating to watch the effects of altitude, how it picked one person and not the next. Over the past few days, we had seen many climbers turning back, unable to continue. But as we ascended higher, there were more. It plays with your mind watching this happen. I wasn't sure whether to feel grateful or guilty that I felt fine, or to worry whether altitude sickness was about to hit me as well. I decided to feel grateful for feeling well for as long as it may last, and to enjoy every moment that I could.

We climbed for hours. Tony was feeling well too, in the sense that he wasn't affected by the altitude, but his shoulder was starting to trouble him. An old injury was flaring up again. He struggled a little at first, then more and more as we climbed higher. Dennis offered to take Tony's daypack for him, and he agreed, relieving the pain a little from his shoulder. We walked on, but each time I looked back at Tony, his face showed how much pain he was in.

We stopped for water and a rest every so often, and Dennis sat down next to me.

'How do you think we're going?' I asked. 'Are we making good time?'

'We're making really good time,' Dennis said. 'But how's your brother?' I looked over at Tony, sitting on a rock, leaning over with his elbows on his knees.

'He's tough,' I said. 'He's obviously in pain, but he'll keep going.'

'I know climbers like him,' Dennis said. 'He's driven and stubborn, and that alone will get him to the top.' He paused. 'It's just getting back down that's the problem.'

We set off again and continued up the switchbacks. Slowly climbing, one foot in front of the other. It was exhausting. After the gruelling day yesterday, the lack of sleep and the punishing climb, it was extremely difficult. Dennis looked back to check on us.

'Tony!' Dennis shouted, 'Open your eyes!' He was so tired, he was walking with his eyes closed.

We pushed on along a seemingly endless incline. *One foot in front of the other*, I reminded myself, *one foot in front of the other.*

'Anna,' Dennis called out to me, 'what's the name of the point where this path meets the crater rim?' he asked.

'Stella Point,' I answered wearily.

'Look up,' Dennis said. I stopped walking, steadied myself and looked up to see a sign above reading:

CONGRATULATIONS
YOU ARE NOW AT
STELLA POINT 5756M

I could have cried with relief. We were now at the point where our switchbacks had taken us all the way up to the rim of the crater, on top of Kilimanjaro. From here, we walked around the crater rim to find the peak.

I gasped with joy seeing the sign and grabbed Tony. 'We're almost there, we're almost there!' I told him. We stopped here for a few minutes for a drink and a rest, taking in the incredible view of climbers below us snaking their way upwards, only visible by their head torches. A man behind me was vomiting over the edge of the path. Another was crying, holding his head in his hands. A whole group touched the Stella Point sign, took a picture and went straight back down. We had kept a good pace up the mountain and passed many groups, as they cared for the unwell and took others down the mountain.

I'd listened to Mark's stories of climbing Kilimanjaro, looked at the maps and understood the route well before the climb, but I certainly underestimated this last section. Thinking we'd done all the hard work, and now we just walked around the rim to the summit, it sounded easy from here. It wasn't. And possibly because of my optimistic expectations, this was the most difficult section of the climb for me. The rim was quite steep, and the air was so very thin. On the crater rim, the oxygen level is approximately half of that at sea level.

I bent over on my poles for a minute, adjusted my backpack, collected myself, and walked on. It was still slightly dark and hard to see exactly where we were and what we were looking at. The path ahead was all that mattered, and we pushed on. Tony had pain written all over him, but his steely determination pushed him forward. Slowly but surely, we made our way around the rim of the dormant volcano and reached the summit, with its glorious sign reading:

CONGRATULATIONS
YOU ARE NOW AT
UHURU PEAK, TANZANIA, 5895M

We were ready to collapse with exhaustion, but we made it. It was 6am, just as the sun was rising above the clouds. I took off my pack, sat on an icy rock and burst into tears. I watched the sun peak over the clouds and the sky turn beautiful shades of pink and blue. We were the fourth people to reach the summit that day. So for the first few minutes, we had it almost to ourselves. Magical.

I stood again and walked closer to the edge, looking out on the cloud cover below. Somewhere far down there was my family, my home, and the life I'd come to love. I thought of all the hours I'd spent gazing up here to the place where I stood right now. I thought of everything this mountain had come to symbolise for us—the hope, the struggle, the beauty, the failures and the triumphs. I was standing on the top. And it felt incredible. I closed my teary eyes and prayed, gratitude and love spilling out faster than my thoughts could carry them.

I sat on an ice-covered rock and pulled a photograph from the chest pocket of my jacket. The sweet faces of Jabari, Shay and Charlie looked back at me. It was a picture from our final day in Court—my three beauties dressed in their shiny clothes with wide, cheeky grins. I'd sealed it in plastic, and on the back I'd written an inscription. It was part of a Bible verse that I had held onto for the past three years—sometimes with feeble faith and other times with bold declaration.

Immeasurably more than all we ask or imagine. Ephesians 3:20

I had prayed and believed and clung to this verse—that God was powerful beyond what I could ever hope or comprehend. I knew this to be true. He had shown me through numerous seasons of my life in the past. He was powerful and good and faithful, again and again. I held that picture in my numb, gloved fingers, another testament to God's goodness and power in my life, kissed those three cheeky faces and placed it firmly under a heavy rock. A tiny piece of evidence of the story that had unfolded in the shadow of this mountain, now sitting on its summit. More thankful tears, freezing on my cheeks.

A few more minutes passed, just taking it all in. We could see more climbers emerging over the rim in the distance, so we took the chance to take some pictures before it got busy. Taking our gloves off to use the camera was painful from the cold, so we snapped away quickly and returned our icy fingers to the warmth of our gloves.

Surprisingly, there was phone reception on the summit, and I watched tears run down my brother's face as he spoke to his wife, Meg. 'We made it,' he said. 'We're on the summit.'

I called Mark and heard the kids clapping, cheering and yelling, 'We love you,' and 'We're so proud of you, Mum,' from the background.

We stayed on the summit for about 45 minutes, looking around and exploring a little. The sunshine revealed massive glaciers that loomed out from the side of the mountain like icy cliffs, and the incredible crater in the centre. It looked ancient. Dropped down from the rim, nestled lower in the centre of the mountain, there were perfectly circular rock formations, getting deeper in the middle, as if a meteor had flown from outer space, crashed into Kilimanjaro and sent waves of rock rippling outwards.

The summit was everything a summit promises to be: elation, joy, relief, blissful exhaustion, triumph. Now we just had to get down.

Chapter 43

Descent

"You cannot stay on the summit forever; you have to come down again. So why bother in the first place? Just this: What is above knows what is below, but what is below does not know what is above. One climbs, one sees. One descends, one sees no longer, but one has seen."

—RENE DAUMAL

After 45 blissful minutes of soaking in incredible views and the thrill of standing on the snowy peak of Kilimanjaro, the cold became too much, and we turned to descend. Re-energised from our summit experience and our rest at the top, I felt like skipping down the mountain. This was the easy part, right?

At first, it was. We circled the rim again and began to make our way down. Our descent route, which was different to our ascent route, took us down the mountain via the quickest path possible. The top section of the mountain was soft, icy gravel that slid downward with each step. It was great fun, and we slid almost as if we were skiing down. What took us six hours to ascend that morning took us two hours to descend, and we arrived back at our camp from the previous night in good time.

The route we had chosen (the Machame route) is typically completed in either six or seven days. We had chosen the six-day option, which meant we had ascended more quickly (four sleeps on the way up) and would descend the mountain with just one sleep. Some climbers choose to sleep at the camp they had been at the previous night, for just a few hours, before descending the following day. At this point, Tony and I were both feeling well and were keen to descend as quickly as possible.

On the initial descent, Tony had started to feel pain in his toes, where they were butting into the end of his shoes. Once at camp, he removed his shoes to find some blisters appearing and put some Band-Aids on.

After a meal, we got moving again. We were making great time since we had reached the summit so early, and returned quickly. The next section was steep downhill and would continue like this until we stopped at our next camp. Our plan had been to reach this camp by late afternoon, sleep the night, and walk the final hours of the descent the following morning. But by the pace we were going, it looked like we would reach camp by lunchtime.

'How many hours is it from our last camp to the end of the climb?' Tony asked Dennis.

'Only about three or four,' Dennis replied.

'So, if we got there by lunch, couldn't we just walk the rest of the way in the afternoon and not camp overnight?'

'Yeah, we could,' Dennis said. 'It's up to you guys. We'd have to be at camp by lunchtime to make it work, but yeah, we could do it.'

However, as we left the previous night's camp and descended lower, Tony started to feel a new pain. This time, it was his knee. Walking downhill is terribly rough on the joints, and one of his knees was not happy. At first, there was a comment here and there. His blisters and knee were causing pain, but after a few more hours, walking became excruciating for Tony. With every step, he was moaning and hobbling, using his walking poles to take some of his weight and lessen the impact.

We reached our final camp by lunchtime and sat down together for a hot meal in the dining tent. We enjoyed our hot soup and discussed our plan from here. We were both keen to keep going. It seemed strange to camp here when the exit gate was just three or four hours away, and it was only lunchtime. But Tony's knee was the concern. It was a concern whether we stayed the night or not. We feared that if we stopped and stayed the night, his knee would seize up completely, and getting going again in the morning would be too difficult. Tony decided our best bet was to keep going now in the hope he might be able to push through for another few hours. Dennis agreed, and we set off on our final leg.

Tony pushed through valiantly, but he was unable to conceal the level of pain he was really in. Our pace had slowed considerably, and we became concerned we weren't going to make it to the gate by closing time at 5pm. Dennis suggested he stay with Tony and continue at their pace, and one of our other guides would walk ahead with me. That way, I could reach the gate by 5pm and have them wait for Tony and Dennis.

My guide and I walked ahead. We walked for another hour or so and rounded a bend in the path to find a white 4WD with a red cross printed on the side.

It was a shock to see a vehicle up the mountain, but the red cross indicated it was obviously there for a medical evacuation. As we walked past, I wondered what had happened and hoped no one had died, or was seriously ill, higher up the mountain.

My guide and I walked on for another hour or so, then we heard the 4WD approaching behind us. We stood to the side, and the car slowed beside us, revealing Tony in the back seat! The 4WD pulled over to pick us up, and I climbed up towards him.

'Are you alright?' I asked, concerned.

'Yeah, this guy just offered us a ride, so we got in,' Tony replied. Dennis was sheepishly looking out the window. There were a few other passengers in the back as well, and we rode together in the back of the 4WD until we got to the gate.

When we reached the gate, a medic appeared from the building.

'So who's the guy with the wrecked knee?'

I looked at Tony. Tony looked completely confused. When no one else spoke up, it dawned on Tony for the first time that the medivac had been called for him.

'Uh, me?!' Tony replied. Tony looked over at Dennis, who was grinning.

'Well, if I told you I was calling for a car to take you off the mountain, you would have been too stubborn to get in!' Dennis laughed. 'We would have been there all night. You weren't going to make it without the car.'

I threw back my head and laughed and laughed. Dennis was as sneaky as he was perceptive. He'd made a call from his phone, speaking Swahili so Tony couldn't understand, to arrange for the 4WD to meet them. Then when they happened upon it, Dennis acted surprised, as though it was just good luck a car was waiting, and they got in.

Tony's pride took a hit, but at least we made it off the mountain. Truth be told, what we had done over the last 24 hours was incredible. After a full day of climbing, we had rested for three hours, climbed six hours to the summit of Kilimanjaro, and descended the entire mountain (well, almost!) in 12 hours. It was an epic feat and a wonderful adventure. And I was fairly sure it was the first and last high-altitude climb for my dear brother.

We drove the bumpy roads back to my little home. Mark was expecting us home tomorrow, and I snuck through the door and yelled, 'Surprise! We're home!'

Mark gave me a big hug, and we sat on the lounge to tell our long tale. As I was talking, to my complete shock, another of our friends from Australia, Jo's husband, Williams, casually walked in from the kitchen, sat down on the lounge and took a sip from his beer. I jumped out of my chair.

'What?!' I laughed, 'What is going on? What are you doing here?'

'Gotcha again!' Mark laughed, pointing at me.

Williams had flown in not long after Tony and I set off for our climb and had spent the week with Mark and the kids. Tony knew all about it and had kept it a secret up the mountain, but I had no idea. Friends from home are like manna from heaven when living far away. I felt intensely happy sitting back on the lounge, having just summited Kilimanjaro that morning, and now sitting here in the company of great friends hearing news from home. That husband of mine was getting mighty good at surprises.

On the plus side, it appeared Williams had forgiven me for leading his wife and baby daughter into peril on safari. I figured if he'd come all this way to visit, he mustn't be holding it against me too much, although I did notice he didn't bring any of his children with him. Probably for the best.

The following day, Mark, Tony and Williams set out on safari. They enjoyed their own adventure at Tarangire (not in the wet season this time), managing to avoid getting bogged and stranded.

They did, however, encounter a pride of lions at close range as they went to sleep in their tent. In scenes reminiscent of our first safari when Mark and I freaked out about elephants tripping on our tent, Williams' life flashed before his eyes as the booming, guttural roar of lions filled his ears. Before long, he was in the foetal position on the floor of the tent, covering his vital organs and hoping the lions chose to eat Mark before they found him. I can attest to the pure terror of that sound at first exposure. The sheer power and volume of a lion's roar in the wild at close proximity is intensely overwhelming. Even the low grunts, snarls and panting breath is enough to leave you frozen in place. A thin layer of canvas is all that separates you from the great beasts. In time, it becomes awe-inspiring and thrilling, but at first exposure, it certainly feels like imminent death.

Williams made it through the night, uneaten, and in the morning, Mark filled him in on the nature of lions in the wild, and that as far as we know, no lion has ever clawed through a closed canvas tent to eat the occupant, information that may have provided more comfort the night before!

Chapter 44

Dar es Salaam

"You gain strength, courage and confidence by every experience in which you really stop to look fear in the face. You are able to say to yourself, 'I lived through this horror. I can take the next thing that comes along.' You must do the thing you think you cannot do."

—ELEANOR ROOSEVELT

Our final few months in Tanzania were a mix of filling our weekends with all our favourite things, savouring every moment, and sorting the logistics of our return to Australia. We had finished the adoptions, and the last piece of our puzzle was getting all seven of us back home. We needed a specific kind of visa for the children to return to Australia, and there was a list of hoops for us to jump through before they were eligible. For this step, we were dealing with the Australian Embassy based in Nairobi, and from all experiences so far, they had been wonderfully helpful.

To get our papers in order, I needed to take Shay, Charlie and Jabari for a health check. But the only doctor in the country recognised by the Embassy to complete health checks was based in Dar es Salaam. Off I went with three three-year-olds who had barely seen the world beyond their hometown and safari parks.

Going anywhere with toddlers is a challenge, let alone taking three of them across the country by plane. The kids had no memory of their plane trip from Mwanza to Moshi when we first brought them home, so flying was a new experience. I had talked it through with them repeatedly, drawn pictures of planes, and played games to prepare them. But when the day arrived and I walked with them across the tarmac to board the plane, its engines already roaring and creating a wind tunnel as we walked, the kids freaked out.

Charlie, ever a nervous little guy, started screaming first and tried to scale my legs like a palm tree. The other two followed suit and the three of them brought me down like a pride of lions attacking a giraffe. We fell in a bundle on the tarmac, and I hugged them close and tried to shout above the roar of the engines to comfort them. This failed miserably and I saw no path forward other than carrying all three, who clung like koalas, and climbing the stairs to the plane as their screams continued. Quizzical looks from strangers were par for the course for us, but three Tanzanian children screaming while an Australian lady dragged them, unwillingly, onto a plane was next level for onlookers.

Once we entered the plane and the children saw the seats, their screams completely stopped.

'Mumma! There's chairs!' Shay exclaimed.

'Yes, this is where we're going to sit,' I replied, explaining what I thought was obvious.

'We sit here?' asked Jabari.

'Yes!' I replied, 'Here's where we sit!' and sat each one in their seat, buckling them in.

'Oh, we go IN the plane, Mumma! We not go ON the plane. We go IN the plane!' Charlie said with relief.

Only then did I understand their confusion. All that time as I was telling them, 'We're going on a plane,' they thought they were going to ride on the top of it. No wonder they panicked when they saw the plane!

The remainder of the trip was relaxed and smooth, much to the relief of the other passengers. We landed in Dar and took a taxi around town for a few hours attending appointments and getting items checked off our list. The trip was a success at every stop, and I was quite pleased with how well we were progressing. We stayed overnight in a hotel, and the children experienced seemingly thousands of "firsts" as we went, such as riding in an elevator and pressing the buttons that lit up. There was a staircase made of transparent Perspex that we descended at snail's pace as they baffled at how they could stand on something they could also see through. They squealed and giggled and held onto the rails for dear life.

Once our tasks were completed, we headed back to the airport to return home. I was confident this time that the kids would be fine as they were now well aware that we would be going in the plane to fly home. We arrived at the airport in Dar es Salaam and came towards the stepped escalator that would carry us to the first floor. The children had never seen an escalator before, and not realising there would be one in the airport, I hadn't prepared them.

Charlie started crying and clinging immediately at first sight of the escalator, and I knelt down a few metres in front of the escalator to talk them through what this was and allow them to watch others ride up and down safely. But Charlie wasn't convinced and each time I stood to approach, he started screaming again. His distress was unsettling Shay and Jabari, who started whimpering as well. I stopped again, trying to calm them, but knowing we didn't have a lot of spare time, and I didn't know how many other panic moments may lay ahead before we were checked in.

Eventually, once Charlie's screams had lowered to a whimper, I walked them towards the escalator, holding three little hands and gently guiding them onto the rising steps. Charlie's screams returned, so I picked him up and swung him onto my hip while keeping hold of Jabari and Shay's hands as they stood on the step in front of me. Suddenly I felt a strong tug, and Charlie was pulled from my arms. I turned to see a Tanzanian man running down the last few steps of the upward-moving escalator and taking off with Charlie in his arms!

This was a moment of pure terror. I had two toddlers in front of me who had never ridden an escalator and didn't know how to get off at the top, and one child just ripped from my arms. My instinct was to chase after Charlie. I yelled out to the people in front in panicked, muddled Swahili, and left Shay and Jabari as I ran down the escalator. I started crying and screaming out as I leapt down the final few upward-moving steps and ran towards the man I could still see holding Charlie in his arms.

'He's got my child! That's my son!' I screeched out as I ran. Stunned onlookers stood around, motionless. The man was walking now, towards the exit, and I caught up to him, ripped Charlie from his arms, still screaming, and turned back towards the escalator. The man had let Charlie go with little resistance, and although I was ready to fight, I was relieved I didn't have to. I ran back to the escalator to see a kind woman at the top, holding Shay and Jabari's hands while they waited for me. She had heard the commotion and helped them off the escalator. Once at the top, I thanked her profusely, informed airport security, gathered the three children together and hugged them and cried.

I wasn't sure exactly what had happened. I didn't know if the man had tried to abduct Charlie, or what his intent was. I was aware of how the situation may have looked—maybe it looked like I was taking someone else's children against their will, as I didn't look like their mother, and they were distressed. I'll never know. But whatever the intent, it was terrifying, and I kept as tight a hold on those babies as I could until we were safely home in Moshi.

Chapter 45

The Police Report

"A woman is like a tea bag—you can't tell how strong she is until you put her in hot water."
—ELEANOR ROOSEVELT

There was one final document we needed to finalise the kids' visas. One last piece of paper that stood between us and home. There had been so many documents already—reports, letters, certificates, applications, Court papers—and each one we had ticked off. Some were quick and simple, and others were an epic battle. I was hoping and praying this last one would be simple.

It was a Police check. It was done by the local Police station to indicate we had not committed any crimes in Tanzania and had no criminal record. By all accounts, it was simple enough—we applied, paid the application fee, it was sent off, and came back a few days later.

Mark began the process, went to the station, filled in the forms, paid the fee, and had it sent off. A few days later, we received word that the report had come back and was ready for collection. Mark was unable to pick it up, so I went into town to collect the completed Police checks. Mark had given me the receipt so I could show we had already paid, and I drove to the station expecting to run in and out with the certificates. It didn't quite happen like that. It never did.

I entered the Police station and was met by a Police officer at the desk. I explained what I was here for, and he directed me to an office down the hall. Following his instructions, I walked down the hall and entered the first door on the right. There was a second officer sitting behind a large desk. I explained again what I was after. The officer looked at me for a few seconds, then leant back in his chair and rested his arms behind his head. He was clearly contemplating his next move, and the tiny hairs on the back of my neck stood up. I was on alert. There's a level of alertness that becomes standard when living in Tanzania—you don't daydream or lose track of time when you drive. You are always alert. And then there's another level. It comes when you sense something is not quite right.

You're not sure yet, and you aren't ready to turn and run, but you're on edge. Standing in this office, the pause was too long, the officer's gaze too intense, and I was on edge.

'You want to collect the Police checks?' he asked.

'Yes. I've been informed they have arrived here at the station and are ready to be collected,' I said.

'Well, we'll have to see if that's the case,' he replied. 'Take a seat in the waiting room and I'll call for you if I find them.'

I returned to the waiting room, guessing at what this guy was after. Presumably, he wanted money. As long as I was safe, I wasn't going to give him any. We'd already paid. I had my receipt, that was enough. Maybe I was just in a mood, but I wasn't going to let this guy intimidate me into handing over more money. As I waited, I performed my now-instinctual safety checks. I noted the two doors, large windows, good visibility, busy street, and many pedestrians. Each of these earned points for safety in my mind. I was okay for now.

He left me waiting for 20 minutes in the waiting room and then wandered out.

'Your reports have come in,' he confirmed, 'but another officer has them. He picked them up from the post office for you. Come with me, and he will meet us and give you the certificates.'

More hairs standing up.

'That's okay,' I said. 'I can wait here. When he comes back to the station, I'll collect them.'

'He's not coming back to the station,' the officer retorted quickly. 'Follow me, we'll get them now.'

I contemplated what to do. I was confident he was toying with me. And I was confident he could make our certificates disappear and never be found if he wanted to. I needed those certificates—I can't even begin to describe how badly we wanted to get this finished and get home. I just needed these certificates. I decided I'd follow along, for as long as we were in a safe location—busy streets with local women around would be fine.

I paused and held his gaze long enough to let him know I was sceptical, that I didn't buy his story, then I stood and followed him out the door. I walked behind him, not beside him. It felt like he intended to parade me up the street, as if we were together, and I wasn't going to walk beside him. The streets were bustling and busy, which put my mind at ease. He led me up the street, turned a corner, walked through a market, up another street, turned again, and down another street. It was getting ridiculous; my patience was beginning to wear thin.

And then he stopped at a small street-side restaurant. He made his way to a table for two and sat down, indicating for me to sit opposite him.

'Where is your friend?' I asked, without sitting.

'He's coming now. He's on his way,' he replied, laughing.

'Where is he going to meet us?' I asked.

'He's coming to meet us here,' he answered. 'Relax.'

'Then I guess we'll need another chair,' I replied. I narrowed my eyes at him. I wanted to be clear that I wasn't playing, and I wanted him to think I wasn't intimidated. I was intimidated. But I didn't want him to know that.

I pulled up a third chair and sat down. I turned my chair to face outwards and moved it away from the table. This was not going to look like a lunch date. People chatted and ate around us, and I kept my gaze on the happenings in the street, and away from the officer.

To my surprise, the officer called over a waitress and ordered a meal! I kept my body turned and didn't engage in conversation. He waited for his meal.

'What time is he meeting us?' I asked.

'He's on his way now,' the officer lied. I didn't buy it. But I wasn't sure what my next best move was. I hoped to wait him out until he gave in and handed over the certificates.

The officer's meal arrived, and he ate it slowly. We sat in silence, waiting. His phone rang and he answered it, speaking quietly and laughing into the phone. He ended the call with more promises that the other officer would be here soon. He wasn't.

Over three hours had passed since I had arrived at the station before the officer stood abruptly, paid for his meal, and said, 'He will now meet us back at the station.'

Interestingly, he had not received another phone call with any new information about his friend's plans to meet us. Grateful to be moving on, I stood and followed the officer back through the streets and markets, and into the station. He took me straight back to the office I had first met him in. He sat at the desk and opened the top drawer.

'Your certificates are here,' he said, and pulled them out of the drawer without passing them to me. The mood was getting a bit intense. I thought I would try and lighten it with humour.

'Oh,' I said with a grin, 'but your friend is not here? I guess he must have snuck in and put them in your drawer just now.'

The officer looked at me for a second and then smiled slowly. 'I guess so,' he said.

'Now, I will give these certificates to you once you pay the fee. It will be 50,000 shillings.' 50,000 Tanzanian shillings is about 30 Australian dollars. It wasn't much, really, but I still didn't want to pay it.

'I've already paid the fee, and here is my receipt,' I replied.

'Yes, but that is just the preliminary fee,' he stated. 'And now you must pay the remaining 50,000.'

'I won't be paying any more for these certificates,' I said firmly. 'There is no further fee required.'

'Well then, I guess I will just keep them in my drawer,' the officer said and tucked them back away, leaning back in his chair again and returning his arms to their resting position behind his head, a smug grin creeping its way across his face.

I looked him in the eye and contemplated my next move. Should I just pay it? I just wanted to get out of there and take those certificates. But I didn't want to give him the satisfaction of knowing his games were working. He'd paraded me around town for three hours to wear me down and get me to pay him for the privilege. I couldn't do it.

I had an idea.

'Okay, fine.' I began. 'But first let me view the certificates to check they are correct, and you've spelled our names properly. I'm not paying for something that is incorrect.'

He opened the drawer and pulled the certificates out. I wasn't sure if he was silly enough to hand them to me to check, but it was worth a try.

'Yes, yes, check them,' he said, and he placed them in my hands.

I checked them carefully, and then gripping them tightly, I quickly moved back towards the door.

'Thank you very much,' I said quickly. 'They are perfect. I'll leave my receipt by the door.' I grinned cheekily at the officer and tucked them safely into my bag.

The officer sat up in his chair suddenly, realising his error, and then leant back again, laughing loudly.

'Oh, you're good! You're very good!' he said as I made my swift exit. The sound of his laugh was still audible as I jumped into my car, locked myself in and drove away. Relieved and excited to have the final papers in my hot little hands, I sped out of there, heart racing.

Good grief, I was ready to move home!

Chapter 46

The Other Side

"All their life in this world and all the adventures in Narnia had only been the cover and the title page: Now at last they were beginning Chapter One of the Great Story which no one on earth has read: which goes on forever: in which every chapter is better than the one before."
—C.S. LEWIS, *THE LAST BATTLE*

With only a few months left in Tanzania, Mark declared he would never again eat in the school dining hall. We'd spent the past three years eating the same ten or so meals on rotation. No more! We could buy burgers, chips and drinks for the whole family for the equivalent of seven Australian dollars, and this was all the excuse Mark needed to avoid the dining hall.

We had all the visa paperwork completed for Shay, Charlie and Jabari and were awaiting a reply. Unsure of what to expect, and traumatised by all the paperwork debacles so far, we were cautiously hopeful that this one would be quick and easy. There was nothing more to do but enjoy our last few months of life in Moshi.

We booked ourselves solid, fitting in all our favourite things one last time. Amboseli National Park was top of our list. Amboseli is across the Kenyan border, but not too far from us. The classic pictures you see of giraffes and elephants walking across the plains with snow-capped Kilimanjaro in the background are taken from Amboseli National Park. The only thing between Moshi and Amboseli was Mount Kilimanjaro. We would drive around the mountain, cross the border into Kenya, and enjoy our final safari at Amboseli.

Just as we were about to head off on safari, Mark's phone buzzed with a message:

YOUR VISA APPLICATIONS HAVE BEEN APPROVED.

We looked at each other in amazement. Approved? Just like that? No crisis, no delays, no extra fees, no confusing discussions, no begging, no tears—just approved! We jumped up and started screaming, hugging, grabbing the kids and throwing them in the air.

'We've done it!' Mark yelled to surprised little faces. 'We're going to make it home!'

We cheered and giggled and checked the message a few extra times to make sure. The kids carried on playing, quite accustomed to our celebrations of pieces of paper they knew nothing about, and Mark and I stood in shock, looking at each other with intense joy. Everything was done. There was no more paperwork, no more applications, no more approvals, no more waiting, no more praying against another disaster. We were done.

Our trip to Amboseli became a huge celebration. We enjoyed a smooth safari, taking our own classic safari photos, marvelling at the incredible wildlife, and noticing in general how much lighter we were feeling, with the whole adoption process finished. At dinnertime, we were surprised with a beautiful cake delivered to our table, organised by some friends in Moshi, to celebrate our visa approvals.

We sat on the porch of our cabin on that first evening of our safari, with an epic view of Mount Kilimanjaro stretching out before us as the sun went down. As the sun set on the mountain, the warm glow turned the snow pink, and five little Dombkins ran and played and giggled in front of us.

'Hey, An,' Mark said, putting his arm around me as we gazed up at Kilimanjaro.

'Yeah?' I asked.

'We're on the other side of the mountain.'

Chapter 47

Max

"When you leave Africa, as the plane lifts, you feel that more than leaving a continent you're leaving a state of mind. Whatever awaits you at the other end of your journey will be of a different order of existence."
—FRANCESCA MARCIANO

We'd been back home in Australia for two weeks. We had said a teary goodbye to our dear Moshi friends. They sent us off after an emotional goodbye lunch by making a long, winding human tunnel for us to run through, with tears and cheers in equal measure as we boarded the bus to the airport. We cried the whole way, leaving this extraordinary country we had come to love so much and these once-in-a-lifetime friends. After 30 hours of travel with five little ones and 16 suitcases, and a joyful airport reunion with our families in Sydney, we stepped into our new home. I was tired.

The kids ran ahead into the house and lay down on the living room floor. They rolled onto their backs and started doing snow angels.

'This house is so furry!' Shay yelled.

'Oh,' I said, suddenly becoming aware of how much they'd never seen before. 'This is called carpet!' They all ran off to explore the rest of the furry house.

We'd arrived a few days before Christmas, and the reverse culture shock was intense. I ducked to the shops to pick up some gifts, and nearly cried from pure overwhelm. Noise, people, lights, decorations and a thousand shiny things was all too much. This was my hometown. I'd lived here forever, yet it felt so foreign. I was tired.

We revelled in being back with our loved ones, celebrating Christmas with our family, exchanging gifts under the tree, singing carols with our church family, and enjoying getting to introduce everyone to our children, at long last! And then off we went to Queensland for a few weeks of holidays on the beautiful Sunshine Coast. It was glorious and relaxing and all things wonderful. And I was tired.

It's no wonder I'm tired, I thought to myself after falling asleep on the couch at 10am. *I've just moved home from living in Tanzania, adopted three children and am now raising a seven-year-old and four four-year-olds. That's pretty tiring. Anyone would be tired by that, right?* I questioned myself, trying to make sense of my fatigue.

But that afternoon I fell asleep again. I couldn't remember the last time I'd had a daytime sleep, let alone two. And then it hit me. I could remember. I knew this feeling. I was never tired, not like this. Except—

No! I thought. *Not possible. Totally not possible. It's just the trip to Tanzania and all the many children. That must be it. Surely that's just tiring! It's just years of tiredness all coming at me now. That's what this is.*

As hard as I tried to lie to myself, I knew. I knew that feeling. I ducked off to the shops in a panicked daze, came home, and a few minutes later, there were two pink lines staring back at me once again. I was pregnant.

Not possible. I thought again, as the pink lines seemed to laugh at me. *How could this even be possible? We don't accidentally fall pregnant! We can barely fall pregnant with every tracking device, thermometer, and chart known to mankind! I can't be pregnant! Oh my word, I'm pregnant! How old am I? Am I too old to have a baby? I'm thirty-... something? Why can't I remember how old I am? 32? 31? I have no idea. Oh my goodness. Is this some kind of joke? God, are you serious? Have you lost your mind? How on earth are we going to do this? I can't be pregnant. I can't. I have too many children to be pregnant. You can't just have a baby when you've just moved home from Tanzania with five children. Most people we know haven't even met my last three children yet. I can't be having another one!*

I sat in the bathroom in complete shock. I could hear Mark in the lounge room watching the cricket. *What was he going to say?* I debated how long to leave him in his cricket-loving, only-having-five-children paradise before breaking the news. It was his birthday tomorrow.

As I sat looking at those pink lines, my mind went back to all the tests like this I'd taken before. Falling pregnant had been hard for us and I thought of the countless times I'd stared at tests like this, praying and begging for those two pink lines. Squinting a little harder, turning the test on every angle, willing the faintest glimpse of a second line to appear. I thought of the time there were two strong dark pink lines and extraordinary joy, but a little while later there was no heartbeat on the ultrasound. I had kept taking tests, hoping it was a mistake, but the following tests only had a faint pink line, and then nothing.

The memories made my eyes sting with tears, and I held the test close to my belly. *Hold on tight, little one.* I whispered. I could never be sad about a positive pregnancy test. Shocked, for sure, but never sad.

God, I have no idea how we're going to do this. I prayed; *I'm not prepared. But I know you're good. I know your plans are best and if you're making another little Dombkins, I know you'll give us everything we need to raise this sweet baby.*

I came out of the bathroom and just stood there, looking at Mark, with the pregnancy test gripped firmly in my fist.

'What?' he said, looking at me quizzically.

I couldn't find any words. Nothing at all would come out of my mouth. I walked over and handed him the positive test.

'Are you serious?' He jumped up, a huge grin spreading across his face. 'Wait… really? Really? You're pregnant?'

I nodded, searching his face for a reaction.

'This is awesome!' He reached out and pulled me into a hug. His enthusiasm in that moment was everything I needed. If he thought we could do it, I knew we'd be okay.

Two years prior, on a visit back to Australia, Mark had been booked in for a vasectomy during his visit (because, obviously, five children are enough for anyone) but a few days prior to the surgery, the surgeon fell off his bike and broke his arm. The surgery was cancelled. We joked it was a sign from the Lord that we should have another baby.

Mark was quite clucky for a few weeks, cooing over pictures of our friends Paul and Michelle's new baby girl, Rosie. But it was a short-lived moment (because, obviously, five children are enough for anyone!) and on a visit the following year, he tried to re-book the surgery. This time he'd left it too late to book. He missed out again, and we joked that the Lord *really* wanted us to have another baby. Or maybe the Lord wanted us to improve our organisational skills. It's hard to say! Nevertheless, we weren't too concerned as we knew we didn't fall pregnant without extraordinary effort, intense praying, a little begging and some medical magic.

And yet here we were. Two weeks home from Africa, one seven-year-old, four four-year-olds, and one tiny embryo making its presence known for the first time. We laughed and shook our heads in disbelief and checked the test again, and there was no doubt—baby Dombkins number six was on their way.

The first thing I did was call my midwife. Yvonne had delivered Jackson and Jemima, and I knew how hard it was to get into her program. I called her, still in a state of shock and could barely believe I was telling her I was pregnant again. She giggled and celebrated and reassured me she could be my midwife again and all would be well.

Over the next few days and weeks, we shared the news while still in disbelief ourselves, with our friends and family. The responses varied—there was silent shock from my family, laughter and cheering from Mark's parents, screams of joy from friends, and all eventually landed in love and support for our crazy family and this next twist in our wild tale.

Nine months of horrendous morning sickness later, our beautiful little Max entered the world. He was born in such a rush that I ate breakfast at home, gave birth at the hospital, and was back home again for lunch. Mark nearly missed it while parking the car, Meg did miss it while parking hers, and Yvonne calmly caught that baby boy about 30 seconds after rushing me down the hospital hallway and into a birthing room. He was ready to be born, and he was not waiting around for the rest of us to catch our breath.

Once again, I enjoyed the amazing medical care provided completely free of charge in my amazing country. Yvonne came to our home in the days following Max's birth to weigh him, do all the newborn health checks, make sure he was feeding well, and check on me post-birth. We were both completely well, and still, we were cared for.

I watched Shay, Charlie and Jabari enjoy their new baby brother and was reminded again of everything they lacked at this stage of their life. Maybe it was the post-birth emotions, but I teared up constantly as I thought of their hunger and hopelessness at this time in their lives. I wished I could rewind them—take them back to the newborn stage and spend hours just holding them, looking into their eyes and feeding their tiny bellies. I couldn't, of course, but I could bring them into these incredible moments with Max. They were now the big kids, for the first time, and their new baby was so deeply loved. Max completed our family in a way only God knew we needed.

Chapter 48

What About All the Others?

"Your real job is that if you are free, you need to free somebody else. If you have some power, you need to empower somebody else."
—TONI MORRISON

During our time living in Tanzania, we watched, learned and listened to many who call Tanzania home. There is so much to learn, and since we were raising three Tanzanian children, we wanted to immerse ourselves as deeply and widely as we could. Trying to understand our kids' story was top of our priority list, and as we learned, it was apparent that their story was also the story of millions of others. Literally millions of other children shared their path. They were not unwanted. But the life circumstances and lack of support services in Tanzania led to a crisis point, where abandonment was the only option. I found it almost unbearable to think about—to really let myself imagine the pain of those moments, the agony of the process, the unthinkable decisions that led up to a child being left behind. How did any parent survive that pain?

At first, my thoughts returned often to the 50 babies remaining at the baby home in Mwanza. We had seen those little faces ourselves, held them in our arms, played with them in the yard, and then walked away. That thought kept echoing in my mind for years to come: '*What about all the others?'* Each one had their own story, each facing a crisis point that led them there—to be loved and cared for in a baby home, but many would never find a family.

We shared our journey with friends and family back in Australia, and many responded as we did. They were moved by all we shared and inspired to understand more, and to help somehow. We started thinking about how we could help more—what could be done?

Orphanages around the world have a terrible reputation, and indeed many deserve it. Tales of trafficked children, abusive environments, and poor conditions are horrifically common, leading many to call for the closure of all such institutions. But in the absence of a foster care system or a safety net of any kind, where would the abandoned children go? Many countries don't have waiting lists of families ready to take in a child, and government support to help them do so.

In countries like Australia, we say we don't have orphanages, but we do. We just call them "group homes" or other similar, non-specific, non-threatening, under-the-radar names. It's where we put the children who have been so damaged by their trauma and by our systems that every foster placement fails, and we house them together with paid shift workers to supervise them. These are the children our system has failed. These are the children *we* have failed. We've denied them a permanent family and a permanent home, we moved them time and time again, severing their ties to any parent figure. We've had children living in hotel rooms for months or years, with case workers coming in and out to supervise, but no family to belong to. We have a terrible history, a stolen generation, where indigenous children were removed from loving parents without good reason, and we are rightly cautious now. We should absolutely be cautious to remove a child from their family, and we should provide that family every resource possible to overcome the challenges that make their home unsafe. But if we do remove a child, and they cannot return home, we must allow them a new family.

We have many children who have been removed from their birth family, but they are kept in limbo indefinitely. They are not allowed to stay in their original family, and they are not allowed to be adopted into a new family, despite having foster carers who would desperately love to adopt them.

The point we seem to miss is that from the moment a child loses or is removed from their parents, they are in crisis. They're free-falling from the moment of loss until the moment they land in a permanent, loving home. And in that time, they are damaged irreparably. We have scores of beautiful foster families in Australia and around the world that give immense love and support and make every effort to hold that child through their storm, but those parents would agree that a temporary home (as wonderful as it may be) is not enough. That child cannot settle until they find their permanent family. Every child should be able to come home, forever.

There are many adult adoptees in Australia who have been irreparably damaged by adoption. They are angry and hurt, and rightfully so. Their stories are true, their pain is real, and their voices are vital in helping to reform a broken system and prevent us from repeating the mistakes of the past.

There are also many adult adoptees with beautiful stories of successful adoption. Their stories are true, too. Their joy is real, and their voices are vital in teaching us how to do adoption well.

We must be able to hold both—that we have done adoption poorly and we have done it well; that adoption can be a vessel for ongoing trauma, or it can be a vessel for deep healing. Both are true. Those who hold these perspectives are not on opposite sides of a debate—they are on the same team, on the side of the children, advocating for adoption policies that put children first.

The truth about adoption is that we need to do it more, and we need to do it less, at the same time. We need to offer adoption to children who can't return home, and prioritise their need for stability. And we need to offer more support to families at risk of losing their children before it hits crisis point. Adoption can be a beautiful option for a child without a family, but it wouldn't be necessary if their birth family could keep them in the first place. I'm not sure we'll ever get to a place where adoption is never needed—there are circumstances where it's unavoidable. But surely, in many instances, it could have been avoided if there had been earlier intervention.

All these thoughts swirled in our minds as we walked through our adoption process. As those 50 babies at Forever Angels lingered in our minds, along with the millions of others, and the reality of just how difficult it had been to adopt our three became clear, we started shifting our attention from those 50 to the next 50—the ones who were yet to be born, yet to be abandoned. We wondered what might have happened to our kids' birth family if they had been supported from the start. What if our kids' birth parents had known of somewhere to get help? How many of the 50 babies had parents who would have loved to keep them, if only they had the means?

We talked through all these thoughts with Amy—our guru. She knew so many stories like this, understood the complexities of poverty, child abandonment and the Social Welfare system in Tanzania. She agreed that many of the babies who had come to Forever Angels may have had a different outcome if there had been earlier intervention. She told us there would likely always be some that needed a baby home. When tragedy and poverty collide, there will be children orphaned or abandoned.

But she had been developing and testing an idea, an early intervention strategy to support vulnerable women and allow them to keep their babies. Amy's support program had allowed abandoned babies to return to their biological families and prevent some babies from being abandoned at all. We listened and learned and soaked in her words that were so full of hope.

In Tanzania, 20 women a day die in childbirth, leaving 20 newborns at risk of abandonment. Twenty every day. They are at risk of abandonment because there often isn't a way for their family to keep them. Without a breastfeeding mother, there is little hope for survival. Formula milk is available but priced so highly that even Mark and I were unable to afford it when we brought our three babies home. Our babies were old enough for cow's milk, so this wasn't a problem for us, but for those living in poverty, it simply isn't possible.

Additionally, fathers left with newborn babies are generally unable to stay home from work to care for the child. No work means no pay, and this would put the whole family at risk. As a result, many of the 20 motherless babies are abandoned. They are not unwanted; they are just unable to be kept. Can you imagine the heartbreak? It's so far from our experience that it's barely possible to imagine, but if we let ourselves try to go to that place—to attempt to comprehend the experience of holding a dearly loved baby in our arms, looking into their trusting eyes, feeling their tiny fingers grip around our thumb… and knowing we cannot keep it. Can you imagine?

Amy's idea was great, but the Tanzanian government provided no funding for such projects. There simply was no support available to families in need.

We began by sharing what we saw and learned with our close family and friends, who were as moved as we were. We ran small fundraisers, with generous donations from people we loved dearly. That money was able to support a few more families to keep their children. Their stories were spine-tingling. A mother with triplets who survived childbirth but was so malnourished herself she was unable to breastfeed. Three babies who would have been given up, despite having a loving mother who desperately wanted them. Amy's program provided formula milk for the triplets, education and training for their mother, and assistance setting up a small business selling fruit and vegetables from her home. She could feed her babies and earn an income.

She kept them, and they kept her.

And we kept telling stories. We kept talking about how a little support could completely change the lives of a family. And as we told stories, we found more people who wanted to join us. And as more people joined us, we could support more families. The potential of what could be done with more funding was incredible, and before long, our sporadic fundraising attempts led us to create Forever Projects—a charity devoted to raising funds to keep these babies in their families.

Chapter 49

Shakuru

"How lovely to think that no one need wait a moment, we can start now, start slowly changing the world! How lovely that everyone, great and small, can make their contribution toward introducing justice straightaway... and you can always, always give something, even if it is only kindness."

—ANNE FRANK

Across the ocean, another baby was born. Baby Joseph was born around the same time as our little Max. He was born to Shakuru, a busy mum juggling a big family and all the challenges of life in a small village in Mwanza. He became the youngest of five siblings. Shakuru was just like me, only on the other side of the world.

When Joseph was born, Shakuru's milk didn't come in. She tried in vain to feed him, but there was simply nothing there. No one came to check in on her, and without enough money for formula milk or to pay for a hospital visit, Shakuru and Joseph hit a crisis point. Shakuru was terrified. A few years earlier, Shakuru would have been forced to make a choice no mother should have to make—to watch her baby die in agony, or to secretly abandon him to a baby home, knowing she would be jailed if she was caught. Either way, she would lose him. But things had been changing in this town, and for this family, there was hope.

The fundraising efforts of Forever Projects had provided funding for Amy's program, and Shakuru was directed to Forever Angels, where, instead of abandoning baby Joseph in desperation, she was empowered to keep him. She was given formula milk to save his life. She came to a weekly gathering to meet other women like her and receive training in newborn care, nutrition, and business skills. She was given a small amount of money to start her business, and she bought a sewing machine. She had already been to a sewing school and had the skills to tailor clothes and a talent for creating her own designs. With the sewing machine, she was able to work from home, caring for baby Joseph herself and sewing to earn an income. One year later, she was completely self-sufficient, supporting herself, growing her business, employing more staff members and providing for her family.

As Forever Projects grew and our fundraising capability increased, we were able to empower Amy and the local teams. The impact on the community spread quickly. What was first a small trickle with a few families in a pilot program became a flowing stream. The program was having an amazing impact. Women in the program were able to support others at risk in their villages, taking their new knowledge home to share with others. All it cost was $1200 Australian Dollars for a woman to complete the program. $1200, 12 months, and a woman could keep her baby and support herself and her whole family, independently from that point on.

The numbers of babies in the baby home began to decrease as more families entered the program. The malnourished children's ward at the local hospital, that had always been overflowing, was now empty. Empty! I could barely believe it when I heard that news. I had been to that hospital myself and seen the look of hopelessness in the faces of those mothers and babies, and to think they were now being cared for was completely overwhelming.

The program was working, and the impact on the community was so powerful that the next step became scaling the program to new locations. If it could work in Mwanza, there was no reason we couldn't see the same impact elsewhere, with the right teams in place. Amy's network of connections across the country was vital in identifying new locations—we needed reputable baby homes with a proven history of honourable practices and committed local staff with deep knowledge of the needs of their communities.

One by one, we started the program in baby homes across the country. First in Geita, then Arusha, then Tanga, then Dar es Salaam. In total, across the five centres we've now seen over 2,500 babies come through the program, stay with their families, and live independently of financial support. 2,500! As I think about that number, it takes my breath away. I think back to that moment of leaving the baby home carrying Shay, Charlie, and Jabari in my arms, turning around to see those little faces remaining. '*What about all the others?*' was the thought that entered my mind that day, and it had lingered and pestered and prodded ever since. The joy of knowing there is now somewhere to go, someone to help, and the bright hope of life together for those families brings tears to my eyes.

Shakuru's business has continued to expand. As this story is being written, she is working on her next move. She plans to train other women in her community to sew, to give others the same support she was once given. One of the rooms at Forever Angels that once had every wall lined with babies' cots is now empty, as the number of babies requiring care in the home has reduced. That room may be the one she uses to teach other mothers to sew. Can you imagine? The very space that once housed abandoned babies could now contain a group of strong, hard-working mothers, learning new skills that will change their families' future, all while their babies stay safely in their care. Goosebumps.

There is so much hope for what we can achieve together in the future. If this project can work in multiple cities across Tanzania, we know it can work further across the world. Our goal is to continue to expand, uniting people like you and me with people like Shakuru to change lives and families around the world. And the beauty here is that we need each other, because changing lives across the world changes us, too. It changes our families, our children, our workplaces and our communities when we give and serve, when we challenge ourselves and open our hearts to care about others, when we look these tragedies in the face instead of averting our gaze, and when we find the courage to lean in and care deeply.

In the past, we've called countries like Tanzania "developing" and our own "developed", and while there may have been some economic truth to that, there are many more ways in which "they" are more developed than "us". The families in this program have taught us they are rich in culture, storytelling and honouring their elders; they support each other, sharing all they have and knowing their neighbours deeply; they grieve together, celebrate together and connect deeply with each other; they have a strong work ethic, and sacrifice for their children and their families; they are able to value humans over possessions and each other over their things.

We have much to offer—our time, our skills, our finances, and our love—but we have much more to gain. We are not the saviours, we're the students. We get a small insight into the lives of incredible women and families whose strength and determination inspire us to grow. If we let them, it's they who are saving us.

In my home, baby Max was growing well, learning to walk, smiling and giggling in a stable home with his birth family. In Shakuru's home, baby Joseph was growing well, learning to walk, smiling and giggling in a stable home with his birth family.

He wasn't another number in an orphanage. He was loved and cherished. And all it took was a small amount of funding, a supportive community, and a woman who did what we all do—work hard for our family by any means possible.

She kept him, and he kept her.

Home, forever.

Epilogue

"Vulnerability is not winning or losing, it's having the courage to show up and be seen when we have no control over the outcome. Vulnerability is not weakness, it's our greatest measure of courage."
—BRENÉ BROWN

We step through the door of the baby home once more. My children, once-chubby toddlers, are now long-limbed, athletic nine- and ten-year-olds. Some of the staff immediately recognise them and come running, greeting them with awkward hugs and wide smiles. Shay, Charlie, and Jabari are unsure. Tentative. My heart is in my throat.

We've been planning this trip for a year. It would be the first time that the kids and I have returned to Tanzania since moving home. It's been both thrilling and agonising to plan. Shay, Charlie, and Jabari barely remember anything from their life in Tanzania, and we felt for a while that it was time. They needed to return and see their home. We speak about it constantly in our everyday life. It's so firmly entrenched in the fabric of our family, and yet it was a distant memory for them. We wanted to bring them back, to have the sights and smells and sounds come to life for them. But there was no small amount of trepidation.

It felt in some ways like returning to the scene of a trauma. Our memories were such a mix of elation, terror, joy, and wanting to rock back and forth in the corner. I wasn't sure how I felt about coming back myself, and the thought of preparing our children for this moment was paralysing at times. I did my research, and it didn't help. It was quite difficult to find stories of other adoptees who returned to their home country as children. Many that I asked had never returned themselves, even as adults. Some advised against it, suggesting it would disrupt and unsettle their life in Australia and their connection to us. Others encouraged the idea, but few had any real experience or wisdom to share.

I lay awake many nights leading up to this trip, praying, wondering, hoping, planning. Talking it over with God. *How were the kids going to respond? Was this the right thing to do? Was I doing enough to prepare them? How could I possibly prepare them?! What if they hated it? What if it was all too much—too confronting, too painful, too foreign? What if they wished we never took them? What if this undid everything we'd been working towards for years? What if they couldn't tell me how they felt—if they were hurting on the inside but unable to say it out loud?*

The fears were many, but our gut feeling remained. It was time. They needed to go back. We all did. And so, standing in the doorway of the baby home, watching my children stiffen as they hugged strangers, I held my breath.

They took a few tentative steps inside the doors, and their eyes moved upwards to see walls covered in pictures of each baby who had lived in this place. Following the faces along the wall into the next room, they found their pictures. Their tiny baby faces stared back at them. Shay's face erupted into a grin. Charlie stared as if in shock. Jabari's picture was there too, although he only stayed here for a week. He giggled at his image, high up on the wall. They were three of a sea of faces looking back at them—each face with a story of their own. Some returned to their biological family, some were adopted into new families, some moved on to older children's homes, and some didn't survive. Each one loved, cared for, and remembered in this place.

They cautiously walked further into the baby home, peering around, trying their best to take it all in. And then they met the babies. A group of little ones were playing with toys on a colourful woven mat. I put my arms around Shay, Charlie and Jabari. 'Hey guys,' I whispered, squeezing them in close, for a Titanic moment, 'This is where we first met!' I kissed their foreheads and squeezed a little tighter.

We wandered outside to the playground and saw the older kids running around—a busy bunch of children climbing, swinging and playing. Charlie looked back at me, cautiously. 'You can go play,' I said.

Still barely daring to breathe, I watched them with intense respect. They left my side and slowly walked over and began to join in. It didn't take long. Within minutes, they were piggybacking children, pushing them on swings, and climbing on the playground. Their faces started to light up with genuine engagement. Something was happening. Caution turned first into curiosity, and then into courage. It was like watching the birth of something new. Expressions on their faces emerged that I'd never seen before—some kind of mixture of intrigue, joy, and camaraderie. They were captivated and completely at home.

Each in their own way, they delighted in these precious children, who were living a life that was once theirs.

Charlie had endless energy for running laps of the playground with a grinning child bouncing on his piggyback, some almost as big as him. Hour after hour, he never tired. Shay found the cuddly toddlers and quickly had a gaggle of children climbing into her lap for a hug. Jabari found the tiny baby room, and dimples I never knew he had appeared on his face as he smiled, held those babies, tickled their tummies, and rocked them to sleep.

I sat in the tiny baby room with little Harriet in my arms, and Shay, Charlie and Jabari around me, each with a baby cradled carefully in the crook of their elbows. The picture was breathtaking. Shay and Charlie were now sitting in the very place they lay as newborns, only now they sat here—strong, healthy, and with all the love in the world for the tiny ones in their arms. One of the mamas met my gaze, my teary eyes giving away my thoughts.

'I remember your babies,' she said quietly, 'They lay right here.' She smiled warmly, patting the mattress we were sitting on. 'They were so small when they first arrived, their little heads the size of the palm of my hand.' I looked deeply into her kind eyes. This woman knew my babies before they were my babies. It's an anomaly known well by any adoptive parent, and the feeling is just as surreal with each encounter. There's a part of our children's lives that existed before they were ours. It's unknown to us, but there are strangers in the world who hold those puzzle pieces. There are memories, photographs and shared experiences—moments and connections between our kids and others that we know nothing of. Those memories belong to the people who filled the gap—the time between our children losing their first family and finding ours.

This mama was one of them. She fed my babies, changed them, rocked them to sleep, and held memories of their life before I knew them.

'Shay was always sucking her thumb, right from the start. And then later she would suck her thumb on one hand and twirl her hair with the other hand.'

'Yes, I remember,' added another mama. 'And Charlie would only drink half his bottle of milk, but Shay, she would drink...'

'One and a half!' they said in unison and broke out into giggles. I laughed with them, amazed at the details they remembered. They knew Shay and Charlie so well—each memory so precise and accurate. I knew their memories were true as this was exactly the way they came to me. I have a hundred photos of Shay sucking her thumb while twirling her hair.

I sat quietly for a few minutes, baby Harriet sleeping heavily in my arms.

I contemplated what it was like for these women to do this job—to come in every day and give themselves to these babies, knowing they may care for them for a few weeks or a few years, and then ultimately let them go. They saw the joy of babies returning to their biological families, or finding new homes, but they also dealt with the tragedies of life here. They held babies in their arms as they died, planned funerals, and comforted each other in their grief. To love these babies was a risk. To know them deeply and connect with each one was incredibly vulnerable. I could hear in the way they spoke about my children, and the joy they showed in seeing them again, that they had allowed themselves to really know and love them.

Trying my best to keep my tears to a trickle and not break down completely, I said, 'Thank you. Thank you so very much for loving them so well, before I could.'

My shaky voice couldn't get out much more, and I was mercifully engulfed in a hug from each side, my tear trickle becoming a stream. I was intensely grateful for these women, for their devotion to my babies, for the genuine love they gave, and for their unreserved bear hugs while I sobbed my eyes out.

All six of our kids loved being in the baby home. Their response was everything I had dreamed of but barely dared to hope for. It was going to make the next few weeks so much easier. At every possible chance, they wanted to go back. We had deliberately not planned much for the next week, so we could take their lead and listen to what they needed. And every morning, the first question was, 'Can we go to the baby home again today?' Oh, my heart, how I loved those words.

Over the week, with more and more visits, their questions started coming. We had told them their story a thousand times, and they always listened but with little interest, like they were humouring us. Now, being here in this place, it was like the pieces all started coming together.

On our second day, we went to visit Babu. He knew we were coming, and we knew he'd be thrilled to see the kids again. We piled into the 4WD and travelled the dry, dusty roads out to the house Babu shared with his new wife. Pulling up out front, we spotted Babu hard at work in his garden. Seeing our car, his face lit up and he ran towards us through the cassava plants. Mark jumped out and they hugged like long-lost friends. I opened the back door, and the kids piled out. Seeing Shay, Charlie and Jabari, Babu rushed over and pulled the three of them into a huddle. He bent his head down to their height, arms stretched around all three, and held them tight. Delight covered his face. He held them like this for a few minutes, looking each of them in the face, kissing their foreheads and speaking softly in their ears. It was just beautiful.

Babu looked well, and although he was in his mid-70s, he was maintaining his home and garden beautifully. Babu was using the land surrounding the house to grow all kinds of vegetables and fruits. Rows of well-maintained crops stretched across the front yard.

We met Babu's new wife, and they welcomed us into their home. My mind wandered back to the place Babu lived when the children were left with him, the small, dark concrete room that used to be home. His new home was full of life. There was light, a beautiful cool breeze, lush gardens, and four good-sized rooms. Babu was using two to live in, and the other two he was renting out as an income stream.

Babu's front yard also held Bibi's grave. She had passed away four years prior from stomach cancer and was laid to rest here in Babu's garden. We stood around her grave with the children, remembering her love and devotion to them, and telling them once more the story of how she saved their lives.

Sitting in the living room, we shared a watermelon, and the children asked Babu the questions they had been planning to ask. I giggled to myself, listening as their questions unfolded. There were two categories: 1) general likes and dislikes, and 2) deep questions about their past. There was nothing in between.

What's your favourite food? Did you like to play soccer as a child? Has our birth mother ever come back? What do you love to grow in your garden most? What is your favourite fruit? How long did our birth parents stay before they left us? What's your favourite colour? What's your favourite animal? Were you scared we were going to die? What do you like to do in your spare time? Do you know Jabari's birthdate? Do you like music? Do you know which twin was born first?

This question was a big one. Charlie asked it, and I knew he was dying to be the 'older' twin. We had never known before, and we had always told them they were the same age and who was born first was of little consequence. But as they entered primary school, it became a regular topic of conversation. In fact, I would often be walking through their school and have other students run up to ask me which twin was born first. Somehow, it mattered, and not knowing was driving them crazy. Because Shay was taller, most kids put their money on her, which she quite enjoyed. Poor Charlie hated this, and I knew how much he wanted to be the older twin. 'Are you sure you want to know?' I asked him, 'What if it's not you? Do you still want to know, even if it's not you?'

'Yes, I want to know,' he said firmly. He was willing to take the gamble. I looked over at Shay.

'Do you want to know?' I asked her.

'Yep!' she answered, confidently.

'Are you both sure?' I triple-checked.

'Yes!' they agreed. I turned around and nodded to Mark, who translated Charlie's question to Babu.

'Do you know which twin was born first?' Mark asked.

Babu nodded. I felt sick. At least when we didn't know, they could both believe it was them. Someone was about to be bitterly disappointed.

'It was Shay,' Babu said. 'I remember her mama telling me that the girl had been born first.'

'Are you sure?' Mark checked.

'Yes, I'm sure,' Babu replied.

I turned around to look at the kids. They had understood Babu's answer. Shay was smiling a little, but being careful not to rub it in, which I was thankful for. Charlie looked devastated. I felt for him deeply. These were big moments for our kids—listening to their story, told in person for the first time in their memory. It was all becoming much more real to them as they saw and heard it for themselves. Some things were interesting, new and exciting, while others were harder to swallow.

Throughout the course of our time with Babu, we were able to confirm many parts of the story as we knew it and find out some new pieces of information.

Before we said our goodbyes, I asked a question I'd been thinking about for nine years.

'Babu, what was it like for you and Bibi on the day you decided to give the children to us to raise? Was it a sad day? Was it a difficult decision? What was it like for you?'

Babu smiled and shook his head. 'It was not difficult; it was a very happy day. We just wanted them to live, and we wanted them to be together. We prayed for a year for someone to come, for the children to live. We were watching Jabari die, Bibi was sick, and even with help we couldn't raise them.' Babu reached forward and took Mark's hand, cupping it between his own. 'When we heard that you would take all three together, we were so happy. It wasn't a sad day; God had answered our prayers. We were both very happy.'

As I write this, I'm sitting by the beach in Zanzibar. It's the last day of our return adventure. Tomorrow, we fly back to Australia and return to normal life. But we're all a bit different. This trip has moved us all. I wouldn't call it closure—that sounds too final, and we're on a much longer journey. It's been more like living the final paragraphs of a multi-part series. It's the end of this chapter, of this book, but the next book starts tomorrow.

What I have loved most is watching my children step into their own story. Ever so carefully, like trying on an expensive outfit. They've listened and watched and then slowly taken their own steps forward. They've been brave and vulnerable and open. They've been curious and honest and expressive. They've engaged deeply and allowed themselves to be changed. I am so proud of them.

I watch them walking together down the sand towards me, the sunset colouring the sky behind, giving their faces a soft glow. I'm overwhelmed once more with gratitude for the family we've become, for the journey we're on. Happy tears (my new best friends) glisten in my eyes once more.

Let's go home.

Afterword

The Story Before the Story

"My story is important not because it is mine, but because if I tell it anything like right, the chances are you will recognise that in many ways it is also yours. Maybe nothing is more important than that we keep track, you and I, of these stories of who we are and where we have come from... because it is precisely through these stories that God makes himself known to each of us most powerfully and personally."

—FREDERICK BUECHNER

I'm sitting on a softly patterned upholstered chair in an auditorium filled with strangers. The mood is serious, but warm. There is pain in the room, but also strength. This is a recovery meeting. I have deep respect for the men and women seated around me, for their stories, their courage, their commitment to turning up and doing the hard work. Some are recovering from addiction, some from childhood abuse, some from a lifetime of domestic violence, and others from perfectionism, eating disorders, workaholism or deep shame. Everyone in the room has a story, and everyone is here to learn, to grow, to continue in their recovery.

A woman on the platform greets the crowd as the chatter around me quietens. She welcomes us all, shares some words of hope from her own story, and then welcomes me up to speak. It strikes me as I stand how much younger I am than most in the room. They have vast chapters of life lived beyond mine—marriages and children and careers and adventures I'm yet to embark upon. I wonder what 20-year-old me has of value to share and wish I was hearing their stories. I want to hear them all.

But whether I like it or not, I'm standing on the stage with a quiet audience before me. I flatten my notes on the podium in front of me, take a breath and begin to speak. I tell them my story. I tell them about childhood sexual abuse and the impact it had on my life. I tell them about shame and confusion and all the ways I tried to cope but made it worse. And then I tell them about healing and hope.

I take them back to kindergarten me. I'm five and scared, but I keep a song in my mind about Jesus and climbing mountains, and it becomes my comfort and prayer in the worst moments.

When something seems
Too hard to handle
Too big to conquer
Too far away to touch
Remember this
He'll never leave you
He won't forsake you
He's your strength and he's your song

So sing and start to say
I'm climbing my mountain, step by step
I'm climbing my mountain, day by day
I'm climbing my mountain, all the way
I'm climbing my mountain, I'm gonna make it

One step at a time
With Jesus by my side.

(One Step at a Time—Debby Kerner and Ernie Rettino—arrangement muddled by five-year-old me).

I'm little but my faith is strong, and my God is real. He is my confidant and friend, the only one who knows my story, and as my song promised me, He never leaves or forsakes me. I begin to realise something then that I come to understand more and more over time: that actually, He feels like home. And where He is, home is - then, and now and forever.

As I finish, I thank my audience and return to my seat. I struggle to place the emotion I feel. There's a swirly mix of bitter and sweet. I believe in doing this, in sharing my story, because I know how much it means to me when others share, how much I learn and how it feels to know there are others with a story like mine. I believe the more we talk, the more we break the silence, the harder it is for abusers to succeed. And that maybe if the adults can talk, we can help give voice to our children. So I speak on days like this because I believe in doing it. But it's not easy.

And as I sit there, a new thought emerges. I become aware that while I will always believe in telling this story, it's not the only one I want to tell. This is a story of things that have happened to me, largely beyond my control. I'm in the story, as the survivor of those events, but I didn't choose this story. It just happened to me.

I start to wonder, for the first time, what story I would choose to tell. The excitement of this thought travels through my body, leaving a trail of goosebumps on my skin. I close my eyes for a moment, and in my mind, I see a large open book resting in my lap. It's heavy, leather-bound and opened to the last page. I read over the words on that page, written in my own handwriting. And then I close the book, hug it closely to my chest and return it to the shelf. Beside me, I see a new leather-bound book. I lift it up, place it on my lap, open the first page and write *Chapter One.*

I wonder, dear reader, what your story holds, what mountains you've climbed and are climbing today. I wonder what heavy books you have laid open before you and if any of those books are ready to be closed, honoured and placed on a shelf. I wonder if there's something in you longing to open a new book and enter a new story.

Take a pen, strap on your mountain boots, and pray your guts out. I know you won't regret it. I want to hear your story.

Acknowledgements

Thank you firstly to Mark, who holds our family together with bad dad jokes, relentless positivity and the kindest heart. It's the greatest joy to live every day of this life we've chosen together with you.

Our friends and family – we are so blessed to be deeply known and loved by you all. Thank you for cheering us on, praying for us, loving our kids, setting us straight, listening to all the crazy, and just walking alongside us.

To our church community (past and present) who have shaped our faith, shown us Jesus and taught us to hear the cry of the oppressed. Our life is an expression of our faith, and our faith has been grown in friendship with you.

To Amy and the Forever Angels staff – thank you for your vision, your love, your dedication to the women and children of Tanzania, for saying "yes" when our tiny premmie babies needed your help, and for loving them so well before we could.

To our Forever Projects community – to every person who has helped raise 2.5 million dollars by using what's in your hands to make a difference. We love your hearts. We're so glad to be in this together.

To our Forever Projects Core Community, who fund all our overhead costs, allowing 100% of every other donation to go directly to women and babies in Tanzania – you've been our friends, our advisors, our cheerleaders and our backbone. None of it is possible without you. We're proud to know humans like you.

To our Moshi friends and ISM community – our life in Moshi was made so wonderful by you. We are so grateful for your friendship during those years – weren't they the best?

To Deborra-Lee Furness and all at Adopt Change – thank you for your dedicated advocacy for adoption reform in Australia, for giving voice to vulnerable children and refusing to accept poor policy. Thank you, Deb, for your beautiful words in support of this book, for being brave and self-less with your life and your work, and for your generosity in amplifying the work of others.

Thank you to those who have brought this book into being – to Caroline Baum for being its biggest champion, to my literary agent Jeanne Ryckmans for finding it such a perfect home, and to my publisher Bonita Mersiades at Fair Play Publishing for bringing this book into the world. Thank you all for taking a risk on a newbie like me, for believing in this story, and for walking me through each step to get it out there.

Thank you to Ben Hawkins for my beautiful cover design, Imogen Baker for your early look over the manuscript, Adrian Lammers for your magical photography, and Scott Harrison for your encouraging words, and the inspiration that charity: water is to us and to Forever Projects.

To Babu and Bibi, for your courage and persistence that saved your grandbabies lives, and for not giving up until they found a forever home. You'll always be their heroes, and ours.

To our children's birth parents – we will never really know all you went through, or what it was like to lose your babies. We hope one day you'll know they survived and they're amazing. You'd be so proud.

And to the God I love, it's all for you.

MORE REALLY GOOD BOOKS FROM FAIR PLAY PUBLISHING

The Bipolar Runner

Jumping Jack

A Secret Grief

Light and Shadow

Hear Us Roar

Radicalised by FIFA

www.fairplaypublishing.com.au

PEPPER PRESS

www.ingramcontent.com/pod-product-compliance
Ingram Content Group UK Ltd.
Pitfield, Milton Keynes, MK11 3LW, UK
UKHW021833270726
14058UKWH00001B/135